REPUBLIC
# P-47
## THUNDERBOLT

# REPUBLIC
# P-47
# THUNDERBOLT

## The Operational Record

## Jerry Scutts

Motorbooks International
Publishers & Wholesalers ®

This edition first published in 1998 by Motorbooks International,
Publishers & Wholesalers, 729 Prospect Avenue, PO Box 1,
Osceola, WI 54020, USA.

© Jerry Scutts 1998

Previously published by Airlife Publishing Ltd, Shrewsbury, England.

Library of Congress Cataloging-in-Publication Data available

ISBN 0-7603–0578–1

Printed and bound in England.

# Contents

# Acknowledgements

Among those helping to create this record of one of the most famous aircraft of the Second World War, the author was pleased to draw upon personal recollections, printed data and the photographic collections of a number of individuals and agencies. These include Martin Bowman, Don Campbell, Jim Crow, Harry Holmes, Philip Jarrett, Jack Lambert, Ron MacKay, Brian and Brenda Marsh, Bruce Robertson, Philip Savides, Andy Thomas, Richard L. Ward, Military Aircraft Photographs, the United States Air Force, and Republic Aviation. Among the printed references consulted were those by Frank Olynk, Roger Freeman, Don Woerpel, Bill Colgan, Ken Rust, Ernest McDowell, David Weatherill, James Fielder, Gary Fry, Gene Stafford, William Hess, Geoff Thomas, Victor Flintham, Dan Hagedorn, John Rawlings, and Wg Cdr C.G. Jefford.

A special thank you is extended to Peter Cope  for his recollections of flying the Thunderbolt in Burma.

# Introduction

Startling many observers by its sheer size when it was first flown as a new interceptor fighter for the U.S. Army Air Corps in 1940, the Republic P-47 Thunderbolt eventually showed that it could more than hold its own in combat with smaller, seemingly far more agile fighters. By the early 1940s, the international vogue was for fighters with the smallest possible airframe, which is what P-47 designer Alexander Kartveli originally aimed for.

But with the need to adopt a very large air-cooled engine to obtain the necessary horsepower and incorporate a turbo supercharger – the first fitted in a single-seat interceptor – Kartveli was obliged to significantly scale up his design; adding essential war equipment boosted weight but with a 2000 hp Pratt & Whitney Double Wasp pulling it along, the P-47 could absorb higher weight and still turn in a good performance. Most designers have to address the often conflicting balance of power-to-weight ratio and, even though Kartveli more or less built a weight spiral factor into his fighter, the P-47 was destined to get even heavier as the war progressed. To illustrate just how much bulk a single late-war model P-47N pulled into the sky on take-off, one has only to compare its weight statistics with those of contemporary fighters. Numerous examples can be quoted but, for brevity, one P-47N weighed as much as two fully loaded Messerschmitt Bf 109Gs.

Size ultimately became an asset to the P-47 rather than a drawback. Airframe strength meant that the aircraft could lift an impressive ordnance load for ground attack work and, as ably demonstrated on many occasions, a big, strong structure could protect the pilot very well in the event of determined attention by the enemy or in a crash landing. Pilots walked away from some amazing Thunderbolt wrecks and the aircraft regularly returned to base with incredible battle damage.

Second World War air combat wrought many changes in pre-war doctrine regarding the deployment of fighters. Range quickly became a highly desirable asset, as did the ability to haul drop tanks, bombs and rockets. Many fighters designed as interceptors of enemy bombers ended up combating other fighters or attacking targets on the ground. In the overall dimensions department, the P-47 remained in a class of its own throughout the Second World War; as a fighter it also compared more than favourably with any other type in the Allied inventory and it carved out an enviable combat record, excelling, as did many other aircraft types, in a variety of roles for which it was not primarily designed.

*The Seversky P-35 represented the Republic forerunner's first successful bid for a military contract. The 1st Pursuit Group flew P-35s in typical late-1930s bare-metal finish with fuselage badges, in this case, the Snow Owl of the 17th Pursuit Squadron. The unit was further identified by a white cowling ring. (A. M. Chappell)*

# 1
# Kartveli's Heavyweight

When Russian emigré Alexander Seversky established his own aviation concern in the U.S.A. in 1922, the seed that would ultimately grow into a range of highly effective interceptor fighters was sown. About ten years later, Seversky reinforced the design expertise of the company by securing the services of another Russian, Alexander Kartveli. Together these two men designed, built and flew a number of advanced prototypes, beginning with the SEV-3 amphibian of 1933. The BT-8 trainer came along two years later and with it Seversky's first Air Corps contract, for thirty-five examples of an aircraft that had itself been an outgrowth of the SEV-3.

Seversky aquired his own manufacturing facility in 1935 and although this site, at Farmingdale on New York's Long Island, was to become synonymous with aircraft construction for over fifty years, the early period was far from easy. Despite some export success, Seversky failed to interest the U.S. government in a true combat aircraft until a replacement for the Boeing P-26 pursuit was sought by the Air Corps. Tenders for a P-26 replacement were sought in 1935, and as Seversky had for some time aimed at winning a production contract for a pursuit aircraft, he entered the SEV-2XP for an evaluation of new types to be held at Wright Field that June. When this machine, yet another upgrade of the original Seversky design, crashed *en route* to the test airfield, luck had not entirely deserted the determined Russian. The Air Corps allowed the competition to be postponed to give Seversky time to rebuild his entry, as otherwise there would have been but a single contender, the Curtiss P-36.

The prototype P-35, alias the SEV-1XP, was a single-seat reworking of the 2XP, the original entry for the A.A.C. competition. Its revised lines and retractable undercarriage showed how fortuitous the accident to the 2XP had actually been. Cumbersome by comparison, this two-seater would probably have been no match for the Curtiss entry. As things transpired, although the P-35 proved slightly faster than the P-36 and the Air Corps was at last looking favourably on Seversky, Curtiss protested that the delayed competition had given their far smaller rival an unfair edge. The Air Corps again deferred a decision, until April 1936.

In the ten months between the two pursuit competitions, Consolidated and Vought had entered the picture with the PB-2A and V-141 respectively. Both were rejected.

After a favourable Air Corps evaluation of the SEV-1XP, Seversky was awarded a contract for seventy-seven aircraft on 16 June 1936. All were designated P-35 except the last example, which incorporated some significant design changes and became the XP-41.

In attempting to design a new pursuit for the Army, 'Sasha' Kartveli faced a considerable challenge. The Air Corps had for years been strongly orientated towards the bomber as the primary weapon in future conflicts – fighters or 'pursuits' were considered almost an unnecessary luxury at a time when military budgets were severely restricted. Kartveli was not, therefore, alone in working hard to tailor the official requirement to something the conservative Air Corps chiefs would accept – and which his concern could build in high numbers, if required. Fortunately, Seversky had foreseen the need for high-volume production and the Farmingdale factory had ample space available.

Although their design horizons were largely unrestricted, U.S. military aeronautical engineers of the 1930s were projecting ideas for machines that would only become operational at least two years or more in the future and perhaps be engaged in conflicts that may or may not involve the United States. Those were challenging, stimulating times; innovations in military aircraft design were gaining ground in all sectors of the industry and being incorporated in a range of new types that were setting world standards.

But as to actual military involvement of the United States on an increasingly unstable world stage, there was much debate. Many people would not entertain even the possibility of physical involvement in 'foreign wars' and, even when conflict broke out in China in 1937 and in Europe in 1939, the isolationists continued to hold sway. Selling arms to support one side or the other was entirely different; the U.S. always had had its business interests very much to the fore and aircraft manufacturers had to be commercially viable to survive the financial strictures of the previous two decades.

Foreign customers had, therefore, placed orders for U.S. combat aircraft in substantial numbers by early 1939 but deliveries had not all been completed by the time the European war began that September. It was only when reliable news on what the *Luftwaffe* had done to Poland filtered back to America that a few far-sighted people in the industry began to realise that modern war, if it involved the widespread use of air power, had suddenly and quite dramatically changed. Reports of the indiscriminate use of air power by the Japanese in China added fuel to the fire.

Some individuals consequently took steps to modify new designs or prototypes to meet current requirements. These had apparently changed so fast that pessimists could foresee that a slow, ill-protected aircraft with restricted ability to deliver ordnance over any distance could now be obsolete even before it left the drawing-board. Or maybe not. Who really knew what kind of fighter and with what capability would be needed by Air Corps pilots and aircrews of the future? Even in 1940, the U.S. Army had only vague, largely outmoded ideas on what actual combat would demand of American military aircraft. The notion that air power would primarily be required to support troops in the field

was about as far as it went.

Pitched into this melting pot, probably the biggest crossroads for aviation since the Wright brothers, were designers such as Kartveli, Ed Heinemann of North American, Peyton Magruder of Martin, and many more. These men would gain initial wartime contracts for their respective companies by concentrating on aircraft which they knew how to design and build and which did the job, at least in peacetime. American aircraft, while they had some serious drawbacks in terms of armament, were in many design details right up-to-date and, most importantly, they usually proved to be highly adaptable. Yet the new American heavy, medium and light bombers and fighters met relatively tight parameters built on company experience and budgets.

Manufacturers were answerable to their shareholders and any new designs submitted would hopefully bring forth lucrative military contracts and, at the same time, beat their competitors. Before the United States entered the war, the traditional builders of single or multi-engined aircraft tended to win contracts in the categories they were familiar with. Most companies, both large and small, soon branched out into other areas which spawned a plethora of experimental bombers, attack types, fighters and seaplanes. Often, these remained purely experimental, 'one off' prototype examples but, in general, the war stimulated the industry like never before.

### SEVERSKY INTO REPUBLIC
While Seversky was in England to promote his ideas, he was voted out by the board of directors and Wallace Kellett appointed head of a new company. Seversky was persuaded to accept a cash settlement to relinquish his position and in October 1939 the Republic Aviation Corporation was formed. The restructured company was changed as little as possible and Alexander Kartveli remained as chief engineer. Seversky had achieved much by continually and economically modifying existing single-engined aeroplanes. In designing the forerunners of the P-47, neither the Republic management nor Kartveli saw any reason to change to anything more complex, particularly as the company had found a niche as a military supplier with the

*Top: Dubbed a 'convoy fighter' due to it having a substantial range, the 2PA was a ingenious reworking of the XBT – Seversky did not believe in building numerous expensive prototypes!*

*Above: The P-43 Lancer was another generic link between the early Seversky designs and the P-47. The family likeness to the big brother Thunderbolt was quite evident in this diminitive pursuit aircraft. (P. Jarrett)*

P-35. But equally, Kartveli knew that successfully creating a fighter acceptable to the Army presented many pitfalls.

The choice of powerplant for any new fighter was, of course, critically important but selecting the most reliable liquid-cooled or air-cooled unit at a time when U.S. manufacturers were promoting powerful new engines with significant increases in output over what had gone before, was not at all easy. For one thing, few of the promising engines of 1940 had been thoroughly proven. Both radial and in-line engines had merit for fighters and both appeared to be equally reliable, but good performance depended very much on the weight and size of the airframe they would be fitted into.

Initially Kartveli had envisaged a lightweight interceptor fighter with the smallest possible airframe built around the new V-12 liquid-cooled engine being developed by Allison. And when the resulting Seversky model AP-10 was examined by the Army Board at a meeting in August 1939, its potential seemed clear. Kartveli was asked to develop it, working in conjunction with Wright Field engineers.

At that point, some limitations in the AP-10 emerged. When the Army wanted provision to be made for bomb racks and other modifications, the weight of the aircraft inevitably rose, from 4600 lb to 4900 lb, although the original armament, two fuselage-mounted machine-guns, remained unchanged for a time. The AP-10's estimated top speed was 415 mph at 15,000 ft.

A contract covering two prototypes of the modified AP-10 – which had in the meantime become the XP-47 – was drawn up but rejected by Washington. Among the reasons was that the aircraft's armament was now considered to be too weak and its top speed too low. In January 1940, Kartveli agreed to a redesign under a new contractural agreement – but then Republic ran headlong into those war reports from Europe. The Air Corps immediately drew up a list of modern innovations that had to be incorporated into any new U.S. design, particularly self-sealing fuel tanks and armour plating. The perpetual challenge of the right power-to-weight ratio had rarely been more closely studied.

To discuss this whole matter, the Air Corps convened a special board, the members of which realised that a number of current fighter proposals would be rapidly outclassed should they ever actually see combat as designed. The XP-47 was among them and the board also voiced concern that Kartveli and other designers were placing too great a reliance on using Allison engines. Kartveli forestalled the possibility of the XP-47 being cancelled by turning his attention to installation of the Pratt & Whitney Double Wasp.

As any air-cooled engine would have been far too bulky to fit the original lightweight XP-47, the Double Wasp being particularly massive, Kartveli created a completely new airframe around this engine. On 12 June 1940, Republic officially submitted the XP-47B. Air Corps observers noted some very desirable features for a new fighter, particularly the armament of six 0.50-in Browning machine-guns. Few fighters anywhere had such heavy firepower and Kartveli had made ample provision for two more guns to be fitted in the spacious wing bays, which did not incorporate any fuel cells.

The estimated performance of the XP-47B, which included a top speed of 400 mph at 25,000 feet with a climb rate of 5 minutes to 15,000 ft, was also encouraging. Even though the weight of the Republic design had risen dramatically, to an amazing 11,600 lb gross, unprecedented for a single-seat fighter, the Air Corps felt favourably inclined towards the aircraft and approved it for production on 6 September 1940. The contract called for 773 production P-47Bs.

Kartveli had realised that his new interceptor fighter's altitude performance would be best achieved by the installation of a turbo-supercharger. In an age when bombers were still believed to be virtually invulnerable to interception – much less destruction – by fighters, he was not alone in striving to solve what amounted to an unknown equation – how could the modern fighter reach the bombers' altitude in time to attack them before they inevitably annihilated their target?

Supercharging appeared to be the solution. But the extensive intake and exhaust ducting required for such a system to function efficiently demanded an aircraft with a fuselage section substantially deeper and longer than that of the XP-41, the generic link between the P-35 and P-47, taking in the P-43 along the way. Not that installing a supercharger in the XP-47 was easy; Kartveli's team was obliged to adopt an unorthodox approach to the problem by positioning the main unit in the rear fuselage, with the intake for the air duct mounted under the engine along with the oil coolers. Exhaust gases were piped back separately to the turbine and exhausted via a waste gate in the fuselage underside, ducted air being fed back to the centrifugal impeller and returned to the engine under pressure. When all that had been achieved, the XP-47B looked distinctly pot-bellied and the fuselage had 'stretched' to more than 35 feet compared to the P-43 which was less than 28 feet overall.

A Seversky/Republic family likeness remained however, even though what finally emerged from the Republic factory was one of the largest single-seater pursuits U.S.A.A.C. officers had ever seen. Size, however, did not appear to matter overmuch to the Army – performance was what counted.

## FIRST FLIGHT

Huge it may have been but on completion the XP-47B (serial no. 40-3051) looked every inch the modern – even futuristic – interceptor with the promise of an outstanding performance. In an age when many air arms throughout the world were still operating biplane fighters as first-line equipment, the prototype Thunderbolt looked potent indeed, with its attractive elliptical wing, enclosed cockpit canopy and massive propeller. The effect of sleek streamlining was enhanced by the high polish given to the natural aluminium airframe, which was almost devoid of markings.

Of semi-monocoque, all-metal stressed-skin construction, the XP-47B was powered by an eighteen-cylinder Pratt & Whitney Double Wasp R-2800-35 engine rated at 2000 hp. The engine drove a Curtiss Electric propeller of 12 ft 2-in diameter, the first four-bladed unit fitted to a US fighter.

Pilot entry on the prototype and the first two production P-47Bs (41-5895 and 41-5896) and the final B model (41-6065) was via a port side car-type door similar to that of the Bell P-39 Airacobra and British Hawker Typhoon. This cumbersome and heavy mode of entry had obvious drawbacks and was soon dispensed with. The last of this quartet of P-47Bs was rebuilt as the pressurised XP-47E and fitted with the conventional sliding cockpit hood, a modification almost certainly carried out on the other two P-47Bs.

*Finally there was the XP-47, A.A.C. serial No. 40-3051. Not applied prior to roll-out, the number was added later, as was the camouflage. The window aft of the canopy was also changed. (P. Jarrett)*

Aft of the engine bay and forward of the cockpit, the XP-47B had a main fuel tank with a capacity of 205 U.S. gallons. In addition, a 100 gal auxiliary tank was situated aft of the rear wing hinge support bulkhead. For the maiden flight the actual fuel capacity was 297 gallons of 100 octane gasoline. Oil was carried in a 28 gal fuselage tank. Loaded weight of the aircraft in preparation for the first flight was 12,500 lb without the pilot.

Having been completed and rolled out at Farmingdale on 2 May 1941, the XP-47B remained outside Republic's Hangar 1 and was, somewhat casually, merely parked by the perimeter fence and tethered to a concrete block. Fortunately, the weather remained fine during the intervening period and on 6 May the XP-47B took off for the first time in the hands of Republic test pilot Lowery Brabham.

When he lifted off in the shining prototype, which was still devoid of any national insignia, Brabham had no inkling of trouble. The aircraft flew well enough until the cockpit began to fill with smoke. No test pilot will abandon a prototype unless there is absolutely no chance of saving it without risking his life, and Brabham had the additional worry that, if he did bale out, the important XP-47 programme would inevitably be delayed. Republic would have precious little flight data until a second machine was completed – and the pilotless fighter might fall on downtown Long Island, with disastrous results.

As the flight continued, Brabham was relieved that no flames appeared and he elected to stay with the aircraft to eventually clock up about 20 minutes' flight time. Making notes while the smoke continued to seep into the cockpit, he explored the aircraft's handling characteristics in order to detect the slightest sign of damage that might have been the cause of the smoke. There appeared to be none but it was clear that the XP-47B could not be landed back at Farmingdale as the runway there was unpaved and in places dangerously soft from recent rains. An ideal alternative was nearby Mitchell Field, New York, where Brabham carried out an uneventful landing.

The XP-47B was returned to Republic after several weeks at Mitchell Field and on subsequent test flights it recorded much pertinent data, including a preliminary true air speed of 412 mph at 25,800 ft. No formal speed runs were actually made with the prototype, as the 400 mph plus figure had been verified in the official contract. The prototype was not delivered to Wright Field but retained by the manufacturer on bailment contract, primarily to use as a test vehicle to eliminate any problems that might have arisen prior to production start-up.

Retention of the aircraft at Farmingdale did not, of course, prevent Air Corps pilots from flying it, among them Major Marshall 'Mish' Roth of the Experimental Aircraft Division. His report was highly enthusiastic, particularly in regard to the suprisingly good rate of roll that was found to be possible with such a large aircraft.

Although the XP-47B only existed for a little over a year, it had helped to prove that Kartveli's brainchild had the potential to be a useful combat aircraft, superior in performance to both the P-39 and P-36/P-40, the only alternative single-engined fighters available to the Air Corps at that time.

As testing of the early P-47s proceeded, shattering setbacks for what would soon become the Allied cause, made grim headlines. German dominance of the continent of Europe was all but complete in a catologue of military disasters. And in December 1941, the world knew America was also at war following the Japanese attack on Pearl Harbor.

**SETBACKS**

A state of war in the US brought an urgent need for modern combat aircraft to re-equip all the military services, which were rapidly expanded to absorb a huge increase in new combat aircraft. Republic's most important contribution to a rejuvenated Air Corps appeared to be shaping up, although a few troubled months lay ahead. With production of the P-47B started, aircraft were routinely test flown from Farmingdale, which was also being developed with new concrete runways and taxiways.

On 26 March 1942, George Burrell, Republic's chief test pilot and Operations Manager, took off from a paved runway in the fifth production P-47B (41-5899). Burrell was flying above cloud and just beginning some manoeuvers to determine the cause of a

*Showing off its distinctive elliptical wing and characteristic 'staggered' arrangement of the machine-gun blast tubes, the Thunderbolt prototype existed for some two years before being lost in a crash. (U.S.A.F.)*

previously reported malfunction, when the entire tail section of the aircraft broke away. The stricken fighter plunged down and eventually came to rest on a golf course near Mitchell Field. Burrell managed to bale out but he was too low for his parachute to deploy fully and was killed on impact.

Fortunately, most of the P-47B landed intact and prompt action by firefighters enabled an examination of the wreckage to determine the cause. It was eventually traced to weakness around the tailplane attachment point. But that was not all. On 1 May, another P-47B suffered some damage while in a dive. This one landed safely but with its fabric-covered elevators and rudder in shreds. The trouble was put down to compressibility effects.

Republic initiated remedial work on the P-47's rear fuselage structure and confirmed the need to fit metal-covered control surfaces as soon as possible. But strengthening the Thunderbolt's airframe could only partially overcome the problems associated with high-speed flight. Republic was certainly not alone in being relatively unprepared for the effects of such natural phenomena, but quick and easy solutions to the problem were hardly to hand. The remedial work the company carried out on the early P-47s as compressibility damage occurred was the best that could be done in the circumstances, considering the urgent need to get the new fighter into service.

A further untimely crash was to occur on 8 August. Test pilot Filmore 'Phil' Gilmore strapped into the XP-47B which was still cloaked in the olive drab and neutral grey camouflage paint applied for a 'photo call' for *Life* Magazine photographers back in February. In the meantime, the XP-47B had joined Republic's Experimental Flight and among other modifications, had been fitted with various different engines. Gilmore had flown it on a number of previous occasions. A considerable amount of tuning and tinkering had been necessary to induce the Double Wasp to deliver the advertised 2000 horsepower, but it rarely obliged. Gilmore had had the XP-47B's turbocharger regulator adjusted to give increased manifold pressure to compensate for varying atmospheric conditions prevailing over the U.S. East Coast in August.

As the Thunderbolt prototype climbed, so did the manifold pressure indicator. The gear was still coming up when the indicator passed the red line. Gilmore released the gear retraction handle which interrupted the retraction cycle – and stopped the tailwheel directly in the path of the jet blast from the supercharger turbine, whereupon wheel and oleo proceeded to melt.

The climb-out continued at about 160 mph I.A.S. but upon reaching about 12,000 feet Gilmore sensed a tail heaviness. Speed fell off and he was acutely aware of having no control response. There was certainly no elevator control and precious little reaction to any retrimming. And the angle of dive was increasing. It was time to get rid of the canopy, just in case.

Gilmore saw the A.S.I. reading 420-430 mph, jettisoned the pilot's door and the attached part of the canopy and unwisely pulled his parachute ripcord. The chute billowed too quickly and some panels were torn out of it under the extreme air pressure. But Gilmore dropped away as the XP-47B continued its dive into the waters of Long Island Sound.

Phil Gilmore's injuries were not serious and his test report proved invaluable in enabling further refinements to the early Thunderbolts to be made although such work naturally took time and inevitably led to delivery delays. Due primarily to the time a water recovery would have taken, the XP-47B was left where it came down.

Standard service testing of the P-47 was carried out at Wright, Patterson and Eglin Fields, a combat evaluation test on three P-47C-1s fitted with metal-covered control surfaces being conducted at the latter facility in October 1942. Among other performance figures, this test recorded an impressive top speed of 427 mph but Army Air Force (which the Air Corps had become on 20 June 1942) officials were of the opinion that the P-47C needed a far better time-to-climb performance. Pilots, too, felt that in taking 7 minutes to reach 15,000 feet the P-47 was hardly outstanding for a new interceptor fighter.

This problem was addressed by Republic. A slow climb to altitude was a relatively unimportant drawback the company had little choice but to accept and it remained with the P-47 for much of its service life. Airframe weight was such that little could be done apart from ensuring that the engine gave maximum output. During the war, the P-47's ability to climb did indeed become a source of controversy, the rate improving and declining depending on model and engine rating to the point that the P-47N would take just over 14 minutes to reach 25,000 ft. Little did the A.A.F. officials realise that in the P-47C they were looking at one of the best climb rates of the entire Thunderbolt series, rather than the worst.

It was, incidentally, C. Hart Miller, Republic's Director for Military Contracts, who thought up the name Thunderbolt for the XP-47 and thereby initiated a company hallmark – Thunder would be perpetuated in the names of aircraft throughout the company's subsequent military programmes.

# 2
# America's Guardian

While the possibility that the United States would be bombed by the Axis powers became increasingly unlikely after Hitler had attacked Russia in June 1941, the threat nevertheless had to be addressed for the foreseeable future. Also, Japan's aggression in China had, since 1937, bought a gradual deterioration in relations with America, and future military operations in the Pacific region could certainly not be ruled out. The Army Air Corps therefore maintained a substantial home defence force, which included the P-47 interceptor fighters of the 56th Pursuit Group.

Having been activated at Savannah, Georgia on 15 January 1941 and equipped with P-39 Airacobras and P-40 Warhawks, the 56th Group (comprising the 61st, 62nd and 63rd Squadrons) completed its early training and moved later that year to Charlotte, North Carolina and Charleston, South Carolina.

Before the Japanese attack on Pearl Harbor, some A.A.C. fighter units had already been moved overseas, primarily to meet any threat to the Philippines. This movement continued at a more modest pace as friendly territory fell to the new enemy and nothing short of an Allied disaster unfolded in the Pacific. When the Japanese reached a limit to their conquest in New Guinea there was a chance to reinforce the area and build up base facilities in Australia.

Early in January 1942, the 56th was on the move again, but not to a war zone. It continued on home defence duties and by mid-year had dispersed its squadrons on three airfields on the U.S. East Coast – Bendix, New Jersey, Bridgeport, Connecticut and Farmingdale. Initially the 61st F.S. was assigned to Bridgeport, the 62nd to Bendix and the 63rd to Farmingdale, but some interchanging followed and for a time the 62nd was also based at Wilmington, South Carolina. A headquarters was established at the municipal airport at Bridgeport but this facility had a relatively short runway and most 'first time' check flights were made from Bradley Field at Windsor Locks, Conn., which had a runway over one mile long.

Republic rolled out the first two P-47Bs in March 1942 and these machines were duly test flown by company and Army pilots to ensure that they met the performance figures achieved by the XP-47B. In most respects they did although the addition of military equipment had inevitably increased airframe weight by some 650 lb compared to that of the prototype. But apart from taking about two minutes longer to reach an altitude of 15,000 feet, the P-47B was actually faster than the XP-47B, being capable of 429 mph in level flight.

Production delays resulted in there being only four P-47Bs on hand by May but these served to introduce the 56th Group's groundcrews to the intricacies of the new type, particularly the engine and supercharger. While the cowling access panels exposed virtually all the innards to the Pratt & Whitney engine, thereby making maintenance reatively easy, the same could not be said of the aircraft's hydraulic system. With its myraid lines and electrical cables linked to numerous cockpit controls, this appeared quite daunting to the novice pilot.

New pilots were also quite intimidated by the mass of controls – which subsequently led a British observer to liken the P-47's cockpit to a church organ with its rows of push-pull levers. In fact, many of these switches and controls were supplemental to basic flight instrumentation and everything tended to become clear once the pilot had had a chance to familiarise himself and had actually flown the P-47 a few times.

*A P-47B (41-5931) flown by the 56th Pursuit Group in the U.S. during 1942. The aircraft has the earlier forward-angled radio mast, a black serial number and a plane-in-squadron number on the cowling and fin. (P. Jarrett)*

In March 1942, the 56th Group had witnessed the arrival of the man who would lead it through its toughest early period of combat in Europe. Captain Hubert Zemke had returned to the U.S. after a period of instructing in Russia where he had checked out pilots on the P-40 before stopping over in England. Zemke had taken the opportunity to make a close study of the R.A.F. operational methods under war conditions and as the 56th's group operations officer, he was able to pass on his valuable experience to pilots of the three squadrons. On 16 September, Zemke replaced Colonel John Crosswaithe as group commander.

Being based cheek by jowel with the Republic factory meant that when it was decided to re-equip the 56th with the P-47, its pilots hardly faced a long delivery flight. It was actually no accident that part of the group was at Farmingdale. The official view was that the P-47 had so many new features compared to existing fighters that its merits or otherwise could only be determined by experienced service pilots flying it on a regular basis.

And so it was to prove; after checking out the first pilots, the 56th carried out innumerable practise interceptions which, although somewhat irksome to the individuals involved, were valuable training for eventual combat. The pilots built up flying hours and, most importantly, the 56th became thoroughly familiar with the Thunderbolt under peacetime conditions in which new tactics could be tried out and some of the technical problems, inevitably associated with any new aircraft, overcome.

Republic also gained much from these months prior to any P-47 entering combat. Together with reports from Europe on what the modern fighter needed to survive in a shooting war, the company amassed a considerable amount of data from the 56th Group's early operations with the P-47B. These were ultimately incorporated into modifications and changes on the production lines, each with an ever-increasing number of Technical Bulletins which were distributed to all Thunderbolt users throughout the war years.

Operating from Bridgeport's long runway undoubtedly assisted the 56th's trainee pilots for the P-47B required at least a half mile take-off run to safely clear a 50-foot obstacle. The airport runway gave plenty of margin for error.

Elsewhere in the States, some of the first

groups that would eventually represent the fighter cadres of the largest air force the world had ever seen, were being formed or had begun training. Those units in existence in 1942 generally trained on aircraft that they would not, due to a number of circumstances, actually fly in combat. Many of those destined to later re-equip with the P-47 invariably trained on P-39s and P-40s. Thunderbolts arrived later as output increased with most examples of the early models prior to the P-47D being used only for training rather than combat. It understandably took time for the A.A.F. to make firm decisions on which unit would operate which type of fighter in which theatre of operations – during the first six months of war, hardly anyone knew what was wanted.

Whatever happened, America had many allies and commitments around the world; these needed assistance and protection to fight the axis powers. A major part of that help would come through air power, the provision of which would need thousands of new pilots and aircrew under an expanded air training organisation. To train enough fighter pilots for all the war theatres was a massive task requiring the formation of a number of full A.A.F. fighter groups which would function as

replacement training units (R.T.U.s). These units were to remain in the Zone of the Interior (Z.I.), as the United States became known under wartime military acronyms, for the duration of the war – or for as long as the need for new pilots lasted.

A total of thirteen groups were eventually equipped with the P-47 for training purposes during the Second World War. Unlike operational fighter groups which usually had a basic complement of three squadrons, with a fourth occasionally attached primarily for in-theatre training, the Stateside training units could have a strength between one and six squadrons, four generally being most common. With the war winding down and the majority of combat groups trained and posted overseas, most P-47 training groups were deactivated late in 1944.

**NEW CHALLENGE**
While there were encouragingly few fatal accidents during the early months of training, some familiarity with the P-47B led the pilots of the 56th into a hitherto unknown area of flight conditions. Being young, carefree and, of course, indestructible, the pilots began 'wringing out' the P-47 to see just what it was

*Part of the total of 171 P-47Bs built at Farmingdale, 41-5963 has the black serial number applied to these early models and a distinctive camouflage demarkation line. (M.A.P.)*

capable of. The trouble began when they climbed to maximum altitude and threw the machine into a power dive. On occasions, the aircraft grimly lived up to its meteorological namesake and went straight into the ground.

Some time passed before it was realised that a high maximum diving speed plus the aircraft's airframe weight built up too much momentum and that on the way down the P-47 encountered compressibility. Air pressure built up to the point that at 500 mph no fabric-covered control surfaces could cope with the imposed forces and were simply torn away, invariably leading to a fatal crash.

Much has since been written of this early realisation that manned flight was entering hitherto unknown realms, and the fact that P-47s were dived at near or above 'sound barrier' speeds (at least as far as the A.S.I. needle on the instrument panel was concerned). But all that could be done in 1942 was to post warnings in each Thunderbolt cockpit advising the pilot that the aircraft should not exceed 300 mph in the dive and that violent manoeuvres should be avoided.

Such restrictions could not always be followed to the letter in combat, but it was realised that prompt and correct elevator control was the secret of avoiding the onset of compressibility. Unlike test pilots, combat pilots rarely if ever have a need to throw their machines into high-speed power dives from a very high altitude and to hold or steepen the dive angle for thousands of feet. Metal-covered control surfaces and stronger trim tabs were better able to withstand extreme air pressure than fabric-covered surfaces and these were fitted on the P-47C pending a full revision of the elevator control system in later models.

During the Thunderbolt's service test period, thirteen pilots were killed and forty-one P-47s lost. Although the number of aircraft write-offs was high, many pilots had walked away from crashed Thunderbolts. They owed their lives to its tough construction and the cushioning effects of the supercharger plumbing that ran below the cockpit floor was particularly appreciated in belly landings.

After completing 171 P-47Bs, Republic tooled up for the improved P-47C-1 and completed the first example on 14 September 1942. Among other advances, this outwardly similar model introduced linked throttle, engine rpm and supercharger controls so that the pilot could control these functions by moving a single lever. Four-point suspension shackles for the carriage of a belly tank holding up to 200 U.S. gallons of fuel (mainly for ferrying purposes) were also introduced. The P-47C-1 had a revised oxygen system which included an additional bottle located in the leading edge of the port wing and an A-17 turbocharger regulator. Accumulating data on the combat needs of a modern U.S.A.A.F. fighter resulted in the P-47C-2 which followed the 112 examples of the P-47C-1 into production and incorporated all the revisions introduced on the C-1.

The P-47C-2 was the first of the Thunderbolt series considered suitable for a war role. It had metal-covered rudder and elevator surfaces and improved controls as well as the necessary shackles for a belly tank, as fitted to the P-47C-1. Revised engine mountings introduced on the P-47C-1 had extended the space occupied by the engine alone to six feet from front to rear and lengthened the Thunderbolt's nose by 13 inches compared to that of the P-47B. The fuselage was now 36ft 1in long nose to tail and this was to remain unchanged for all subsequent first-line models. The P-47C-2's supercharger controls were also revised, with an additional gate just aft of the cowling attachment line and a circular exhaust port aft of this, an arrangement that was standard on all subsequent production Thunderbolts.

After 128 P-47C-2s had been completed, Republic built 362 P-47C-5s which were similar to previous models apart from some changes to radio equipment and the aerial mast aft of the cockpit. Earlier aircraft had had the mast sloping forward but the P-47C-5 introduced a straight mast.

Republic then moved on to a third main production model which, with numerous detail changes, would represent the bulk of wartime Thunderbolt output. This, the P-47D, proved remarkably adaptable to some quite drastic modifications, all of which served to make the aircraft one of the most important in the Allied inventory. Production was initiated at Evansville, Indiana in December 1942 with a batch of 114 aircraft designated P-47D-RAs without any suffix number. The powerplant

*A P-47C of the 61st Fighter Squadron at Mitchell Field with flight commander's red fuselage stripe and red cowling band. A straight radio mast was introduced on this model. (P. Jarrett)*

was the R-2800-21 rated at 2000 hp and the aircraft was otherwise similar to the P-47C.

The P-47D-1, also powered by the R-2800-21, had additional cowl flaps – a total of twelve – to improve cooling. These extended down the sides of the cowling to below the wing leading edge to show five when the aircraft was viewed in profile, rather than the three of earlier Thunderbolts. The aft edge of the two lower flaps, which were smaller in area than the others, had a distinctive 'cutout'. Again, this feature became standard on the 105 P-47D-1s and on all subsequent models.

Additional pilot armour was provided in the cockpit and minor changes were made to the radio and aerial, the fuel system, the method of oxygen operation, and the accessory compartment. Armament was specified as either six or eight 0.50-in Colt-Browning M2 machine-guns with a maximum of 425 rpg. On 305 gal of internal fuel and carrying 200 gal in an external tank, the P-47D-1 had a normal range of 400 miles at 25,000 ft. This translated into an endurance of 1.3 hours although it should be stressed that individual aircraft could differ by a considerable margin in this respect.

Evansville built 200 and Farmingdale 445 P-47D-2s which, apart from a further revision of the fuel system during the output of the latter batch, were similar to the P-47D-1. These were followed by 100 P-47D-3s which incorporated all previous changes, and 300 P-47D-5s which were also similar. Only 299 D-5 airframes were released for service, however, as Republic converted the last P-47D-5 (42-8702) into the XP-47K.

All 200 P-47D-4s were also built at Evansville, these being followed by 350 P-47D-6s which had B-7 two-point bomb/drop tank carriage fuselage shackles, normal bomb weight being a maximum of 500lb. This Thunderbolt model was also capable of carrying 75 gal, 108 gal, 110 gal, 150 gal or 200 gal drop tanks on the belly shackles. The 250 P-47D-10s had a revised hydraulic system including flap controls and a G-23 General Electric supercharger.

Significant 'under the skin' changes were made to the P-47D-11, 400 examples of which were completed. With the introduction of water injection for the R-2800-63 engine, pilots could call on a few minutes' extra boost in combat, a highly popular modification. A 15 gal tank containing a mixture of water and alcohol was located in the accessory compartment and operated automatically by a lever on the throttle. Overall performance of the P-47D-11-RE remained much the same as that of earlier models although maximum speed, 433 mph at 30,000 ft, was marginally better.

*Top: Bad radio-interphone reception plagued the early P-47s and in an effort to eliminate it, 'whip' aerials were tested on this D-2 model. In the event, the troubles were cured and most service P-47s continued to use an aerial mast.*

*Above: These P-47Bs from the 61st F.S. are led by 56th Group Commander, Hub Zemke, whose aircraft is identified by the fuselage stripes (red, yellow and blue front to rear), the number '1' and a red, yellow and blue segmented cowl ring, these being the colours of all three group squadrons. (U.S.A.F.)*

Evansville's 250 P-47D-11-RAs were similar to those built at Farmingdale, the latter plant following on with 496 examples of the P-47D-15-RE. Another important change on this model was the introduction of wing pylons to enable either ordnance or drop tanks to be carried in addition to a load on the belly shackles. Some internal wing structure modifications were made to allow for wiring and 'plumbing' of the new racks which were positioned outboard of the gun bays. The availability of three hardpoints brought the

P-47D's maximum external fuel capacity to 375 U.S. gallons and the bomb load to a maximum of 2500 lb in various ordnance combinations.

There followed 254 P-47D-16-REs which had provision for 100/150 octane fuel, and 29 P-47D-16-RAs and 250 P-47D-20-REs all 279 of which were powered by the R-2800-59 engine with a General Electric ignition system. These aircraft introduced a longer tailwheel oleo leg and detail changes were made to the tail of the wing pylons. The last P-47D-20-RE (42-76614) was reconfigured as the XP-47L.

The line continued with 187 examples of the P-47D-20-RA, 216 P-47D-21-REs which had manually-operated water injection via a button-switch on the throttle lever, and 224 P-47D-21-RAs. During production of D-21s at Evansville, the first Thunderbolts left the factory devoid of camouflage paint, 'natural metal finish' being introduced from 13 February 1944 in line with U.S.A.A.F. directives.

Not having to apply paint other than the national insignia, airframe warning stencilling and an anti-glare panel forward of the windscreen, not only saved manufacturers a considerable number of man-hours but brought an improvement in performance. An estimated 40 lb of paint was required to completely camouflage a P-47 and this saving could obviously be turned into increased performance, modest though the gain was. Not all commanders wanted bright silver aeroplanes that could be seen for miles, however, so some P-47s were subsequently painted at depots. Others were given top coats of camouflage by tactical units in the field.

The 850 P-47D-22-REs had Hamilton Standard Hydromatic 'paddle blade' propellers of 13ft 1in diameter and A-23 turbo-regulators. The 889 P-47D-23-RAs had Curtiss Electric propellers with slightly shorter, 13ft blades. The final batch of P-47D-23-RAs also brought to an end the production of Thunderbolts with the original razorback fuselage configuration. Curtiss had already completed 356 P-47Gs in five batches which were equivalent to the P-47C and early Ds built by Farmingdale and Evansville.

## FIRST OVERSEAS

With output of Thunderbolts steadily rising during the remaining months of 1942, many people were anxious to know exactly how the aircraft would fare in combat. The 'Germany first' policy adopted by the U.S.A. in agreement with Britain had enabled the establishment of a strategic Army Air Force in England. In December a batch of 88 P-47C-2s was loaded aboard freighters. These machines, part of a total of 200, were the first to be issued to VIII Fighter Command.

Preparing Thunderbolts for an Atlantic crossing involved the removal of wing and tail surfaces and thoroughly protecting the airframe against salt water corrosion. A plasticised composition called Paral-tone was sprayed over all exposed surfaces, joints being sealed by tape. Fighters, due to their modest size, could be carried either in holds or on the decks of freighters, secured on suitable planking built over any suitably flat surface. It all depended on available space aboard the individual cargo ships few of which were allowed to leave U.S. ports less than fully loaded. Deck cargo would sometimes consist of a couple of aircraft to complete the manifest. Other ships would have the bulk of their load made up by complete aircraft and spare parts.

Once the convoy had reached the U.K., P-47s and other U.S. aircraft were offloaded on to lighters and ferried ashore to be moved by road to special depots for the removal of the Paral-tone. This involved about 40 man-hours per aircraft, personnel working with a degreasing compound of hot paraffin to soften the coating for final removal of the 'skin' with the aid of scrapers and scrubbing brushes.

At locations such as Speke in Liverpool facilities were available to fit U.S. aircraft with U.K.-compatible radio sets and other items before they were flown to operational airfields for further preparation prior to combat. It was fortunate that the need for such servicing had been foreseen and appropriate steps taken to establish a comprehensive support service for the Eighth Air Force. With much initial help from Britain, this organisation soon grew out of all recognition in terms not only of size but of expertise in all areas of aircraft engineering. The P-47 would absorb a considerable amount of these resources during the war years.

While their aircraft were shipped, the personnel of all three squadrons of the 56th Fighter Group embarked for the sea crossing to England. Before too long, P-47 combat reports would be to hand.

# 3
# Escort Fighter

With England as the cornerstone of the United States Army Air Force's European Theatre of Operations, heavy bomb groups had begun attacking the European continent on 17 August 1942. Daylight precision bombing of key industrial centres, both in occupied Europe and in Germany was believed to be the way to inflict significant damage on the Nazi economy and to fatally weaken its ability to wage war. Using the B-17 Flying Fortress and B-24 Liberator, VIII Bomber Command further believed that the heavy machine-gun armament of these bombers would be enough to ward off enemy interceptors and ensure that the campaign was conducted within a reasonable percentage of loss.

By the end of the first few months of operations, German flak was perceived to be the greatest threat to the heavy bombers but there came a gradual realisation that however heavily armed bombers might be, German fighters could still shoot them down. The A.A.F. therefore took steps to create a fighter force to fly escort to the bombers as far as their fuel capacity would allow. The need for such operations had hardly been foreseen in any air arm before the war and once again the A.A.F. was starting more or less from scratch.

Again the Eighth Air Force appreciated the valuable local assistance it received from the British. It saved time, for example, to base VIII Fighter Command's operational methods on those of the R.A.F.; British airfields and much support equipment would also be used, as would the established system of R.A.F. ground control and air-to-air communications. Combat flying 'tours' were also modelled on those adopted by R.A.F. Fighter Command and U.S.A.A.F. fighter pilots undertook duty of 200 hours' flying time in the combat zone as the baseline tour.

Having taken a long, hard look at the fighter options open to it, the Eighth's fighter commander, Brig-Gen Frank O. D. Hunter, was forced, in consultation with A.A.F. Chief 'Hap' Arnold, to reject all but one type. Neither the P-40 Warhawk nor the P-39 Airacobra had the performance to fight the FW 190 and Bf 109 on equal terms in the escort role, the Spitfire had too little range and the P-38, the initial 'ideal' choice, was in too short supply. That left the Thunderbolt. This was also viewed as far from ideal because of its range but the P-47 was available and would continue to be in increasing numbers. Unlike the P-38, there was no call to send P-47 units to the Pacific theatre where long range, preferably with the safety factor of two engines, was of paramount importance.

It was therefore decided that the first three fighter groups to form the nucleus of a P-47 escort force in England would be the 4th, which was then flying Spitfires and had seen a considerable amount of combat, plus the 56th and the 78th. These two would make their combat debut as part of the Eighth.

It was in Britain that the P-47 met its critics, both British and American, head on. R.A.F. pilots who had flown against the *Luftwaffe* firmly believed that the nimble FW 190s and Bf 109s of the *Jagdwaffe* required an equally agile opponent – their Spitfires were the machine for that job, not a great heavy beast like the Thunderbolt. The Americans who had yet to give the P-47 the acid test, could only highlight the positive qualities of the Republic fighter and await results from their first missions across the Channel; only time would tell.

Major Cass Hough, test pilot and engineer for VIII Fighter Command, was the man largely responsible for ensuring that the U.S.A.A.F. went into action against the

Germans with equipment (invariably modified rather than to U.S. factory specification) that would stand up to the test of European combat. Hough virtually rewrote the book on the performance of the P-47C prior to any Thunderbolt flying combat operations; he found an aircraft much to his liking and one that he estimated as having great potential.

There was much more pre-combat work to be carried out on the P-47 than anyone realised, least of all Republic. Not that the type was alone in having to have its command and communications radio sets changed to operate on U.K. wavelengths and generally to comply with R.A.F. ground station practice. All American radios had to be modified before any Thunderbolt went into action as part of an extensive field test programme which also included the results of British investigation into the effects of compressibility.

During the course of 1943, comparative tests into fighter performance at transonic speeds at the Royal Aircraft and Armament Establishment at Farnborough would establish that the critical Mach number of the P-47 was low at 0.74. This compared to that of the Spitfire which was 0.88. The lack of a Machmeter to inform the pilot that the airflow was about to break away and induce a shock stall which caused loss of lift and increased drag, was a considerable drawback to Second World War fighter pilots. The critical Mach number was that at which the fighter's nose went down and the pilot experienced increasingly heavy stick forces. Trying to bring the aircraft back under control quickly brought about physical exhaustion – the point determining the critical Mach number. Little could be done at the height of a war to entirely eliminate this problem, apart from constantly emphasising to pilots the dangers of exceeding the posted limitations of the P-47, particularly during a power dive from high altitude.

In England, the P-47C was also flown in mock combat with the two principal German fighters. Fortunately for many inexperienced A.A.F. fighter pilots, the RAF maintained flying examples of both the FW 190A and Bf 109G and VIII Fighter Command's Thunderbolt evaluation included detailed comparison tests with both German interceptors. Despite British scepticism over the P-47's capability, the resulting performance figures were quite encouraging. They showed that provided air speed was maintained, the P-47 could catch both enemy types in a chase even though it lacked good initial acceleration; the FW 190 could also dive away from the P-47C at altitude but the latter's good power-to-weight ratio enabled it to close rapidly. At height, the Thunderbolt had the edge over the FW 190 and Bf 109 but it was at a distinct disadvantage lower down, particularly below 15,000 ft. Both enemy types could outclimb the Thunderbolt with considerable ease and the absolute ceiling of the Bf 109 was significantly better.

In general, it was felt that the average P-47 pilot could meet his German opposite number on more or less equal terms but the American had ideally to maintain his air speed, preferably above 250 mph A.S.I., at all times and use his fighter's weight to maximum advantage. In this latter respect, the Eighth's fighter pilots were occasionally to be marginally assisted by their adversaries, for it was a favourite *Jagdflieger* tactic to power dive away after attacking bombers, seemingly oblivious to what was on their tail. This manoeuvre stemmed from combat with Spitfires, early marks of which found it difficult to catch the 190 in a high-speed dive.

German pilots had grown used to assuming that they would not be overtaken by enemy fighters – and old habits die hard. But time and again, American fighter pilots observed that the Germans failed to realise that nothing could dive as well as a P-47 and that indulging in a tail chase was often fatal to the hapless *Jagdflieger*.

Theatre training on the P-47C was initiated at Debden, Goxhill and King's Cliffe, respectively the first U.K. home bases of the 4th, 78th and 56th Groups. Of these, Goxhill was a training establishment and the 78th would, soon after completing the in-theatre course, move south to Duxford, Cambridgeshire.

By the spring of 1943, the time when American heavies could have American fighters escorting them on a regular basis was fast approaching. But in reaching that historic milestone more subtle difficulties had to be overcome. Considerable American prejudice against the P-47 came from the 4th and 78th pilots, all of whom had previously flown entirely different aircraft. The men of the 78th

*Training was the lot of many razorback P-47s and this 25 July 1944 photo includes a P-47C-2, (41-6275/G76), a P-47D-RE (42-22352/G71) and a P-47D-11-RE (42-175489/G55) serving as gunnery trainers, with four guns apiece instead of eight. The fuselage letter/number code indicated the base. (U.S.A.F.)*

bemoaned giving up their P-38s even though they had never used it 'in anger' but with the Lightning gone, a great effort was made to master the Thunderbolt. The 4th was more sceptical.

To ex-R.A.F. Eagle squadron pilots, the only replacement for a Spitfire was a more powerful Spitfire. Such individuals made up the bulk of the 4th as they had also flown only fighters fitted with liquid-cooled engines. The P-47's radial engine would be something entirely new to them and few could deny that, compared to a Spitfire, the P-47 looked very sluggish

indeed. In some respects it was – but how much of a drawback the Republic fighter's substantial size and weight would be in combat was a question nobody could really answer.

That left the 56th. With some ten months of experience of flying the P-47 behind it, the personnel (both air and ground echelons) of the group had some advantage over the others – at least they believed in the aircraft and knew its capabilities and weaknesses.

But far worse than any human predudice or technical drawback with the P-47, flying from

*The first P-47s in England had to run the gauntlet of R.A.F. criticism; the British were amazed by the Americans developing such a massive single-seat fighter. Painted on this P-47C-2 assigned to the 4th Group is a temporary I.D. number which was soon replaced by code letters.*

England brought a huge 'x-factor' into the equation – weather. And plenty of it. Few American flyers had ever experienced the cold and all-pervading damp of a European winter, and certainly not flying through it with people trying their best to kill them while doing so. As the P-38 pilots and groundcrews would discover later in 1943 when the P-38 reacted adversely to the conditions prevailing over Europe, so too did the P-47 pilots and engineers find that the 'fair weather' aircraft being manufactured in the U.S. were at a distinct disadvantage when flying from England. Their charges had to be protected, particularly against damp.

Moisture in the ignition systems of the Pratt & Whitney radial gave considerable trouble before a reliable damp-proofing compound was developed to protect the spark-plug leads. The Thunderbolt's ignition system also played havoc with radio communications, a 'chain reaction' problem that was not initially realised. Pilots found that high cockpit noise levels made it almost impossible to talk to one another in the air. This problem was reduced but it persisted until later P-47 models incorporated pressurised magnetos to eliminate it.

To offset these drawbacks there were numerous good points about the P-47 that endeared it to pilots who were not ready to condemn it out of hand or to make unfair comparisons with other types. The Thunderbolt was easy to fly, it did everything the pilot told it to do and it was found to be very stable, particularly in high winds. Its seven-ton bulk enabled it to withstand the kind of buffeting that unnerved many pilots flying lighter fighters. And the phrase 'any crash you can walk away from' could have been invented for the P-47.

Training invariably led to accidents and crash landings and pilots had only to witness a few wrecked Thunderbolts to know that, if the worst happened, they would have a high chance of surviving a crash. All that plumbing, necessary for the turbocharger, running below the cockpit area gave an excellent cushioning effect if the aircraft had to land on its belly. It might not have seemed the most positive attribute for a fighter but combat proved that the survival rate for downed P-47 pilots was gratifyingly high – and there were few complaints about that.

### ACID TEST

While the Eighth Air Force's early daylight missions were mainly to targets in occupied

France, its bombers were quite capable of attacking Germany but no British fighter could effectively escort bombers that far. Used to being escorted by R.A.F. Spitfires, the bomber crews had little choice but to accept the situation as it prevailed into early 1943. A ray of hope that the much-vaunted Lightning, which had begun arriving in Britain in the autumn of 1942, would be their long-range escort, came to nothing, at least not at that early stage. By November, the P-38s been assigned to the Twelfth Air Force in North Africa. Operation *Torch* and 'Junior', as the new air force was nicknamed, appeared to be taking almost everything the VIII Bomber Command needed, including some of its experienced groups.

As German fighter opposition to daylight air raids grew in intensity, the A.A.F. urged that more P-38s be dispatched to England and enough were made available for a number of new VIII Fighter Command groups. In the meantime, the daylight bomber offensive from England was to be maintained despite the voracious demands of *Torch*, which had also left the 4th Fighter Group as the only fully operational American fighter unit in the U.K. When the Eagles became the first in-theatre Eighth Air Force fighter group to convert to Thunderbolts, the worst fears of some pilots were confirmed.

Probably not fully appreciating that the P-47 was the only escort fighter the Army had apart from the P-38, some of the men who would be the first to fly it in action remained firmly unimpressed. For the 4th, the switch to an American fighter coinciding with the remustering as personnel in the U.S.A.A.F. certainly did not help. Not everyone wanted to change either aircraft or uniform, although all agreed that A.A.F. catering was far superior to that otherwise found in wartime Britain.

Some pilots regarded the P-47 with a mixture of awe and apprehension, many sharing the jaundiced view of their British colleagues that something that big could surely never 'mix it' effectively with the German fighters. Others were more positive. Something that helped this situation was the healthy rivalry that grew up among professional equals. Rumour had it that there was nothing to flying a P-47 when experienced pilots such of those of Hub

Zemke's outfit were in charge – and they had not even flown it in combat. There arose a determination among the 4th Group pilots that if the 56th could do the job with the damn Thunderbolt, so could they.

That such rivalry needed to be fed by proven demonstrations of prowess in combat could only be to the detriment of the *Jagdwaffe*; R.A.F. Fighter Command had, since the early part of 1941, been taking the war to the enemy across the Channel with the object of drawing German fighters up. The American fighters would fly missions basically similar to the *Rodeo* (fighter sweep) and *Ramrod* (bomber escort) sorties made by Spitfire squadrons. There was one important difference: whereas the R.A.F. flew operations with small formations of light bombers such as Blenheims acting as little more than bait to entice enemy fighters up to do battle, the U.S.A.A.F. fighters would be over the continent primarily to protect large numbers of heavies. The bombers were out to smash vital German industry to the limit of their range, a threat the German high command could hardly fail to take seriously. Persuasion to attack the American heavies would rarely be necessary.

Early on, VIII Fighter Command's lack of any fighters with extra fuel tankage restricted escort missions being flown much beyond Paris if an imaginary, radiating circle was drawn out from their U.K. bases. The P-47's internal fuel capacity offered precious little reserve for combat. Even though the aircraft had been provided during development with the capability to carry external fuel tanks few examples had been shipped to the combat zone. The trouble was that reliable jettisonable tanks were simply not available in the numbers that would soon be required. And drop tanks were not designed to be reuseable. Therefore, any victories P-47s claimed against the *Luftwaffe* fighter force could only occur if the enemy was bent on shooting down B-17s or B-24s early in their mission, or when they were about to clear continental airspace on the way back to England. Placing themselves within range of the U.S. escort made little tactical sense, for many chances for combat would occur once the P-47s had turned for home on the outward leg. Bases in northern France, Holland and virtually right across the Reich could thus be alerted in ample time to meet the threat.

*Eighth Air Force technical trouble-shooter Lt-Col Cass Hough with part of his flying unit at Bovingdon. Hough took to the P-47 and flew this D-6 (42-7921) and others in an ongoing programme to sort out its problems. This photo was taken at the time of the award – believed to be August 1943 – of the D.F.C. to Hough for 'independent flight research', the press 'slug' hinting that the decoration was partly for flying faster than sound in the P-47 and P-38. Without understanding the implications, this was believed at the time.*

What the early P-47 pilots did realise, either through fact or rumour, was that they would be up against the best fighter pilots in the *Luftwaffe*. Across the Channel, JG 2 and JG 26, both flying the FW 190A, had achieved a worrying level of superiority over the R.A.F. Spitfire Mk V. This problem had been addressed with all speed and the newer Mk IX which the 4th had briefly flown had redressed the balance. But the fact remained that the Germans had the potential to cause havoc among the lumbering

B-17s that made up the bulk of the Eighth Air Force in the spring of 1943.

The German pilots' main targets would remain over their home territory for hours, unprotected by American fighters and naked to highly efficient flak batteries. Using an efficient map reference and radio control interception system, the *Jagdwaffe* could afford to treat the whole process of interception in an almost leisurely fashion, selecting their altitude with care and forming up in substantial numbers before bringing the maximum weight of fire from their guns to bear on whole formations of heavies at once. They could land, refuel and replenish their ammunition and make further attacks, and land at basically stocked secondary aerodromes scattered across Germany.

In evaluating the P-47 for service in the E.T.O., VIII Fighter Command could hardly have failed to notice that the new fighter bore a superficial resemblance to the Focke-Wulf 190. Bomber gunners confirmed that one radial-engined fighter looked much like another over a relatively short distance and in the heat of action they had precious little time to distinguish friend from foe. Eighth Fighter Command, therefore, issued instructions on 20 February 1943 that all P-47s in the E.T.O. were to have recognition markings in the form of white bands painted around the nose and tailplane. These bands were remarkably effective, with the white offering high contrast to the olive drab and grey paintwork worn by all Thunderbolts. Coupled with the U.S. national insignia on all four wing surfaces of P-47s, they certainly helped to reduce the 'ours or theirs?' confusion bomber crews and fighter pilots might otherwise have had in greater measure.

## COMBAT DEBUT

On 10 March 1943, the 4th Fighter Group's 334th Fighter Squadron put up fourteen P-47s to fly *Rodeo* 179, the first Thunderbolt show in the European Theatre of Operations. Lt-Col Chesley Peterson led the uneventful sweep which took in parts of the French and Belgian coastlines before returning to Debden. The 334th had been taken off operations in mid-January and stood down for forty-five days in order to convert 4th Group pilots to the Thunderbolt, a process that was achieved with few hitches. In that time, eleven pilots each received about 30 hours' instruction on the new type; each of these individuals returned to his respective squadron to have two pilots assigned to him to continue the teaching process.

The first few P-47 operations from England in the spring of 1943 were valuable without being overly dangerous. Enjoying some safety in numbers, the pilots flying these 'coat-tailing' sorties obtained their first sight of enemy territory and, on occasion, experienced German flak at first hand, although this was usually too far away to cause undue nervousness. Shakedown missions were an ideal introduction to combat as, though they were often uneventful, all guns were loaded and pilots were as ready as they would ever be to fight if the enemy appeared.

Reaction from the German fighter force to American fighter formations was less than immediate. It was 15 April before each side clashed. The encounter resulted in victory number one for a 4th Group P-47 pilot, an event that was duly celebrated back at Debden. The group had met with FW 190As from either JG 2 or JG 26, the two German units, that with various reinforcements from other *Jagdgeschwader*, were to 'hold the line' against Allied daylight incursions of the continent until well into 1944.

Numerous Messerschmitt Bf 109s, in F and G model form, would also be put up against P-47 groups. A fighter renowned for its high-altitude qualities, the Bf 109 had the measure of the early Thunderbolts in this respect but it shared the American aircraft's slightly poorer performance at the lower altitudes where both types fought on more or less equal terms. But as was always the case in fighter versus fighter combat, so much depended on the skills of the opposing pilots that mere comparisons often meant little. The point was that all three fighters were basically very sound designs with a performance well up to the standards prevailing in 1943. It was the human factor and tactics that usually made the difference.

In terms of armament, despite the Germans' use of heavier calibre guns, American pilots found that the battery of eight 0.50-in Browning machine-guns was more than adequate against both the Bf 109G and FW 190A. Capable of an outstanding performance, particularly in its rate of roll, the FW 190 was the more agile and heavily armed element of the crack German fighter duo. Yet even though the FW 190 generally carried two 20mm cannon and four 7.9mm machine-guns, the cannon were relatively slow firing with a modest number of rounds while the machine-guns used rounds only marginally heavier than those of rifle calibre. In comparison, American machine-guns were of a calibre that slotted between a light machine-gun and a cannon; more importantly in combat terms was the fact that the pilot could pump them out in a steady

*Although the P-47 was not quite the Spitfire replacement pilots of the 4th Group expected, Thunderbolts helped build the group's early reputation. At Debden in 1943 a 336th Squadron line-up included P-47D-6 VF-O Donnie Boy, the personal aircraft of Don Gentile coded VF-T (42-8659) a P-47C-2. Nearest the camera is the P-47 subsequently flown by 'Red Dog' Norley, although here it is clearly the earlier mount of another pilot. Unfortunately the full name is unreadable. (U.S.A.F)*

and often deadly stream with a 'spread' better than that of the FW 190. Mixed armour-piercing and incendiary rounds were usually loaded into the wing troughs of the P-47 with tracer as required for visual sighting purposes. Ammunition mixes could be varied at the descretion of individual pilots.

If the P-47 pilot learned the vital lessons of using short economical bursts, could use a reflector sight properly, judge range correctly – and get in close enough – he could often obtain enough lethal hits on either of the German fighter types to send it down. Nobody ever said it was easy but the 'fan of fire' possible with the M2 Brownings often was enough to at least inflict damage and deter an enemy pilot, perhaps unnerve him enough to feel it prudent to break off combat and land. If his machine had been damaged, and he failed to get airborne again in time to attack the bombers, then the whole point of the exercise had more or less been achieved.

In the early days of fighter escort to the Eighth's heavy bombers German pilot quality was such that the choice to indulge in fighter versus fighter combat could often be dictated by the *Jagdwaffe*. It was bombers they wanted, not American fighters, if there was the luxury of choice. Of course 'flyer's luck' might desert

individual *Experten*. If they, the cream of the pre-war trained *Luftwaffe*, were killed or incapacitated and their leadership qualities denied to the less experienced, then the American bomber crews' passage would be that much safer. And more importantly, the gradual weakening of the *Luftwaffe* would eventually work against the fighter force as its commitments in other theatres of war grew.

But even as the 4th Group landed from that milestone first mission, which did not seem much like that at the time, the victorious pilot, Don Blakeslee, was still less than enthusiastic about his mount. Learning that the 190 kill had been made in a dive, the public relations men asked the 4th's boss to elaborate, leading Blakeslee to comment that the P-47 'ought to dive – it certainly couldn't climb'. It was the 4th that dubbed the P-47 the '7-ton milk bottle' and this monicker soon turned into 'milk jug' then simply, 'Jug'. Other 4th Group pilots grew to like the Republic monster but Don Blakeslee remain unconvinced.

And there was a debit side to the 10 March mission. Three P-47s failed to return. One was shot down and the loss of two others was attributed to engine failure, the first of several experienced by Thunderbolt groups during this early period of operations. The prime

31

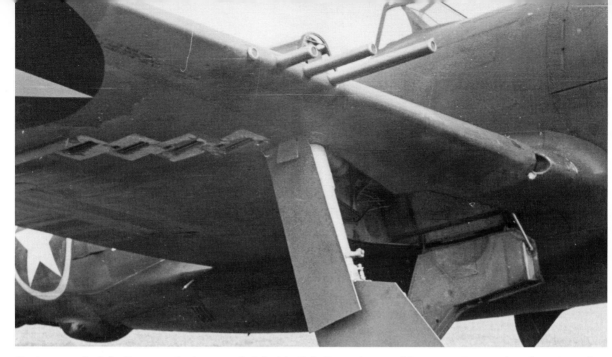

*Business end of the P-47 was its battery of eight M2 Colt-Browning machine-guns. Even reduced to six or four guns the aircraft remained lethal to almost any adversary. Spent shell cases exited through the four underside wing slots.*

cause was traced to pilots selecting incorrect engine pressure settings which brought about high manifold temperatures that could in turn lead to catastrophic failure of cylinders or pistons. In the excitement of combat, pilots were understandably apt to select wrong settings that could ultimately wreck an engine and it was seen that any effective remedy had to be automatic rather than manual. Republic consequently embarked on a series of system modifications to prevent pilots selecting a dangerously high manifold boost by mistake.

In April 1943, the first examples of the better armoured P-47D-1 models arrived in Britain. On the 13th of the month, both the 56th and 78th Groups flew their first 'official' operational missions following a number of theatre orientation flights, so by the end of April VIII Fighter Command had around 120 operational P-47s on hand. Preparations were made to send the embryo P-47 groups on their first full bomber escort mission.

### ESCORT DEBUT
On 4 May 1943, all three P-47 groups made up a force of 117 aircraft, the 4th and 56th flying cover to three groups of B-17s attacking targets in the Antwerp area while the 78th shepherded Liberators and Fortresses on a diversionary raid in the vicinity of Paris. It was recorded as the first *Ramrod* for both the 56th and 78th Groups. Although these R.A.F. operational codenames were convenient, the fact that they were numbered consecutively from the days when only British operations were flown meant they were getting a little confusing, particularly as the Americans had not yet flown missions into double figures. During the last weeks of April, U.S.A.A.F. fighter sweeps had been recorded as *Rodeos* 204, 208 and 211. Eighth Fighter Command reverted to logging fighter missions by Field Orders and 4 May's activity was otherwise more conveniently abbreviated to F.O. 10.

The 4 May mission alerted the *Luftwaffe*, which appeared in modest strength. One German fighter was claimed as a victory by a 4th Group pilot and one P-47 was listed as missing in action (M.I.A.) when it went down into the sea. No B-17s or B-24s were lost to enemy fighter attack – although as was becoming usual whenever the *Luftwaffe* engaged and the heavies opened fire, claims for ten enemy aircraft shot down were filed by bomber gunners.

It was 14 May before the 78th from Duxford scored its first victory, while escorting bombers attacking targets in the Antwerp area.

The honour went to Maj James Stone, 83rd Fighter Squadron C.O., who was credited with the first of five Focke-Wulf 190s shot down that day. The 83rd's Capt Elmer McTaggart nailed another, as did Capt Robert Adamina of the 82nd Squadron to make it three for the Duxford group.

Don Blakeslee despatched his 190 north of Knocke and 1st Lt Aubrey Stanhope (335th F.S.) made it two for the Eagles. Five probables and nine damaged claims filed by pilots from all three groups were officially allowed, all the opposing German fighters being FW 190s. Unfortunately, this success was offset by the fact that three Thunderbolts were lost, all of them from the 78th Group.

Early bomber escort missions were interspersed with fighter sweeps. These could have various objectives, including being of a diversionary nature designed to draw the *Luftwaffe* away from activity elsewhere. Eighth Fighter Command also sent fighters on high-altitude patrols designed to catch *Jagdwaffe* formations forming up prior to the arrival of the heavies in a particular sector. Such operations yielded a handful of victories for the P-47s and almost inevitably losses, not all of which were the result of enemy action. Accidents were a part and parcel of combat operations and these would continue to be a source of fluctuating aircraft readiness rates although the P-47 was no worse in this regard than any other type.

The Germans now showed some signs of intercepting fighter sweeps whereas before they appeared to be conserving their fighter strength solely for the bomber force, but enemy reaction remained unpredictable. Fighter groups would fly missions with little or no sign of German fighters in one sector whereas other American formations might have a tough time, having run into substantial numbers of *Luftwaffe* aircraft, all of which appeared to be flown by the cream of the *Jadgwaffe*.

It was surprisingly easy to miss rendezvous points, even with large formations of heavy bombers. It was just as easy to bypass a large-scale air battle if it was just out of range and taking place over a cloud-shrouded point of the continental land mass which was still relatively unfamiliar to most U.S.A.A.F. pilots. Some participants wondered how they could possibly have missed such action when they were flying over a similar area at much the same time but it continued to occur.

When the *Luftwaffe* did appear, numerous Thunderbolt pilots were legitimately able to open fire. Even if they hit nothing, letting off the battery of fifties at the enemy for the first time was a milestone every novice fighter pilot had to pass. If he inflicted some damage on the enemy, that was an important boost to his confidence which helped him to lose the apprehension that was naturally felt by almost every man before experiencing combat.

But even if nothing came of the resulting actions and losses on both sides remained light, the pace of the bomber offensive and the German reaction to it was gradually increasing. On 13 May, VIII Bomber Command

*Fighter affiliation for the new P-47 groups in the E.T.O. included mock combat with the two principal German fighters, examples of which were maintained by the R.A.F. This view shows one of the 56th Group's 63rd Squadron P-47s racing an FW 190A-4. (P. Jarrett)*

*Far more pro the P-47 than its 4th Group rival, Hub Zemke's 56th assumed the racy nickname 'Wolfpack' and went on to get the best aerial victory ratio of any fighter group in the E.T.O. Aircraft of the 62nd Squadron were photographed during a formation practice with an accompanying Liberator in the spring of 1943. (U.S.A.F.)*

strength was doubled when the 4th Bomb Wing with B-17s began operations. In addition, the 3rd Wing, flying B-26 Marauders, also made its combat debut. Fighter escort had become an integral part of this substantial daylight striking force and it too would continue to grow in strength.

## THUNDERBOLT BACK-UP

As increasing numbers of new P-47s arrived in England, older, less capable models were used, in common with other first-line aircraft types in the E.T.O. and elsewhere, for a host of second-line duties. Aircraft were always in demand for training, routine patrols and searches for airmen downed in the sea, and individual pilots invariably built up their flying hours by volunteering for such sorties. Later on, war weary P-47Ds were used for a more direct search and rescue role in the E.T.O. when specially equipped fighters joined the 5th Emergency Rescue Squadron at Boxted.

More aggressive fighter patrols were also flown by the Eighth's combat groups. These were usually devoid of any bomber-protection element and to some pilots were a welcome break from routine. They tended to be either very small – half a dozen aircraft was quite common – or the Thunderbolts would go out as part of a large joint force with R.A.F. fighters. These missions were often very substantial. On 7 June 1943 VIII Fighter Command dispatched 143 P-47s to join Spitfires in engaging enemy fighters in the Pas-de-Calais area. No enemy fighters were

seen by any of the participating pilots.

Such missions were nevertheless useful in that they fostered the already good level of cooperation between the R.A.F. and the U.S.A.A.F. and they certainly helped to reduce the grim incidents accruing from faulty aircraft recognition. There were numerous wartime losses to friendly fire on both sides. Although it was a problem that was never completely cured, joint service operations could not but help American pilots, many of whom were used to flying in the wide, open spaces back home, understand that some parts of U.K. airspace were getting mighty crowded with people who were all on the same side.

During May 1943, a more formalised Thunderbolt pilot 'school' was established at Atcham near Shrewsbury to act as an Operational Training Unit to speed through pilots newly arrived from the U.S. in operational procedures unique to the European theatre. P-47C and D models were used by the component 551st and 552nd Fighter Squadrons and the unit eventually trained many thousands of pilots from the Eighth and Ninth Air Forces.

Although A.A.F. pilots arrived in the U.K. well able to handle a combat aircraft, the Atcham course was equally important – if not more so – in honing the vital skills, passing on that extra 'ten per cent' they would need in combat. The course also ensured that front-line groups got replacement pilots who needed the very minimum time to become effective additions to the fighting team.

# 4
# Summer Aces

On 12 June 1943, the 56th Group broke a period of little action with a single aerial victory. The Wolfpack sent out forty-eight aircraft with forty-eight from the 4th on a high altitude sweep of the Blankenberge-Calais area. It was one of two similar fighter missions of the day, the second being handled by the 78th. Fighter units were by that time generally sending out morning and afternoon missions, primarily to offer the bombers penetration and withdrawal support.

Few enemy fighters were seen but Capt Walter Cook shot down an FW 190 to record the group's first confirmed kill. When Cook fired at the Focke-Wulf from 300 yards' range, the results were spectacular – hits along its nose were followed by sections of the left wing breaking away. This was believed to have been part of the aileron. The American's fire in all probability killed the German pilot, for he did not appear to take any evasive action. The Focke-Wulf was last seen in a dive, described by eye witnesses as 'uncontrollable'.

The following day, the Wolfpack scored again. Hub Zemke, at the head of the 61st Squadron, swept the Gravelines-Bailleul-Knoke area and came up on a section of four FW 190s of 10/JG 26. Zemke turned the number four German fighter into a ball of flame, fishtailed his rudder to slide behind number three but transferred his position to the number two 190 which presented a better target. Another huge sheet of flame left little doubt that that particular fighter would never fly again. Robert S. Johnson, then a 2nd Lieutenant, opened his personal record in similar spectacular fashion. A 3-second burst promptly exploded his victim which fell northwest of Ypres.

A week of low-key sweeps followed during which the Thunderbolts continued to suffer a number of annoying malfunctions, particularly radio interference, engine troubles and, more seriously, malfunctioning guns. The latter problem tended to be traced to jammed rounds, there being a number of items such as rivet heads and a protruding separator mechanism in the original gun bay design that needed minor modification at unit level.

The *Luftwaffe* had long been wise to the pilot and aircraft attrition that could be suffered from intercepting Allied fighter sweeps and the *Jagdflieger* often chose simply to stay on the ground when American escorts were over the continent. But on 22 June, there was more action when all three P-47 groups flew to bring the bombers back from the Antwerp area. Both the 4th and 78th Groups were in the right place and the boys came home with four and three victories respectively. The Duxford Thunderbolts scored one more on 24 June during another sweep.

American pilots were getting to know full well how tough a fighter the P-47 was and, on 26 June, at least one German pilot, again from JG 26, realised the fact, too. Having staged through Manston to top up the tanks, the Wolfpack put forty-nine aircraft over the continent. After a long pursuit during which he repeatedly tried to shoot Robert Johnson's badly damaged P-47C (41-6235) out of the sky, the FW 190 pilot finally gave up, his ammunition exhausted. Johnson made a successful three-point landing and examined his machine. Both pilot and groundcrew were amazed at how much punishment the P-47's airframe had absorbed while continuing to fly. Cannon shells and machine-gun bullets had jammed the canopy of the Thunderbolt, had ripped into the armour plate, and generally torn up the wings, tail and fuselage. Bob

Johnson reckoned he never had a closer call in his entire combat career.

He went on to reach ace status in October. In his first few months on operations, Johnson flew various 'personal' Thunderbolts, including the P-47C-2, C-5, D-5 and D-10. Serviceability obviously reflected the state of flight line availability of particular aircraft to the extent that pilots occasionally flew a slightly older model if their regular aircraft was off the roster for some reason.

Incidentally, the 56th Group's other famous Johnson, Jerry W., began combat in a P-47D-1, then flew a number of missions in an older C-5 – and this was far from untypical. One of the other reasons for switching aircraft subtypes was that squadron pilots often flew the first available machine. If it happened to be the regular mount of someone else who might have been away on leave and it failed to return, there was nothing anyone could do about it. But groundcrews did try to ensure that individual aircraft assigned to pilots were available because it quickly became common knowledge that no two aircraft from a mass production line handled exactly the same – indeed, there could be quite marked differences that an experienced pilot would notice. Other machines would exhibit inherent problems, probably only minor and merely irritating in themselves, which nevertheless could cause a slight, highly unwelcome distraction in combat.

Apart from the gratifying air combat success, 26 June was a black day for the 56th, one that transpired to be the second worst of the war in terms of pilot losses for the group. Four pilots were killed in combat with II/JG 26, five aircraft were lost and a sixth P-47 was damaged beyond repair. Losses had to be accepted and, to lessen their impact, there were positive signs that the American fighter force in England was gradually gaining strength, giving it out to the *Luftwaffe* about as much as it was taking. On 29 June VIII Fighter Command was delighted to announce that Capt Charles London of the 78th Group had become the first P-47 ace in the E.T.O.

London made ace by shooting down two Bf 109s (the only two German aircraft to go down during the day's mission) attempting to attack the heavies which were out after airfield and marshalling yard targets in France. London

was flying his personal P-47C-5 (41-6335) named *El Jeepo*. In contrast to other pilots, he was able to fly that one aircraft throughout his tour with the 78th.

With the first few months of combat behind them, the Eighth Air Force's Thunderbolt pilots were much more aware of the capabilities of their 'ship'. They now knew what it could do and could look the doubters squarely in the eye. That said, many of them were sceptical of Republic and Wright Field technical directives which seemed too conservative in their estimates of how the P-47 would perform in combat. In particular, the official fuel consumption figures did not tally with what the pilots were getting on missions and it became widely believed throughout the operational squadrons that if the technical manuals had been followed to the letter, the aircraft would hardly have had enough fuel to fly a fighter sweep, let alone bomber escort.

Experience had also proved that better understanding of engine operation, particularly low rpm and high manifold settings, increased range, if only by a few miles. Pilots came to realise that if they did not take these things to heart they could, at best, face a long ride home after being fished out of the sea.

In general, the P-47 groups enjoyed high morale, none more so than the 78th. Energetically led by Col Arman Peterson, the former P-38 group had taken to the P-47 and successfuly clashed with the *Luftwaffe*'s best. And claiming the first ace in the tough combat arena of the E.T.O. did nothing to dimish that infectious American eagerness. But the 78th Group's confidence was adversely affected on 1 July when Peterson was lost. At 29,000 feet over Holland, the group C.O. called in a flight of FW 190s and dived to attack. None of the enemy aircraft were apparently hit on that first pass and Peterson made a zoom climb into the sun, supposedly for another try. Then his Thunderbolt (42-7948) simply disappeared.

The worst aspect of the affair was that no other pilot really saw what happened to Peterson. Despite the pilots carrying out a thorough search of the area of the North Sea where his Thunderbolt had probably gone in, nothing more was ever heard of the popular group C.O.

## MORE VISION

Combat operations had revealed some of the drawbacks associated with the P-47 but the aircraft was generally proving to be reliable. The groundcrews won high praise for their airframe repair work and technical expertise in keeping the mighty Pratt & Whitney radials running smoothly. From their standpoint, Republic's big baby was healthy enough — provided it was nurtured carefully and constantly monitored for any sign of malfunction.

From the pilots' viewpoint, the high razorback rear fuselage of the early model P-47s created a 20° blind spot immediately aft. This was partially overcome by fitting rear-view mirrors to the windscreen framing. But in the spring of 1943 the opportunity arose to significantly improve the view from the P-47's cockpit. In England, Hawker Aircraft had developed a teardrop-shaped 'bubble' canopy for the Typhoon to similarly overcome the poor view aft on early production aircraft. A pattern canopy was shipped to the U.S., presumably as a separate item, as a complete Typhoon (MN235) was not sent across the Atlantic for evaluation until 24 March 1944. The canopy may well have been part of an exchange, for Napier received some useful American machine tools for use with the troublesome sleeve valves of the Typhoon's Sabre engine at about the same time.

The canopy was fitted to P-47D-5-RE (42-8702) which was redesignated the XP-47K; the Typhoon and P-47 were not too dissimilar in terms of size and the fuselage contours in the cockpit area of both fighters was close enough to enable Republic to test-fit the bubble canopy. Some reshaping along the lower edge of the canopy was necessary for a snug fit on the slimmed down Thunderbolt fuselage but the work was completed without delay.

The XP-47K first flew in its new configuration during July 1943 and test pilot

*Along with white theatre identification bands to prevent them being mistaken for the FW 190, the Eighth's P-47s were soon adorned with names and artwork as pilots personalised the aircraft they flew regularly. This P-47C-2 of the 63rd F.S. was the mount of Lt W.J. O'Connor with his wolf mascot* Slipstream. *(U.S.A.F.)*

*For all its enthusiasm and effort, the 56th had to concede first ace honours to the third P-47 group in the Eighth Air Force, the 78th at Duxford. This 83rd F.S. machine was pictured at Ridgewell, Essex, home to the B-17s of the 381st B.G., during 1943. Fighters put down at bomber bases for a variety of reasons, but tactics conferences and weather diversions were the most common. (via Ron McKay)*

reports showed a vast improvement over the razorback in terms of vision. Republic introduced the 360°-view canopy on the P-47D production line, beginning with the 1700th airframe. This and all subsequent aircraft did not receive a new model number but remained P-47Ds, the -25 production blocks onwards having the bubble canopy. The new model was to have been the P-47L but in the event only one experimental aircraft was so designated and Republic's next P-47 model letter was M, the penultimate version.

Recontouring the P-47D's fuselage centre section enabled the manufacturer to increase the capacity of the main fuel tank from 205 U.S. gal to 270 U.S. gal, which was a worthwhile gain. To offset that was the fact that the loss of fuselage depth aft of the cockpit could occasionally lead to reduced directional stability, causing the airflow to break away. It did not appear to be a universal problem but one that seemed only to arise with individual P-47s. To overcome the problem, Republic developed a slim dorsal fin section that fitted in front of the fin leading edge and ran forward to approximately the position of the radio mast, effectively filling the gap created by the down-curve towards the fin of the recontoured fuselage. Dorsal fins were incorporated during production on the P-47D-35 and D-40.

**MORE RANGE**
In the E.T.O. range remained the big challenge and VIII Fighter Command was exploring ways to overcome this major stricture on its operations over the continent. Instructing pilots to nurse their engines and follow proven procedures to obtain maximum fuel economy was good advice as far as it went but such careful husbandry was not — and for obvious reasons could not — always be followed. The easiest way to boost range was to position the fighters as close as possible to Europe and forward airfields on the English coast began to be used on a regular basis.

Manston was the nearest to the enemy coast and became the Eighth Air Force's main diversionary airfield. It was well equipped to replenish the internal fuel load of a P-47, which was burned at 100 gallons an hour in cruising flight. As combat manoeuvring quickly raised consumption to 300 gallons an hour, the topping up process was very useful. From Manston, fighters were well positioned to fly to their bomber rendezvous points in France, while the airfields located in East Anglia were used for escort missions to Holland and later Germany.

Taking off with full tanks gave the Thunderbolts the maximum time on the other side of the Channel — but this was still measured in minutes if fuel burn was raised by air combat. Having each P-47 carry more fuel on every mission was the only real answer. But developing suitable fuel tanks to boost the range of the P-47 took a considerable time and it was not until 28 July 1943 that the A.A.F. could announce that single-seat fighters had penetrated the airspace over the Reich. Admittedly the groups involved had not been able to fly very far into Germany but early results showed that this was more than compensated for by the element of surprise they had achieved.

On that date, the 4th's P-47Ds had carried an early type of flush-fitting belly tank which theoretically held 200 gallons of fuel. In reality, these unpressurised, U.S.-manufactured tanks leaked badly in some instances and others were found to transfer fuel correctly only at altitudes below 20,000 feet. But even if their capacity was considerably less than the maximum, every gallon helped and, by utilising careful throttle settings, the leading aircraft on the mission were able to reach and cross the German border in the vicinity of Emmerich. Flying a morning withdrawal support mission with their bulbous fuel tanks, quickly nicknamed 'babies', the Eagles surprised the *Luftwaffe*.

The bombers they were briefed to link up with were nowhere to be seen but another group of B-17s was soon spotted, being badly harassed by forty-five to sixty enemy fighters. The 4th again took on the FW 190s of JG 26, the battle plan being for the Americans to position P-47s above, below and in front of the Forts to block the *Jagdflieger*'s carefully selected intercept paths. Two FW 190s were shot down in the air battle that gradually took the B-17s out of harm's way near the German border and across The Netherlands. A milestone of considerable significance had been achieved by VIII Fighter Command.

To make belly tanks more efficient, the redoubtable Cass Hough developed a pressurisation system that utilised the exhaust from the Thunderbolt's vacuum pump. Using 75 gal metal teardrop tanks developed for the P-39, this system successfully transferred fuel at altitude and enabled the P-47D to operate 280 miles from England. First operational use of these tanks came on 22 August when the 4th flew the day's mission with the teardrop tanks attached to B-7 racks.

Arranging the delivery of enough P-39-type tanks from America initially proved difficult and a paper-composite tank, based on that designed for Hawker fighters, was produced in England by Bowater-Lloyd. These 108 gal cigar-shaped tanks enabled P-47s to penetrate Europe to a distance of about 325 miles.

If the early P-47 models had drawbacks, they – and all other Thunderbolts – had one asset that endeared them to fighter pilots: an unparalleled ability to destroy enemy aircraft. Eight 0.50-in machine-guns represented a broadside which was more than enough to inflict fatal damage on the lighter FW 190s and Bf 109s on numerous occasions.

Encouraging as the first P-47 operations were, A.A.F. planners issued some operational orders that tended to restrict pilots' freedom of action. Perhaps mindful of the fact that the *Luftwaffe* fighter force based in northwestern Europe outnumbered the total strength of the trio of first-line Thunderbolt groups by approximately three to one, orders were issued for the U.S. fighters to stay with the bombers at all times and not to operate much below 18,000 feet. Pilots appreciated that the bomber crews felt far more comfortable if they could actually see American fighters but, equally, they felt that such tactics handed the initiative too much to the enemy and ignored the dictum that the best form of defence is attack.

A broader interpretation of the orders than had been intended was therefore soon condoned by squadron and group commanders. It was not a new problem and escorts and escorted had to reach a compromise until later in the war when there were enough U.S.A.A.F. fighters to maintain station in set height bands in relation to the bombers for the entire mission.

Two days after the 4th's first incursion into German airspace, the 78th got into the thick of the action with, it is believed, fighters of JG 1 and experienced the almost hand-in-hand jubilation and sadness of war. On the positive side, Eugene Roberts came home with a score of three, the first triple to be scored by a pilot in VIII F.C. Quince Brown achieved another first by carrying out a portentious strafing attack *en route* home to Duxford – and another 78th C.O., Lt-Col Melvin F. McNickle, was lost by the group hardly before he had any chance to make his mark. It took relatively little for a group to believe that such ill luck would continue to dog it and adhere in the form of a jinx. Having lost two commanders in a matter of weeks, the 78th began to wonder.

## QUARTET OF GROUPS

In August 1943, a fourth P-47 group, the 353rd arrived in the U.K. to occupy Metfield in Suffolk. The group comprised the 350th, 351st and 352nd Squadrons, and, by mid-month, it had completed its first shakedown missions. Hub Zemke had led the group on the first sweep, with Philip Tukey taking the second. Group C.O. Joe Morris, headed up the third mission on 14 August, it being none too soon at that point in the bomber offensive to have new fighter groups operational.

On the 16th, there was a curtain-raiser to the main event on the following day, the first anniversary of the Eighth Air Force's first daylight raid on Europe. No less than 180 P-47s from the 4th, 56th and 353rd Groups flew to rendezvous with the bombers over the Elbeuf, a northwestern suburb of Paris. The 353rd was briefed to stick close to the bombers but the pilots reacted quickly to an initial interception by ten FW 190s plus Bf 109 'singles' and 'doubles' whose target was obvious. A running fight developed between the P-47s and both types of German fighter

over the French capital and its outskirts – which must have given heart to those Parisians who appreciated which side was getting the worst of things.

Col Morris was among the pilots who was credited with a 'damaged' FW 190 that day, as was future ace Glenn Duncan of the 352nd Squadron. But Morris was flying one of three P-47s which failed to return. He had last been seen diving after a 190. Another latched on to his tail but was shooed away by the C.O.'s wingman who pulled up with plenty of altitude to spare. When he looked around, Morris's Thunderbolt was nowhere to be seen. Morris survived the crash of his P-47 and eventually returned home.

The day's combat honours went almost entirely to the 4th. Among the victors were Howard 'The Deacon' Hively who got a 190, Jim Goodson who came home with two FW 190s destroyed plus a damaged, and a damaged claim against a Bf 109 was confirmed for one Don Salvatore Gentile, about whom more – much more – would be heard later.

Joe Matthews of the 4th crashed, evaded capture and later got back to Debden to have his kill confirmed, while the sole 56th loss, George Spaleny, was made a P.o.W. Final figures of eighteen destroyed, one probable

*A standard P-47D of the 353rd Fighter Group bearing the short-lived red outline to the national insignia. The aircraft, from the 350th Squadron, carried one of the first belly tanks issued to the Metfield, Suffolk-based group.*

and eight damaged made the 16 August Paris show one of the best days so far for the Eagles.

## DOUBLE STRIKE

On 17 August, the first anniversary of the start of A.A.F. daylight bomber operations from England, the bold 'double strike' on factories at distant Schweinfurt and Regensburg was laid on. A milestone in more ways than one, it was the deepest incursion into the Third Reich that VIII Bomber Command had yet attempted, the targets lying far beyond effective fighter escort range.

American fighters would cover the initial stages of the mission and protect the bombers during the last few hundred miles as they come home to their English bases. Accordingly, the 56th was part of a maximum effort of no less than 240 P-47s which flew to provide penetration, general and withdrawal support. Hub Zemke had fifty group aircraft under his command as he flew at the head of the 62nd F.S. Taking off at 09.22, the fighters made their first crossing of the German border at Eupen in Belgium and about an hour later they picked up the B-17s *en route* to blast the Messerschmitt plant at Regensburg.

From 26,000 feet, the fighter pilots watched their 'Big Friends' fly on. There was nothing more they could do to protect them from what everyone knew was to come. At least those particular B-17s would not have to face the ordeal of the *Jagdwaffe*'s wrath twice over the main hotspots of Germany and Holland for Zemke's fighters had covered that part of the force which was bound, after bombing one of the principal Bf 109 assembly lines, for North African bases. Back on the ground, the fighter pilots would have several hours to 'sweat-out' take-off time to cover the withdrawal.

This second mission of the day took the form of a *Ramrod* that combined the aircraft of the 56th and 353rd Groups to cover the withdrawal of the Schweinfurt force. It took off at 15.20 with Zemke again leading the 62nd Squadron, Capt Francis S. Gabreski the 61st, and Philip Tukey the 63rd, a total of fifty-one aircraft.

Belly tanks were dropped from 20,000 feet near Antwerp at 16.05 hours and the Thunderbolt formation climbed to 26,000 feet. The bombers were met at 16.21 about 15 miles east of Eupen. They were still being attacked by enemy fighters. Weary bomber crews, shocked at the ferocity and duration of the *Luftwaffe*'s reaction to the long-range attacks, were mighty glad to see Thunderbolts primed to take some of the heat off, however long they had had to wait for them. Knowing why did not make the waiting any easier.

P-47s from all three Wolfpack squadrons positioned themselves above the B-17s, the U.S. pilots estimating the opposition at some fifty to sixty German fighters, mostly FW 190s and Bf 109s, although six Bf 110s were also observed. Some of them were using head-on attacks against the long-suffering Fortress crews, an attack profile that was widely reckoned to be absolutely deadly.

Such runs at high closure speeds took cool nerve on the part of the *Jagdflieger* but often paid dividends, their cannon and machine-gun fire invariably wrecking the bombers' engines and killing or incapacitating the flight crews. And, as the Eighth's then current Fortress combat model, the B-17F, was least well protected from head on attacks, the whole business carried a marginally smaller risk to *Jagdflieger* being shot down by return fire. Thus the timely intervention of the 56th saved many American lives, instrumental as it was in deflecting numerous German attacks.

If they succeeded in breaking up the German formations on their initial organised passes, the American fighter pilots – and the bomber crews – had to contend with repeated attacks by relatively small numbers of FW 190s and Bf 109s. Reforming in strength took the German fighters precious time and was rarely accomplished in the heat of an air battle. Having thus evened the odds a little, the American pilots bored in close to be certain of a kill, a tactic that paid dividends but took considerable nerve. Maintaining a collision course with an enemy aircraft until the last possible moment, with the assurance that the 'other fellow' would break first, seemed like a deadly game of chance, but it often succeeded. In personal terms, some of the future aces of the 56th did well on 17 August by claiming a box score of 17-1-9 (destroyed – probable – damaged).

The 353rd Group opened its score with one victory. Having flown its first full group mission (actually the third in the E.T.O. in which P-47s from Metfield had participated) on 14 August, the 353rd flew two more on the 13th and one on the 16th. To fill the gap created by the loss of Joe Morris, Maj Loren G. McCollom, Executive Officer of the 56th Group, transferred to Metfield to lead the 353rd. There were more enviable tasks than leading a group of men who had so recently lost a most popular C.O. on a mission that in anyone's appreciation was going to be rough. Fortunately 'Mac' was up to the challenge.

The 17 August mission was also the 353rd's first belly tank show and after the almost routine return to base of a few aircraft with malfunctioning tanks, McCollom led thirty-two Thunderbolts as withdrawal support for the bombers as they crossed the Belgian coast. 'Mac' set a fine example by nailing a Bf 109 at close range, 150 yards, the first confirmed air combat victory for the 353rd. An afternoon mission that day failed to find any enemy aircraft, a situation that would prevail for the Metfield Thunderbolts for three more missions. Few more forceful demonstrations of the urgency of 'all the way' fighter escort were needed than the epic Schweinfurt and Regensburg raids which despite part of the bomber force flying south and not having to face alerted defences a second time on the way home to England, sixty B-17s were lost to fighters and flak in the largest-scale air battle involving the A.A.F. in Europe to date.

In the final stages, the American fighter intervention spread the air battle from Liege to Antwerp, where R.A.F. Spitfire squadrons were able to wade into the mêlée while the P-47s, some now low on fuel and ammunition, headed home.

The 56th had the best day in terms of victories. Capt Gerald Johnson and Lt Frank McCauley gave an impromtu demonstration of Thunderbolt firepower when the 61st Squadron fell on one of the Bf 110 night fighters of I./NJG 1, ill-advisedly sent to intercept the bombers. Right over the last box of B-17s and totally out of their usual operational environment, the inexperienced night-fighter crew stood no chance. Hit simultaneously by streams of rounds from sixteen Browning guns, the 110 exploded. The pieces cascaded down through the B-17 formation and witnesses swore there was complete radio silence for about 30 seconds as every crewman aboard the Fortresses seemed to be watching the spectacle.

Gerry Johnson also caused his own ball of fire, in the centre of which was a Bf 109 that had been intent on the bombers. Hit at 200 yards' range, the Messerschmitt's light structure quickly succumbed to the broadside of Browning fire. Another 109 took a burst from the American's guns at half that distance, rolled over and went down. Lt Harold Comstock of the 63rd Squadron dispatched a Bf 109 and Capt Walker Mahurin, who exploded one FW 190, then shot down a second. Other pilots did well during the series of combats and, although three P-47s failed to return, the 56th was well satisfied with its box score.

August 1943 was been a busy month for VIII Fighter Command as it also saw two more P-47 groups, the 352nd based at Bodney, Norfolk and the 355th at Steeple Morden, Herts preparing to make their combat debut. At the same time three fighter Wings, the 65th, 66th and 67th, were formed to control fighters in the air. Most importantly, with P-47s now equipping six groups, there were enough fighters and pilots available for the combat units to split their strength and fly relay missions in two subgroups. This not only enabled multiple missions to be launched on a single day but it spread combat experience across all pilots in the group relatively quickly. Rotation of leadership slots in the formations also created more able flight and element leaders so that the loss or incapacity of commanders on operations would not create a crisis. Individual pilot fatigue was also reduced.

Bob Johnson of the 56th scored his second kill on 19 August, and 'Gabby' Gabreski opened his own personal account with the enemy five days later. That day, the 78th again upstaged the Wolfpack and the Eagles by taking the honour of having the second P-47 ace in the Eighth Air Force when Eugene Roberts came home with a FW 190 to his credit. Any striving the rival groups felt they had do to catch up and pass this record by the Duxford Thunderbolts was grist to the publicity mill.

## PRODUCTION EXPANDS

With the general success of the P-47 on escort operations in northern Europe, A.A.F. chiefs moved to ensure that sufficient numbers of new aircraft would be allocated to further

*Another Ridgewell visitor, this P-47D hailed from the 352nd Squadron, 353rd Group, based at Metfield. (via Ron McKay)*

groups destined to serve in the theatre. Combat attrition and accidents also demanded a steady flow of replacement Thunderbolts to the fighting units stationed overseas and to meet this demand Republic had opened a new plant at Evansville, Indiana. This and the Curtiss Wright plant at Buffalo had begun producing P-47s in December 1942 and, approximately one year later, the Republic company and its subsidiaries were completing 660 Thunderbolts per month, a daily average of twenty machines every working day.

There was little external difference between P-47Ds built by Republic and Curtiss, the latter being identified by the suffix G, and 354 examples were completed by March 1944, a fairly slow production rate. Most P-47Gs, which were built in five blocks, were assigned to training units in the U.S. and two G-15s were converted to two-seat trainers.

By the late summer of 1943, the Eighth Air Force had achieved much in building a bomber force that was attacking the assigned targets and, it was believed, significantly damaging key areas of German industry. Its bombers had extended their reach and, while suffering some appalling losses, the gradual increase in the numbers that could be sent on each mission and the improvement in fighter escort range was gratifying. There remained

the problem of fighters accompanying the bombers right through to the target area and back, but this was being addressed.

Early September brought Gabreski's second victory (on the 3rd) and Walker Mahurin's third victim went down on the 9th, Bud having scored two on the 17 August mission.

All the groups participated in the 3 September mission which was to escort groups of heavies briefed to attack a variety of targets in France. The Wolfpack's four victory credits were the only ones of the day, the price being one aircraft lost. A sweep to Dunkirk in company with the 78th did not produce any results.

Despite a high level of fighter activity, most of September was markedly uneventful in terms of combat although a small number of fighters became casualties and there were numerous weather-related incidents. Then came the 23rd, a day of action for the 353rd. All Thunderbolt groups participated in an escort mission but only the Metfield group, which used Thorney Island as a forward base to give that much-needed extra combat time over enemy territory, saw the *Luftwaffe* close enough to score kills – five destroyed and two damaged for one P-47 downed by the end of the day's proceedings. Capt Walter Beckham and Maj Glenn Duncan each shot down a Focke-Wulf 190.

*When the red outline fell from favour, it was simply painted over with insignia blue but the outline usually showed through, as evident on* Babe *a P-47D of the 351st F.S., sequentially the second squadron of the 353rd Group at Metfield. (John Campbell)*

More limited action followed until the 27th when the Germans appeared to take great exception to the Eighth Air Force sending its bombers to Emden and the *Luftwaffe* reacted accordingly. The B-17s bombed on pathfinder signal and while the bombing concentration showed that there was much room for improvement this was also the first operational use of H2X radar in the Fortresses and was something of an experimental mission to see how the equipment performed. All six P-47 groups dispatched a total of 262 fighters and of these, the 78th claimed ten enemy aircraft, the 353rd eight, the 56th five and a single fell to the 4th for a combined box score of twenty-four destroyed, two probables and four damaged. Again, forward bases were used to advantage, with the 4th and 78th positioning from Hardwick and Hethel, and for the first time the P-47s used by these groups carried 108-gal U.S. drop tanks into battle.

October began to bring less favourable flying weather, which the E.T.O. old hands had coped with before. The first weeks of the month brought the Wolfpack's scores to a personal level that well reflected the pool of P-47 experience in the group, Dave Schilling, Bob Johnson, Francis Gabreski and Walker Mahurin all scoring confirmed victories. It was not before time that the most experienced Thunderbolt group announced that it had another ace and the honour soon fell on the shoulders of Walker Mahurin who knocked down his fourth, fifth and sixth kills on the 4th of the month. He was followed closely by Dave Schilling who shot down two on 10 October to claim the baseline five. Also fêted that day was Bob Johnson whose two kills gave him ace status.

Autumnal weather had its positive side. It brought a natural and welcome decrease in bomber sorties, as A.A.F. bomb aiming was still entirely visual and required clear visibility if targets were to be hit hard. Many fighter pilots and bomber aircrew welcomed a slackening of pace.

## ANOTHER DEBUT

Thunderbolts of the 355th Fighter Group were not alone in flying their combat debut on 9 September. The pilots, eager to put the first few missions behind them, were frustrated by the weather for some time. Everyone at Steeple Morden who needed to know realised that Maj Philip Tukey was on temporary reassignment from the 56th to give the new group a few helpful hints. When he appeared at briefing, they knew their first *Ramrod* was 'on'. It proved uneventful, take off having been delayed until 18.16 hours. It was the 14th before the 355th flew a *Rodeo*, again with Maj Tukey leading the 357th Squadron.

Joining the established Thunderbolt force on its Eighth Air Force debut mission on 9 September was the 352nd at Bodney. Led as was customary by an experienced officer from another group for its first few shakedown missions, in this case Lt-Col Harry Dayhuff of the 78th, the group had already achieved a high degree of readiness under Col Joe Mason's tutelage. And although the forty pilots were in the combat area merely to offer cover to the 56th and 353rd as they came in

over the English coast between Southwold and Felixstowe, the die was cast. A second operation later that day was cancelled due to the weather. It would be the 14th before the group operated again, flying two fighter sweeps on the same day.

Routine sweep followed sweep with no action for nearly two weeks for the 355th until on 24 September each of the squadrons was stood down for 48 hours to have their P-47s modified to take belly tanks. More P-47D-5s had arrived by 28 September, by which time the group inventory totalled seventy-six aircraft.

On 4 October, the 355th clashed with the *Luftwaffe* for the first time and although Lt Cully Ekstrom nailed a Bf 109, another pilot, shot up by an FW 190, crash-landed his P-47 with fatal results. October 1943 was generally a poor month in terms of flying weather and numerous missions were curtailed or cancelled. Fog kept the 355th on the ground on the 14th, the day of 'Second Schweinfurt' and another round of heavy bomber losses.

The month also saw the first two P-47 aces announced for the 4th when Duane Beeson and Roy Evans received that accolade. Both pilots made the record books on the 8th, Beeson's fifth and sixth victims being Bf 109s while Roy Evans's fifth was a Focke-Wulf. That day's mission was a success because the

*Tucking in close to the wing of a B-24, Lt Charles Reed in P-47D-10* Princess Pat *(42-75185/UN-X) of the 63rd F.S. sees his charge en route to a safe landing in England. Fighter pilots had to judge correctly such close formating, as a bomber slipstream could 'suck in' the fighter and cause a collision.*

4th's intervention and good teamwork broke up the enemy formations and prevented attacks on the bombers.

In the meantime, Phillip Tukey had bidden farewell to Hertfordshire and returned to Essex and the 56th and Lt-Col William Cummings, who had taken command of the 355th in January, assumed leadership of the group, a job he shared during the early days with Air Executive Officer Lt-Col Thomas Hubbard.

Bad weather anchored the 355th to Steeple Morden's hardstands for days on end during that dreary winter but November brought some success when the *Luftwaffe*, equally ground-bound for much of the time, finally appeared. Generally, the going was slow but typical, considering the weather, with a low level of bomber operations and relatively few chances for the fighter pilots to indulge in combat, right up to the end of the year. But this was valuable theatre experience, sometimes without the participants appreciating the fact, for the English weather could never be ignored in planning and executing fighter operations. The 355th would put its expertise to very good use in the coming months but its greatest success would be during a time when the main tool of the trade was the P-51 rather than the P-47.

The fighters escorted medium bombers as well as heavies during this period and the stage was set for some innovations in the deployment of fighters. High command enthusiasm for new ways to reduce the *Luftwaffe* fighter force in the E.T.O. soon led to P-47s flying the first fighter-bomber sorties.

Escort missions for the heavies continued to bring air combat success to Thunderbolt groups and on 5 November the 56th recorded its 100th kill. Not all of the groups found an equal amount of action, even over much the same area of enemy territory on the same day, and there were times when some pilots wondered how the other fellows did it.

The VIII Fighter Command force had been swelled again in August by the arrival of the P-47s of the 356th Group (comprising the 359th, 360th and 361st Squadrons) flying from Martlesham Heath and the 55th in September with P-38s. Both these groups flew their first missions on 15 October, the Thunderbolts of the 356th led by group commander Lt-Col Harold J. Rau, crossing the Belgian coast at Ostend and sweeping the Dutch islands.

The new group escorted B-26 Marauders on 22 October and on 1 November Martlesham was formerly handed over to the U.S.A.A.F. by the R.A.F. although a strong British presence remained. No. 56 Squadron operating Typhoons, continued to occupy part of the aerodrome, as did an A.S.R. detachment with Spitfires and Walrus amphibians.

The 356th's first live rounds were fired not at the *Luftwaffe* but at barges on the Zuider Zee. *En route* home on 3 November the boys caused little damage but a few holes in one pilot's wing showed everyone that this was the real thing. Hits on enemy aircraft were observed 48 hours later when the group drew a bomber escort. Near Gladbach, the P-47s' turn-back point, a brief dogfight enabled Paul Hyde and Bleftherios Vangos to observe hits on a Bf 109 and FW 190 respectively. The 356th had a new C.O. on 28 November, Lt-Col Einar Axel taking the reins when Harold Rau was transferred to a Wing job.

## CAPTURED THUNDERBOLT
Air combat over Europe obviously gave both the Americans and Germans an insight into the capabilities of each other's fighters, but there was no substitute for examination of a captured example. Sooner or later, complete examples of the main operational aircraft were bound to inadvertently change sides. Such machines were evaluated by test and service pilots to give front-line units valuable pointers to the strengths and weaknesses of the bombers and fighters regularly met in combat. Wrecked aircraft gave up some secrets but superficially damaged, otherwise complete examples that could be flown after minor repairs, were highly prized.

Many American pilots new to the E.T.O. were introduced to the Bf 109 and FW 190 which the R.A.F. maintained in flyable condition, and they had appreciated being able to examine their principal German adversaries at close hand and to fly in mock combat with them. No opportunity had, before the autumn of 1943, had been given to the *Luftwaffe* to fly a P-47 but as an increasing number were committed to combat by the Eighth Air Force there was little to prevent one eventually falling into German hands. This first occurred on 7 November 1943. The aircraft, a P-47D-5

(42-8477 named *Beetle*) belonging to the 355th Group, belly-landed near Caen, France, the inexperienced pilot having mistaken the area for southern England.

Ferried to the *Luftwaffe* test centre by Hans Werner Lerche, who had some anxious moments in determining what some of the controls were for, the new acquisition arrived at Rechlin on the 14th. Subsequent flights were generally conducted without mishap by a number of service and test pilots and the data gleaned included a glowing appraisal of the P-47D's excellent high-altitude capability, although the Germans confirmed what many Allied pilots already knew – the Thunderbolt could be a sluggish handful at heights below 15,000 ft. There is also some evidence that compressibility, albeit in a mild, precautionary form struck when Lerche was flying the aircraft, which actually saved his life. He became acutely aware of the deadly effects of oxygen starvation when the P-47 approached its Mach limit with a decidedly drowsy German at the controls.

*Beetle* was to lead an interesting career in the *Luftwaffe*; it probably survived the war and even got to star in a propaganda film. This Thunderbolt was joined by at least three others which were placed 'under new management', and flew a part of the *Sonderkommando* Rosarius, the *Luftwaffe*'s captured aircraft demonstration unit.

The second P-47 to fall into enemy hands was reportedly flown into Rome-Littorio airfield by a black pilot, which could only make it one of the aircraft issued to and flown briefly by the 332nd Group in Italy. This incident occured in May 1944 and the *Luftwaffe* was subsequently to acquire at least one other P-47D for evaluation. Other Thunderbolts inevitably went down in neutral countries as the air war widened in 1944, although few pilots ended up as guests of the Swiss or Swedes as the long-range escort task passed increasingly to the P-51.

As the newest P-47 outfit in the Eighth, the 356th rounded out a momentous year with combat figures of twenty-nine missions flown, six enemy aircraft claimed destroyed, two probables and five damaged for ten P-47s missing in action. Paul Hyde became one of the unfortunate victims in this last category when he collided with a B-24 during formation form-up on 20 December. The P-47 was apparently cut in half by the bomber's wing and the pilot was not seen to get out. Such accidents happened; the Thunderbolt was big and weighty but, caught in the propwash of a heavy bomber, it often stood little chance of avoiding a collision. Fortunately, such comings-together were not always fatal.

**A NEW ROLE**

By the autumn of 1943, a number of steps had been taken to determine the P-47's suitability as a fighter-bomber *per se*, both Hub Zemke and Mac McCollom of the 56th and 353rd respectively having ideas as to how best to deploy the P-47 in a more offensive role. The 353rd reckoned that dive-bombing had considerable merit, assuming that the whole thing would have to be done without the P-47s getting any custom-built sighting aids. It was not long before Metfield airfield began to reverberate with the whine of Thunderbolts practising a new method of reducing the *Luftwaffe*'s strength. Climbing to 18,000-20,000 feet, the pilots dropped 5000 feet before bomb release and pull out. The results seemed to offer a good chance of accurate bombing and a 'live' mission was laid on, a combined force from all the 353rd squadrons inaugurating another first for the Eighth Air Force on 25 November. The target chosen was St-Omer-Fort Rouge airfield.

McCollom led sixteen P-47s of the 351st Squadron, with escort to the bomb carriers provided by the 353rd's two other squadrons. The operational plan was fairly loose, the pilots being briefed to drop their single 500 lb demolition bombs in flights of four on the leader's command at whatever altitude he judged to be the best for useful hits to be obtained. Initiation of the dive was to be from at least 15,000 feet. Disaster struck early. Five miles south of the target, the initial point was passed when the flak started. The boys pressed on, with McCollom rolling into a turn to bring the target to bear. Then he was hit.

A burst got his main fuel tank, tore away part of the P-47's lower fuselage skin and wreathed the aircraft in flames. Time to get out. McCollom left an increasingly hot cockpit which caused him some painful burns and had a long, cool descent to earth. Immediately picked up by *Luftwaffe* personnel, he was to spend some time in hospital having his burns treated before confinement in *Stalag Luft* 1 for the duration of the war.

In the meantime, fourteen of the remaining P-47s dropped their bombs from 8000-10,000 feet. Most of them missed. Three hits were recorded and one pilot was forced to jettison his bomb. Flak damaged six aircraft and, if it had not been the most successful of missions, VIII Fighter Command and the 353rd had some useful practical information. The loss of Mac McCollom was a bitter blow to the entire group but Maj Glenn E. Duncan stepped in to fill the breach most admirably, preventing any damaging loss of morale.

A second experimental mission, intended as an alternative to dive-bombing, was also flown on the 25th, by the 56th Group. Mindful of the lack of a bombsight in his fighters, Hub Zemke reckoned that the answer could be to have them led into the target by a heavy bomber, which had all the sighting and navigational aids as standard equipment. Fighters releasing on a signal by a bombardier riding in a B-24 seemed a way around the problem. But the 56th's first mission was even more of a disappointment than that of the 353rd, as the Liberator crew failed to locate the target. On 4 December, dive-bombing was tried again.

Meanwhile, escort duty continued, albeit at a slightly slower pace compared to the summer months; fighter sweeps, patrols and A.S.R. searches were carried out and personnel assigned to the new groups in the E.T.O. came to terms with the advantages of their posting. While the European theatre was reckoned to be the toughest air front of all regarding the quality of the German opposition, the advantages of living in England compared favourably with any other A.A.F. location outside the U.S.A.

Quaint, rationed and different, definitely full of history and eccentrics, England appeared even a little backward to some young American fighter pilots. But there was no denying that when the weather brightened, it was a beautiful, comfortable place to be, with friendly people more than willing to share their meagre supplies with their cousins from across the ocean. Friendships made in those years endured long past the duration of the war and both nations were the better for that.

*Flights of P-47s in 'finger four' formation. This Luftwaffe-originated placing and spacing for fighters was generally adopted by U.S.A.A.F. groups during the war – and most other air forces since. (U.S.A.F.)*

### EARLY INTERCEPTION

Although the *Luftwaffe* fighter force commanders seemed slow to appreciate that if the *Jagdflieger* hit American escort fighters early enough into their escort mission they would remain a short-range threat due to having to drop their tanks too early, there was an operational requirement to have the evidence of heavy bombers brought down on German soil. An edict that originated with Hitler, it typically failed to appreciate the situation. But the U.S. escort was on occasion hit early, as shown on 11 December when Gabby Gabreski got hit while flying 42-7871, his second P-47D.

All the Thunderbolt groups were out on *Ramrods*, the 56th making a landfall over Tessel Island flying at 30,000 feet. Six thousand feet above, the Germans pounced out of the sun. Drop tanks were punched off and chaos ensued as the Bf 109s divided their forces to engage the 63rd Squadron and maintain a top cover. Although fighters were all over the sky, the 56th had no losses. Neither the 61st nor the 62nd clashed with the Messerschmitts and were not involved in the dogfight. As there was a bomber escort mission to complete, Dave Schilling did his best to marshal his forces and put both squadrons in contact with the bombers. One flight of the 63rd managed to disengage from the fighter mêlée and rendezvous with the bombers but the early bounce had left the P-47s short of fuel. All that could be done was to patrol over Leeuwarden to await any stragglers which might need help. One Bf 109 was claimed by Lt Stan Morell.

The 61st and 62nd had more success in warding off a substantial Messerschmitt Bf 109 reception committee for the bombers. Lt-Col Landry shot down one before the German single-seaters broke off, to be replaced by a trio of a Bf 110 and two Me 410s. Lt Glenn Schlitz made short work of one of the latter. Gone forever were the days when the German twins could attack the heavies without much fear of being destroyed; the survival rate for *Zerstörer* crews soon dropped below the point where they stood any practical chance against the American escorts.

In close fighter-versus-fighter combat the danger of collision was never far away and it is surprising perhaps that more pilots did not run into either friend or foe. As the 61st Squadron, led by Gabreski, initiated a diving attack on a group of enemy fighters, two Thunderbolts smashed into each other during a crossover manoeuvre. Both exploded at 30,000 ft and neither pilot had time to get out.

Gabreski completed the bounce and destroyed a Bf 110. Paul Conger got two 109s, Lt Robill Roberts's score was a Bf 110 plus two Ju 88s damaged, while Lt Sam Hamilton's 'bag' was two Bf 110s.

Lt Joe Powers, who shot down a Bf 109 and a 110, had nothing but praise for the vigilance of his wingman, Lt Marangello. Tasked with watching his leader's tail, the wingman rarely got an opportunity to score victories himself until he became the leader. There were numerous outstanding 'double acts' of this kind, one reason why the American aces had such a high survival rate. On this occasion, Marangello acted as Powers's eyes, for his P-47 had a decidedly rough-running engine. On the way home, a cracked cylinder threw oil all over the windscreen to obscure his vision, not a totally unique occurance with the

*Two 108-gal drop tanks on the wing racks took the P-47 into Germany on escort missions, but tactical targets in France for the Ninth Air Force prior to D-Day lay within normal range. Well decorated aircraft is P-47D-11 (42-75587)* Lil' Sunshine *of the 379th F.S., 362nd F.G.*

*When the time came, the P-47 proved to be a better load-carrier than any other single-seat U.S. fighter, lifting all that was necessary to knock out ground targets. Dive-bombing techniques paid a high dividend for pilots such as Capt Motzenbecker who flew this particular machine, weighed down with a 108-gal centre-line tank and two 500 lb bombs*

P-47's Pratt & Whitney. Powers, hardly able to see out, was safely escorted back to England.

Gabreski himself had a narrow escape; a burst of 20mm cannon fire had not only penetrated the Thunderbolt's supercharger but had all but demolished the right rudder pedal. Gabby had a bruised foot where the shell, fortunately all but spent, had torn open the pedal.

On 13 December, the 359th Group flew its first mission from East Wretham, an uneventful eleven-ship sweep of the St-Omer area. There followed, weather permitting, one bomber support and a fighter sweep until 22 December recorded the group's first mission with one of its own assigned headquarters pilots, Lt-Col Avelin P. Tacon, Jr leading. Maj Luther E. Richmond from the 352nd Group had guided the group through the first few sorties.

By the end of 1943, the Eighth's Thunderbolt groups had scored a total of 436 aerial victories; 136 P-47s had been lost on combat missions, seventy-nine of which were known to have previously been in contact with enemy fighters. Overall, this was a remarkable achievement, with the relative kill-loss figure being two thirds in the Americans' favour. The above figures are not a complete picture of some nine months of combat flying, however, in that they do not take into account P-47s written-off or damaged in accidents in England, nor indeed pilots killed or injured in such instances. Neither have the probable and damaged claims made against German fighters been included, these being substantial on some missions.

But the baseline month-by-month combat statistics proved a steadily rising rate of success in combat for the P-47: from ten kills in May to fifty-five in August and ninety-six in December. November was the best month, with 105 enemy aircraft shot down. While the increasing victory rate was partially reflected in new groups becoming operational, these had had little chance to boost the figures significantly before the end of the year. The lion's share understandably fell to the guns of the 4th, 56th and 78th. Most encouragingly, the combat figures pointed the way forward to an increasing ascendancy over the *Luftwaffe* fighter force and a better protected heavy bomber force.

# 5
# Down on the Deck

January 1944 opened for VIII Bomber Command much as 1943 had closed, with Thunderbolts continuing to protect the heavy bombers as far as their range allowed. Weather still adversely effected fighter operations, both new pilots and veterans alike realising that this was definitely the one big drawback to an assignment to the E.T.O.

Penetration support sorties remained quiet for the 359th Group into the early days of the month but on the 11th, Lt-Col Tacon led sixty-one P-47s on a withdrawal support in the vicinity of Bergen. Bomber rendezvous came almost immediately that nine German fighters were called in. These were chased away and the Thunderbolts shepherded the B-24s to Amsterdam before breaking off to pick up some B-17s. Keeping Me 410s away from their new charges, the East Wretham pilots were jumped by three Bf 109s and one P-47 went down while the trio of enemy fighters made good their escape. To end a less than satisfactory day, a 370th Squadron aircraft disappeared after being last seen entering a power dive, and two Thunderbolts crashed fatally in England on the return.

On 29 January, the 359th's first P-47 victory, a Bf 110, was shared by two pilots. Other victories and losses followed until 22 April 1944, which turned out to be the 359th Group's best day of its Thunderbolt period.

By November 1943, the delivery of P-47s to the United Kingdom, both to combat units and depots, had reached a peak of 1200 aircraft. The groups had a radius of action of 400-500 miles, the majority of aircraft being then able to carry a single external 150-gal tank under the fuselage or two 108-gal tanks on wing racks. Thunderbolts were also being modified to carry bombs on the wing pylons which would enable a far greater deployment of the type on ground attacks in 1944.

Thus far, the daylight bomber offensive from United Kingdom bases had met with moderate success; numerous targets had been hit and the *Jagdwaffe* had not succeeded in breaking up, much less destroying, a single combat box of B-17s or B-24s to the point that the target was abandoned through losses directly attributable to this one cause. Part of the reason was morale: the bomber crews appreciated the fighter support they were receiving and although they knew that the P-47s could not yet fly all the way to the targets, they had ample evidence of how the 'Little Friends' could 'take the heat off' whenever the opposing fighter forces met.

For their part, the fighter pilots were gradually whittling down the cream of the *Jagdwaffe*: it might have seemed to some individuals to be a slow process but it would not stop until the Allied pledge to purge the German tyranny had been achieved. And until armies of liberation could be put ashore on the continent, Europe would remain a front dominated by air power.

In January, the 361st Group occupied Bottisham to became the ninth and last P-47 group to join the Eighth Air Force. The 361st was in fact the tenth fighter group to be assigned to the Eighth, as, since 20 December 1943, the 358th Group based at Leiston in Suffolk had gone operational on escort duty. Commanded by Col Cecil L. Wells, the 358th's three squadrons, the 365th, 366th and 367th, were destined to fly only seventeen missions with the Eighth before being transferred to the Ninth Air Force.

The 353rd Group loaned Air Exec. Maj Ben Rimerman to help initiate the 361st to the challenges of the E.T.O. and to lead the first few shakedown missions. Delaying its debut until weather conditions were deemed to be favourable, the 361st pilots did not get their first look at the coast of France until the 15th when fifty-two P-47s, each fitted with a 108 gal belly tank, patrolled west of St-Omer. There were no incidents and all aircraft returned safely, eight P-47s having experienced the almost arbitrary technical problems.

One of the peripheral problems the 361st pilots and groundcrews had to live with was the fact that Bottisham's main runway had been widened to allow four aircraft to take off simultaneously. A practical move on the face of it, the job had been completed using the ever-useful pierced steel planking. But the surface underneath never seemed to be completely flat and there was nothing like the pounding of coming and going Republic Thunderbolts to keep airfield repair gangs in constant work. Airfields all over the world experienced this problem but the great danger was that the laden fighters would sink in, loosen the planking sections and rupture the delicate belly tanks. Constant inspection and repair of the runway would occupy groundcrews at most airfields using steel mat surfaces.

The first 361st P-47 lost on operations went down on the group's fourth mission on 29 January when flak nailed an aircraft near Amiens but bomber escort missions on the 30th and 31st brought the first victories. Attacked by Bf 109s near Rheine, Germany, the 374th Squadron's Capt Robert E. Sedman and Lt Joe L. Latimer each claimed one each.

The addition of the 361st gave VIII Fighter Command a total of thirty-six squadrons of P-47s at that time; assuming twenty to twenty-five serviceable fighters per squadron, plus a number assigned to headquarters sections and perhaps spares, a maximum effort could see at least sixty-five aircraft on the flightline and ready to go. Allowing for technical malfunction to manifest itself in various forms (when the aircraft were *en route*), each group was able to put up a substantial enough force. And even if a number of aircraft were obliged to abort the mission, a group would rarely be dangerously depleted. Squadron aircraft strength was increased as the war progressed. From an average of twenty-five P-47s in 1943,

it rose to thirty to thirty-five during 1944 and was up to around the forty-two mark by the end of the war. These could only be average figures, as various factors mitigated against even the most orderly delivery chain from U.S. factories to the embarkation ports for shipment to European depots and finally the war zones. Thunderbolt deliveries were erratic at times and in late 1944 some front line groups would experience a severe, if temporary, shortage of replacement aircraft.

But overall, the 1943 build-up had given VIII Fighter Command nearly 500 P-47s – plus the P-38s and the burgeoning strength of the P-51 groups which by the spring of 1944 increased the available total to between 600 and 800 aircraft. The number of fighters operationally deployed on any given day depended on the type of missions being flown, serviceability and weather conditions.

## ARNOLD'S AXE

Despite the U.K.-based fighter force having achieved much in 1943, it did not look that good from Washington. As far as VIII Bomber Command was concerned, 'all the way' fighter escort was a goal yet to be reached; it had not occurred with the P-47 during the critical first half of the year, contrary to hope. A.A.F. Commanding General H. H. 'Hap' Arnold had some harsh criticisms on the way the air war was being run in England: the bombers were not flying enough missions, too many were being shot down when they were operating and too little progress was seemingly being made to keep *Luftwaffe* fighters away from the bombers – because the U.S. fighters were unable to escort them far enough. One report containing some ill-informed criticism of the P-47's capability did not help a difficult situation.

Ira C. Eaker, Commanding General of VIII Bomber Command, tended to concur with Arnold's views but knew many of the reasons for the shortfall. Numerous individuals from Frank Hunter, VIII Fighter Command boss down through Henry Miller, chief of VIII Air Service Command, had virtually accepted the situation concerning the escort problem. With Sir Charles Portal playing devil's advocate on what could and could not be achieved by single-engined fighters, the view was that Hunter certainly had not done all he could

*P-47D-22* Angel Eyes *(42-26272) was the mount of Capt Howard Wiggins of the 361st F.S., 356th Group, one of the Eighth Air Force units that won a high reputation as a close escort group to the detriment of its overall aerial kill record.*

have to push the solution to the P-47's short range. He was replaced by Bill Kepner, indirectly as a result of that failure.

Equally, there is no question that the P-47 had other problems which seemed, at least to those in the U.S., more urgently in need of a solution, particularly those concerning engine performance and radio communications. But almost a year had been spent on developing or adapting reliable drop tanks for the P-47 and only by late 1943 were they available in quantity. While acknowledging that there was a need to have longer range Thunderbolts escorting the Eighth's bombers, the programme to achieve it – such as it was – had a lower official priority in the U.S. than it merited.

Had it not been for Cass Hough and his command working in the front line in England and Col Mark E. Bradley, Chief of Aircraft Projects at Wright Field, who spent months on the problem posed by the P-47's short range, the Republic fighter might not have achieved all it did within its limitations.

The situation was not actually helped by the fact that an order was placed in the U.S. as early as February 1943 for no less than 60,000 tanks of 200-gal capacity, presumably of the bulbous flush-fitting type developed for the P-39. This was, as related, not found to be the most reliable tank when adapted for P-47 use and Materiel Command indicated a preference for an alternative steel tank holding up to 125 gallons. Finalising the design of this and completing what was, even for U.S. industry, a substantial order, Eighth Air Force sought an alternative source of supply in England. The Ministry of Aircraft Production put forward a 108-gal drop tank constructed of impregnated paper, based on an existing design already in limited use on R.A.F. fighters. The U.S. order was then cancelled.

Unfortunately, although the design of the British tank was officially approved for A.A.F. use in June, some time was required to fulfil the order in the quantity (43,200) initially required and by 12 October only 450 tanks had been delivered. By that time, however, the supply of standard U.S.-75 gal, 108-gal and 150-gal fighter tanks had improved and by 10 December about 18,000 had arrived in the U.K. M.A.P. had meanwhile speeded up the British end of things and more than 7500 tanks were in Eighth Air Force depots by that date. In a matter of weeks, there were almost more fighter fuel tanks than maintenance units could possibly fit. But with or without additional fuel carried in external tanks, the P-47's engine still burned 100 octane at an alarmingly very high rate, about which very little could be done. From many standpoints, particularly those of the pilots, the 'babies' had arrived too late.

Other factors had tended to adversely affect any intensive effort to develop the Thunderbolt as a long-range fighter. Some time before the other engineering problems were solved, A.A.F. thinking was turning more to fielding a completely new aircraft for the escort role, preferably one with adequate fuel capacity built in. In some quarters, this appealed more than spending any more time on modifying the P-47. It was seriously put forward at one point that the General Motors P-75A Eagle be rushed into production. Arnold was all for it until Bradley pointed out that the aircraft, the prototype of which did not even fly until 17 November 1943, was a total 'dog', too slow and unstable without a ghost of a chance of fulfilling the range requirement in the timescale required. It was at that point that Bradley revealed a solution – that the P-51 could be made into the escort fighter the Eighth needed.

Despite the critical view of its performance in Washington, the P-47's record was as good as it could probably have been, given that all single-engined fighters were believed to have almost insoluble range limitations. This view tended to be reinforced by bombing missions which had not included any fighter support. Epic raids such as the 8 August Ploesti mission had not done anything for the pro-escort lobby. Even the two Schweinfurt-Regensburg raids which could only be partially protected by fighters, showed that despite heavy losses the bombers did reach their targets and hit them reasonably hard.

Fortunately, it never came to a situation of heavy bombers being totally unable to attack their targets because the German fighters would simply wipe them out if they had no escort. To paraphrase the widely publicised pre-war belief, in the case of the Eighth Air Force, 'some (actually most) of the bombers always did get through'.

To help them do so in 1944 was a fighter whose name would become synonymous with long-range escort. The P-51 Mustang changed all previous notions of how far single-seat fighters could be made to fly. Within a few months, the Eighth Air Force was fighting a different kind of war. William Kepner's VIII Fighter Command quickly developed its operational capability out of all recognition to that existing less than eight months before and the P-47 took on new roles that few could have foreseen in the spring of 1943.

## REBIRTH OF THE NINTH

By late 1943, the P-51B Mustang had gone operational in the E.T.O. with the 354th Group, a tactical unit assigned to the new Ninth Air Force which had been established in the U.K. on 16 October 1943. Confirming fully what engineers at Rolls-Royce, VIII Air Service Command and Wright Field had known for some time, the North American fighter was indeed the answer to VIII Bomber Command's prayers for a long-range escort fighter. Army Air Force chiefs were a little slow to appreciate the fact when they began issuing the new fighter to tactical groups and a degree of wheeling and dealing consequently took place to have Mustangs replace Thunderbolts in the Eighth Air Force fighter groups. Equally, the P-47 was a natural choice for the Ninth, for it was clear that the big, rugged fighter with its air-cooled engine was far better able to stand up to the rigours of ground-attack work than the liquid-cooled Merlin engine of the P-51.

The Ninth was consequently built up with new P-47 groups fresh from the U.S. although during the winter of 1943-4 bomber escort absorbed almost every American fighter in the E.T.O. Full re-equipment with Mustangs, not only of the P-47 groups but those currently flying the P-38, would take many months. By the spring of 1944, the process was far from complete.

With the invasion of Europe tentatively scheduled to take place in mid-year, ground support would require a substantial fighter-bomber force built around the P-47, the most suitable and numerous type then in the U.S. inventory. The pioneering ground-attack work by VIII Fighter Command groups had ably demonstrated the suitability of the P-47 for such a role. The Ninth Air Force would eventually comprise no less than fifteen groups of P-47s.

In the meantime, the Ninth's new fighter-bomber units would, as they arrived in England, spend some months flying cross-Channel sorties from airfields in southern England, striking targets in occupied Europe in company with A.A.F. Marauders and Havocs and taking part in similar tactical operations flown by the R.A.F. Escort missions were something few pilots had expected to be flying but the first two new Thunderbolt groups assigned to the Ninth, the 362nd and 365th, found few difficulties in protecting bombers coupled with being offered a crack at the *Luftwaffe*.

As the 354th settled into its new role as part of the Eighth flying its suddenly highly coveted P-51s on escort missions, VIII Fighter Command was badgered by men like Don Blakeslee of the 4th Group at Debden for the Eighth to switch its P-47 groups to the P-51. Tests had shown the enormous range

*With 1500 lb of high explosive ready for the next target, a P-47D of the 353rd Group awaits its next mission on 11 September 1944. The Curtiss Electric propeller with its paddle blades is well in evidence. (U.S.A.F. 69072 AC)*

capability of the Merlin-engined Mustang, principally through the achievement of extremely low fuel consumption, something around a quarter of that required per flying hour by the P-47's Pratt & Whitney radial. Consequently the 357th Group, the second Mustang unit assigned to the E.T.O. and originally destined to join the Ninth, was exchanged for the P-47-equipped 358th. When the 357th's P-51Bs occupied their base at Leiston, the 'Orange Tails' moved out to the Advanced Landing Ground (A.L.G.) at High Halden, Kent.

## BUZZ BOYS

Pilots of the 353rd Group soon came to realise that their new leader was a tiger looking for something to hunt. Glenn Duncan put a lot of energy into expanding VIII Fighter Command's ability to destroy the *Luftwaffe* fighter force and he put forward the idea of a specialist unit dedicated to ground strafing. The idea was to prevent the Germans hoarding fighters to attack the bombers – if they did not rise to combat the American fighters, the latter would seek out and destroy them on the ground. In line with the policy of achieving Allied air superiority over northwestern France before D-Day, Duncan was given permission by Bill Kepner to head a selected band of volunteer pilots. These were drawn from his own group and the 355th, 359th and 361st groups.

Kepner enthusiastically lent his name to 'Bill's Buzz Boys' which comprised four flights, one from each of the participating groups. Duncan briefed them and led the way in practising strafing in the safe confines of Metfield which once again kept its collective head down as P-47s charged all over the area refining the technique of shooting up ground targets without flying into the ground or any obstacle which had more right to be there than a fighter. It was exciting but demanding work with little margin for error.

The sixteen volunteers reported to Metfield on 15 March. All pilots flew P-47Ds with paddle-bladed propellers and water-injected engines and, with practice over, they prepared for their first mission as the 353rd Group's C Flight. On 26 March, Duncan led twelve P-47s, one flight of four each armed with two M4 fragmentation bombs. To make the mission as representative as possible, the Thunderbolts attacked five airfields – Chartres, Châteaudun, Anet, St-André-de-l'Eure and Beauvais-Tillé. In this way the pilots would need to vary their approach, note a variety of landmarks, the possible natural hazards of low flying and the strength of the German defences. Each target would present contrasting images of terrain as the pilots swept over at zero feet. All details noted would provide valuable intelligence data for future sorties.

In terms of what was to come, the first mission was representative – on the negative as well as positive side. One pilot, Lt Kenneth R. Williams of the 355th, was shot down. Fragmentation bombs were dropped on Chartres airfield and claims were made for one twin-engined aircraft destroyed, one Me 210 probably destroyed, and four damaged. The pilots strafed a large hangar, three blister hangars, one of which exploded, a flak tower and a water tower (at Châteaudun); two buildings were shot up at Beauvais and five aircraft were damaged by flak.

The Buzz Boys flew an escort without carrying out any strafing on 27 March but, on the 29th, seven German airfields were shot up, Duncan himself leading a flight to Bramsche. No enemy aircraft were seen when he got down low, about two miles from the airfield. He noticed with some interest a flak tower where the gun crew clearly had difficulty in tracking a P-47 doing 400 mph at zero feet. Unfortunately for other pilots, the German gun crews would soon learn.

Duncan reformed his flight and headed for Vechta which lay off the starboard side. With three P-47s covering him at higher altitude, the 353rd's boss found a juicy target in the shape of numerous single-engined and twin-engined aircraft parked in front of the hangar line and dispersed around the airfield. Also noted was a belly-landed B-17. Shooting up two Bf 110s, the American pilot observed fire in the second aircraft and some hits on five or six other machines – but noted the difficulty in accurate sighting at his high closure speed. Flak was also trying hard to shoot down Duncan, particularly when he successfully shot up the B-17. Another 353rd pilot, 1st Lt Ken Chetwood, got so annoyed at the way a gun crew located in a flak tower seemed to concentrate on his ship that he promptly dived and thoroughly sprayed the tower until the guns fell silent.

Duncan reassembled his group and pressed on to Twenthe. Adopting a line abreast formation, the P-47 picked targets from the parked aircraft. Duncan ran out of ammunition after a few bursts but some damage was done by the other pilots. Coming off the target, Lt Francis Edwards of the 353rd took a hit in a fuel tank and as they headed out his ship was slowly leaking fuel. But Edwards made it to within 40 miles of the English coast and was picked up by A.S.R.

When the day's total of enemy aircraft was added up, it reached seven destroyed, five probables and nine damaged. Several locomotives, two hangars, six flak towers and other installations had been destroyed, badly damaged or suffered only minor damage from the liberal quantities of 0.50-in calibre ammunition spread around by the strafing P-47s. One fighter had been lost with the pilot safe and four had taken damage.

These early missions also highlighted the difficulty in confirming that an enemy aircraft had been destroyed on the ground. Duncan and other pilots noted that it was perfectly possible to shoot a machine full of holes without it catching fire, invariably because the Germans learned not to leave the fuel tanks full. Only spectacular fires and explosions, visually confirmed by fellow pilots in the formation and on gun camera film, could really determine destruction. Doubt often remained. Despite this, the Eighth Air Force was the only wartime U.S. air arm that allowed its fighter pilots to receive credits for ground claims – due mainly to the hazardous nature of ground strafing.

## TACTICAL DEBUT

While the Eighth was honing its ground-attack technique, the Ninth Air Force Thunderbolt groups continued to fly bomber escort missions. It was March before the 366th Fighter Group became the first P-47 outfit in the Ninth to fly ground-attack sorties. This mission took place on the 15th, the target being St-Valéry airfield on which the 'Hun Hunters' dropped 250 lb bombs.

On 1 April, the Buzz Boys flew their fourth mission, again to targets in northwestern Germany. Another success in terms of enemy aircraft, locomotives and river traffic strafed, there were no Thunderbolt losses. Mission number five was aborted due to poor weather while the pilots were *en route* and the sixth operation, also to German airfields, resulted in another P-47 loss. Lt Clifford E. Carter of the 359th disappeared in the vicinity of Bohmte airfield.

Mission seven took in the Paris area when the strafing specialists provided target support to the 55th Group before disturbing the peace of airfields around the French capital. Hangars and aircraft were shot up, two pilots claiming the definite destruction of one Bf 110 apiece. And that was about the end of the 'buzzing' experiment. Mission eight on 12 April caused some loss of rail transportation to the Germans. In total, the strafing sorties had yielded claims of fourteen enemy aircraft destroyed, six probables and fourteen damaged, all on the ground. Three P-47s had been lost and thirteen damaged for the additional tally of thirty-five locomotives, ten boats, ten hangars and nine flak towers destroyed or damaged. Out of ninety sorties dispatched, eighty-three were effective.

Kepner himself closed this interesting episode by congratulating all concerned with proving that the Eighth Air Force had an additional ace up its sleeve. From then on, fighters returning from bomber escort missions would be free to strafe targets of opportunity anywhere within their range – an additional wound in the *Jagdwaffe*'s side that would continue to bleed freely.

Having also shown that dive-bombing with single-seat fighters could be effective, the Eighth would carry out numerous such attacks in the future using both the P-47 and P-51. All groups participated at various times but, in general, the command relied to a great extent on 0.50-in calibre machine-guns, the majority of ground attacks being made *en route* back to base after escort missions, on which there was no room for anything other than fuel and ammunition.

Ground-attack sorties also saw the trained fighter-bomber pilots of the Ninth flying dive-bombing sorties although they generally adopted a shallow dive approach to the target prior to bomb release. Sighting was via the standard gunsight. Bomb size was initially

*Where bombs might not do the trick, M10 rockets were an alternative. A little inaccurate for some pilots, the 'bazooka tubes' could be well placed, with practise. P-47Ds accepted the weight increase of the full six tubes without difficulty. (U.S.A.F.)*

limited to a pair of 250-pounders, although this was soon increased to two 500 lb bombs and P-47s were cleared to use 1000 lb bombs in May, mere weeks before the Normandy invasion was launched.

By then, the Ninth had been further strengthened by the arrival in the U.K. of five more P-47 groups (the 36th, 50th, 373rd, 404th and 406th) plus one group with P-38s, and all had flown their debut missions by D-Day – indeed the entire tactical force of the Ninth had passed this milestone by the time of the invasion. Pounding a long list of continental ground targets in the huge softening-up process before *Overlord* was launched, the new P-47 groups quickly came to terms with the demands placed upon them,

demands that would become ever more exacting when the time came to provide close support to friendly troops in the field.

April saw the 48th, 371st and 405th Groups flying their first sorties from England. The 405th flew its first mission on 11 April, the 371st opened its book with a sweep over France on the 12th, and the 48th entered combat, also with a sweep along the French coast, on 20 April. These groups were based respectively at Ibsley, Bisterne and Christchurch. It did not take too long for the runways at Christchurch to deteriorate under the constant take-offs and landings of Thunderbolts. The 371st was consequently obliged to share Ibsley with the 48th from 28 April to 14 May until repairs were effected.

*Numerous P-47s damaged in combat or accidents had to be repaired during the war and a huge organisation fed such machines back to the front-line groups 'as new'. This lonely scene marked the end of a rough one to Emden where flak caused P-47D (41-6367/UN-X) of the 63rd F.S., 56th F.G. to belly-in. A Jeep saved the pilot a long walk back through a seemingly endless sea of grass.*

Since the earliest days, the pilots of combat groups new to the E.T.O. had to learn such basic items of information as the distance that the enemy coast lay from their airfields and from the English coast, the radio channels to use in an emergency, the A.S.R. frequencies, and the nature of the terrain where the likely targets were located. And they needed to learn quickly.

New pilots were urged to keep their eyes open and to observe all they could of hostile territory, note prominent landmarks and generally to observe radio silence and practise keeping formation. They also had to lean the correct engine settings for the most efficient operation of the P-47. Pilots who acted as leaders for new groups were drawn from units that had seen combat and were well able to pass on helpful pointers; instilling a high degree of alertness in their inexperienced charges could one day make the difference between life and death.

## BATTLE OVER GERMANY

While the P-47 was beginning what would be an important new role as a ground-attack aircraft, the Eighth Air Force maintained the pressure on the *Luftwaffe* and protected the bomber force, now 'well in the groove' of the strategic offensive against German industry. Shortly before it was due to receive Mustangs, the 361st Group at Bottisham had its best day, one that went down in the Eighth's record books as a high point in its war against the *Luftwaffe*. On 8 April, the group's P-47s used 150 U.S. gal belly tanks for the first time, giving their pilots an extra 50 miles or so into enemy territory.

The 'Yellow Jackets' swept right through to Steinhuder Lake, briefed to pick up B-24s attacking Brunswick. It was during the withdrawal escort that the Thunderbolts caught up with the enemy; intent on the Liberators, the *Jagdflieger* were badly bounced, losing nine fighters shot down

*The starboard wing of* Little Princess *held some interest for the ground personnel of the 353rd Group after the aircraft arrived back from a mission. Many Eighth Air Force P-47s were repainted after delivery in natural metal finish, although the 353rd appears not to have done this to any extent. The squadron was the 350th and Marvin Bledsoe flew the aircraft for a tour in 1944.*

including two that fell in the Dümmer Lake area and two downed in the running fight over Holland that ensued. Lost to the group was Lt Albert C. Duncan, who was killed in action.

Other P-47s of the 361st had been shot down during the hazardous business of strafing, an experience common to all the VIII Fighter Command groups, but overall the P-47 had established the parameters both for its own future deployment in that role and the success of fighter-bomber operations in general. If strafing had to be carried out against alerted enemy defences, a Thunderbolt was probably the best available aircraft for that hazardous duty. For the 361st, the P-47 era passed during May and by D-Day the group was fully equipped with Mustangs.

Numerous changes were made to the P-47 throughout its combat career, many of them of an internal nature 'under the skin' and not intended to alter the aircraft's outward appearance. But anyone walking around the 356th Group's flightline at Martlesham Heath in the spring of 1944 might have noticed a small number of aircraft with six rather than the usual eight guns.

Although its heavy firepower was usually an asset in combat, the P-47 had always been a heavyweight and, as had been predicted when it first arrived in the E.T.O., that could be a distinct drawback in combat with FW 190s and Bf 109s, particularly at low and medium altitudes. Pilots had invariably allowed for the weight factor but the truth was that the P-47D was barely capable of staying with enemy fighters and fighting on equal terms at altitudes above 30,000 feet. That, as the 356th and other groups realised, was where the German top cover of Bf 109s operated. They always had to be wary of a high-speed bounce when the 109s came down.

Lt Ray Withers of the 360th F.S. pondered this question. If the Jug could be modified to mix it with the Bf 109s at their own altitude it would be a definite bonus and perhaps force the enemy to look again at his operational tactics. These deliberations actually stemmed from a successful combat mission flown by the 356th on 13 May. A force of B-24s attacking Pölitz had stirred up three large gaggles of German fighters, all of which were queuing up to hit the Liberators with about forty aircraft in each gaggle.

As the American fighters positioned to ward off the FW 190s, the Bf 109 top cover came down and all hell broke loose. Nevertheless, the 356th acquitted itself extremely well, to the tune of nine enemy aircraft downed for the loss of one P-47. But to Ray Withers, that

was not the point. The bounce by the Messerschmitt top cover had been carried out almost with impunity – the *Jagdflieger* knew the P-47 could barely touch them while they positioned well above the typical combat altitude.

Withers conferred with his squadron C.O., Capt John W. Vogt and the two officers devised a practical remedy: a P-47 could indeed reach 35,000 feet if it was light enough – and the easiest way to do that was to reduce the wing loading by taking out some of the guns and ammunition. With two of the eight guns of the group's P-47D-28s removed, one on each side, and the ammunition load of up to 425 rounds per gun reduced to just 200 rounds for each remaining gun, the wing was made more aerodynamically efficient by stripping the tactical paint from the leading edge of the wing and wax polishing the natural metal surface. This added 6-8 mph to the aircraft's top speed. Finally, groundcrews filled up the four aircraft of Withers's

*For D-Day operations black and white A.E.A.F. stripes adorned all tactical aircraft. This P-47D, named* Peg O' My Heart *with typical 'invasion stripes' stands armed and ready on its English airfield, probably an Advanced Landing Ground, judging by the steel matting.*

'Superbolt' flight with higher octane fuel.

Fortunately, the P-47D-28 operated by the 356th Group already had most of the modifications specified for the later D series Thunderbolt, including the 13-foot diameter Curtiss Electric paddle-bladed propeller for the R-2800-59 engine rated at a maximum 2430 hp. Flight tests at Martlesham were encouraging. The Superbolt not only operated very well at 35,000 feet, but the lighter wing enabled the aircraft to manoeuvre better as well.

Combat debut for the modified P-47s of Vortex Green Flight came on 19 May. The 356th was briefed, with the 56th and 78th Groups, to escort B-24s bombing Brunswick. The weather was perfect and, for the Superbolt operational test, the *Luftwaffe* obliged by turning out in force to harry the bombers. North of Steinhuder Lake, the pilots of the 359th F.S. spotted the Messerschmitt high cover at about 33,000 feet. Ray Withers's flight of P-47s immediately dropped tanks and climbed. Suddenly, the pilots were turning and banking with about a dozen Bf 109s, neither side being able immediately to gain much advantage. Then Withers closed on one very rapidly and fired from about 250 yards. He observed hits on the canopy area – but immediately the guns were fired the P-47 executed two snap rolls and began to spin.

Withers recovered at 25,000 ft and climbed, spiralling up to 34,000 ft to find the three remaining pilots of his flight still going up after two other Bf 109s. Joining the climbing orbit, Withers obtained a good position and sighted on a 109 from 150 yards, altitude 35,000 ft. Obviously badly damaged, the German fighter shed oil and debris and was last seen spinning into cloud at about 5000 ft.

One pilot caught a startled *Jagdflieger* at height and began attacking him, the two fighters dropping to 25,000 ft in the process. The onset of compressibility was little noticed until the P-47's dive momentum built up, which it did very rapidly; Lt Weber experienced its effects as he dived after his quarry but he rode it out and brought his aircraft back under full control at 7000 ft. The enemy aircraft he had been chasing just kept right on, hit the ground and exploded. Green Flight then called it a day and broke off the engagement.

Ray Withers flew four more Superbolt sorties before completing his first combat tour and passing the modified aircraft to another flight. The experiment was a success insofar as the aircraft were not really needed; pilots observed on subsequent missions that the Germans appeared to have been sorely tried by finding 'low level' P-47s shooting them down at their previously inviolate altitude, and modified their tactics. In any event, the air war over Europe was about to change yet again. A much larger shock for the *Jagdwaffe* was just around the corner.

Weeks before the invasion, the Ninth completed its Thunderbolt force by declaring operational five more groups, the 36th at Kingsnorth, the 50th at Lymington, the 373rd at Woodchurch, the 404th at Winkton and the 406th at Ashford. The 50th was one of the first of this batch of new P-47 groups to look over the French coast when a sweep was laid on for the 1st of the month. The same day, the 404th Group, one of those which originally had 'fighter-bomber' in its designation but was changed to 'fighter' when it came to England – to fly fighter-bomber duties – also flew its first mission. The 36th Fighter Group made its E.T.O. debut on 8 May flying out of Kingsnorth. Ashford, one of the Kent A.L.G.s, was home base for the 406th, the 'Raiders'. The group had flown its first sorties over the Channel on 4 May in preparation for an intensive phase of dive-bombing, strafing and armed reconnaissance sorties over Normandy.

Although the A.L.G.s were an inspired idea, they were not intended to house heavy aircraft for a great length of time and, assuming that the invasion went well, it was planned that the Ninth's P-47s would move to bases in France as soon as practicable. In the meantime, the A.L.G.s prevented overcrowding on the more permanent airfields as thousands of Allied aircraft geared up for the invasion. Nevertheless, these conveniently sited temporary airstrips, created with steel plating of British or U.S. origin laid directly over compacted soil or grass, proved invaluable for accommodating the veritable armada of aircraft crowding into southeast England for one of the greatest military operations in history.

# 6
# *Overlord* and Beyond

On D-Day, the huge Allied air umbrella over the invasion beaches included eight groups of P-47s comprising twenty-four squadrons under IX T.A.C. commanded by Maj-Gen Elwood 'Pete' Quesada (supporting U.S. First Army) out of a grand total of thirty-six squadrons, the balance being made up of groups flying P-51s and P-38s. Five P-47 groups with fifteen squadrons were under XIX T.A.C. control (Brig-Gen Otto Weyland) to support U.S. Third Army. This latter force had a total of eighteen fighter and fighter-bomber squadrons, including the Mustangs of the 354th Group. Part of IX T.A.C. was the 365th Fighter Group, the 'Hell Hawks'.

At 05.20 hours on 6 June, the group sent forty-seven Thunderbolts off to dive-bomb a railway bridge and an embankment less than two miles from the town of St-Sauveur-de-Pierre-Pont and a culvert at Couperville. Led by Lt-Col Robert L. Coffey jr, the force included eleven aircraft each armed with two 1000 lb bombs while the rest each carried three 500-pounders. First to bomb was the 388th Squadron. One flight released 1000-pounders on the culvert from 25 feet, the three remaining flights diving from 600-800 feet under the undercast to release the bombs at 100-300 feet. Other pilots saw 2nd Lt Jack Martell drop his bombs from almost zero feet - and there were immediate explosions. Martell had little choice but to fly through the debris, which of course would not have been there had the delayed-action fuses on his bombs worked. Lt Zell Smith saw Martell flying straight at 200 feet with his guns firing and wing root afire. Passing over the target, the P-47 suddenly plunged straight into the ground and exploded. Martell had no chance to escape and was killed in the crash on the outskirts of St-Lô-d'Ourville.

Almost simultaneously, the 386th Squadron was breaking up the embankment at St-Sauveur. Again, a combination of 1000-pounder and 500-pounders did the trick but premature detonation of some of the bombs took down 1st Lt Robert L. Shipe. After running in at deck

*Once the troops had a foothold in Normandy, the fighter-bombers flew over the Channel and landed on the forward airstrips the engineers had prepared for them in double-quick time. The 368th Group's 397th Squadron used Cardonville (A3), close enough to enemy ground positions for the Army to mark the next target on a local map. (U.S.A.F.)*

*Hundreds of rounds of ammunition were used by each P-47 every day for weeks as the invasion front deepened. Keeping the wing bays replenished was a full-time job for the Ninth's armourers – these probably belonging to the 378th F.S., 362nd F.G. – who needed a constant flow of boxed rounds to do their job. Pilots could rely on the goundcrews to help them keep enemy fires burning. (U.S.A.F.)*

level, Shipe's aircraft was not seen again and the other pilots believed that he had run into the blast from his own bombs. Shipe, killed in the crash, was buried by a French family.

The 387th Squadron suffered no casualties at Sauveur and the P-47s claimed four direct hits. Regrouping, the Hell Hawks winged their way back to England and Beaulieu, each pilot concentrating on keeping his aircraft on track along a narrow corridor allocated to the group by invasion planners.

Landing at 07.16, the pilots were mobbed by the ground echelons with all kinds of questions. For once, the flyers were allowed to say what they had seen as the vast armada moved slowly to the coast of France. Overflying the ships, the pilots witnessed a sight they would never forget.

Later in the afternoon, the group went back to France to attack a railway bridge at Oissel.

German engineers had carried out repairs to the bridge and it was believed that this particular span was being maintained in order to move *Wehrmacht* reinforcements up to the battle area. The Hell Hawks ruined the plan. Screaming out of their dives, thirty-six Thunderbolts each dropped two 1,000-pounders on the bridge from 1000 feet. The bridge quickly succumbed. When the pilots turned away, half of the southernmost span was in the river. No enemy aircraft appeared while the group's D-Day missions went ahead but a top cover was maintained, just in case.

By evening of the first day of *Overlord*, IX T.A.C. had pinned its bomb line to the River Aure parallel to the coast between Isigny and Bayeux, 2-5 miles inland. It was this area that would occupy the Hell Hawks and other groups for the next few days.

Casualties continued to put the destruction

5TH AIR FORCE

*P-47D-21, 42-25487 of 311th F.S., 58th F.G.*

*P-47D-28, 42-29080 of 40th F.S., 35th F.G.*

*P-47D-4, 42-22694 of 342nd F.S., 348th F.G.*

# 7TH AIR FORCE

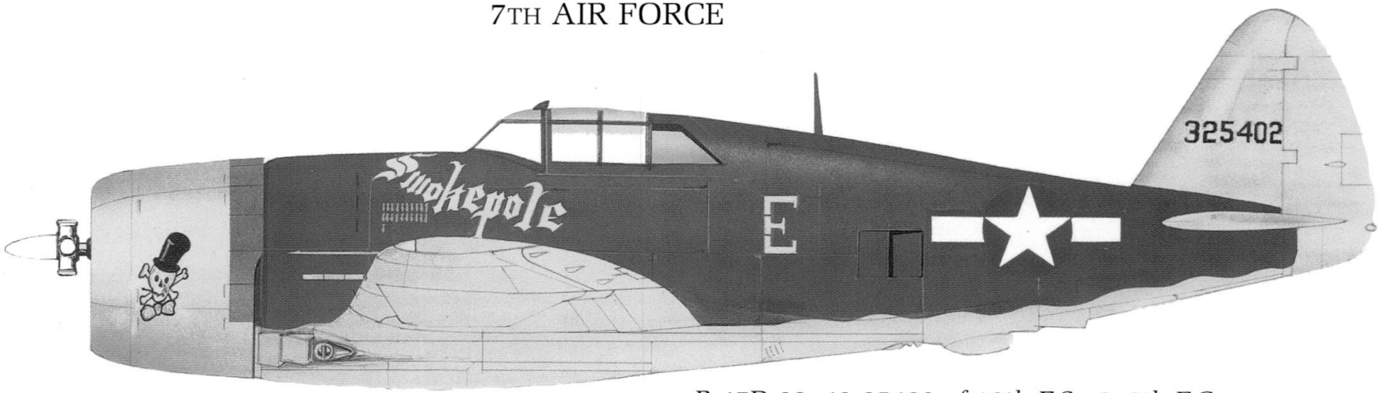

P-47D-20, 43-25402 of 19th F.S., 318th F.G.

P-47N-5, 44-88572 of 437th F.S., 414th F.G.

P-47N-1, 44-87957 of 19th F.S., 318th F.G.

325402

Smokepole

488572

712

MILDRED

05

487957

8TH AIR FORCE

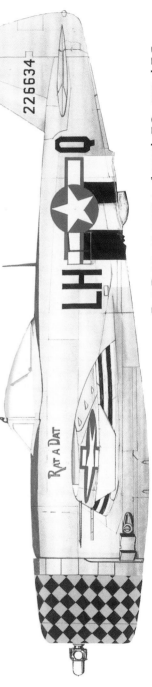

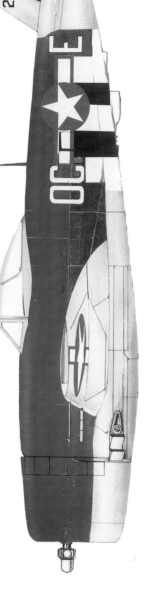

*P-47C-1, 41-6265 of 61st F.S., 56th F.G.*

*P-47D-27, 42-26851 of 359th F.S., 356th F.G.*

*P-47D-25, 42-26634 of 350th F.S., 353rd F.G.*

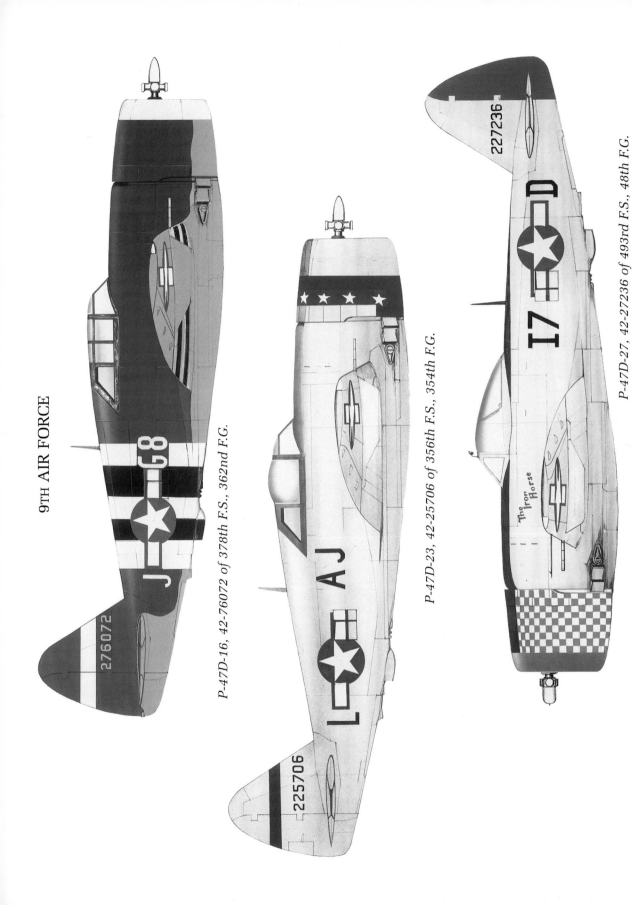

9TH AIR FORCE

P-47D-16, 42-76072 of 378th F.S., 362nd F.G.

P-47D-23, 42-25706 of 356th F.S., 354th F.G.

P-47D-27, 42-27236 of 493rd F.S., 48th F.G.

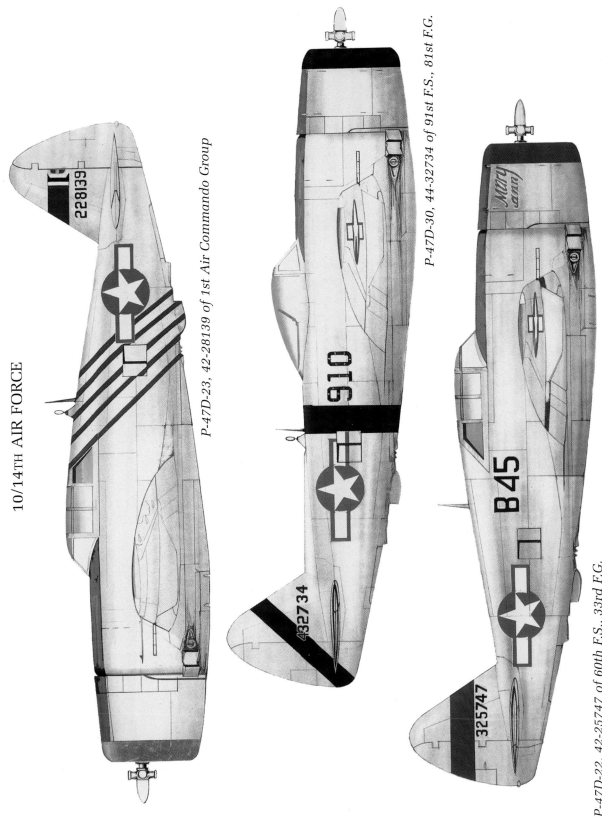

10/14TH AIR FORCE

P-47D-23, 42-28139 of 1st Air Commando Group

P-47D-30, 44-32734 of 91st F.S., 81st F.G.

P-47D-22, 42-25747 of 60th F.S., 33rd F.G.

12TH AIR FORCE

P-47D-22, 42-26368 of 332nd F.G., ex-64th F.S., 57th F.G.

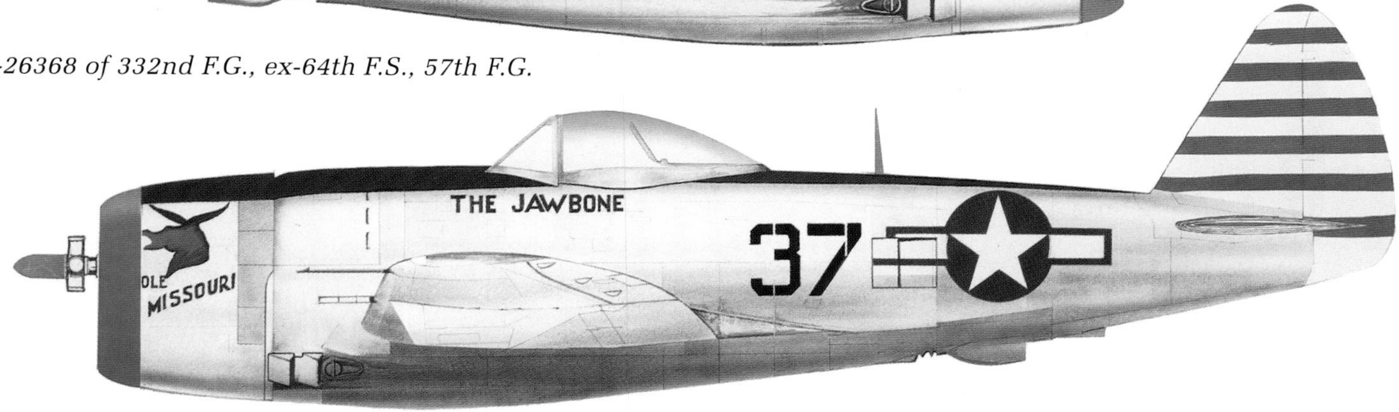

THE JAWBONE

OLE MISSOURI

P-47D-30, 44-32734 of 525th F.S., 86th F.G.

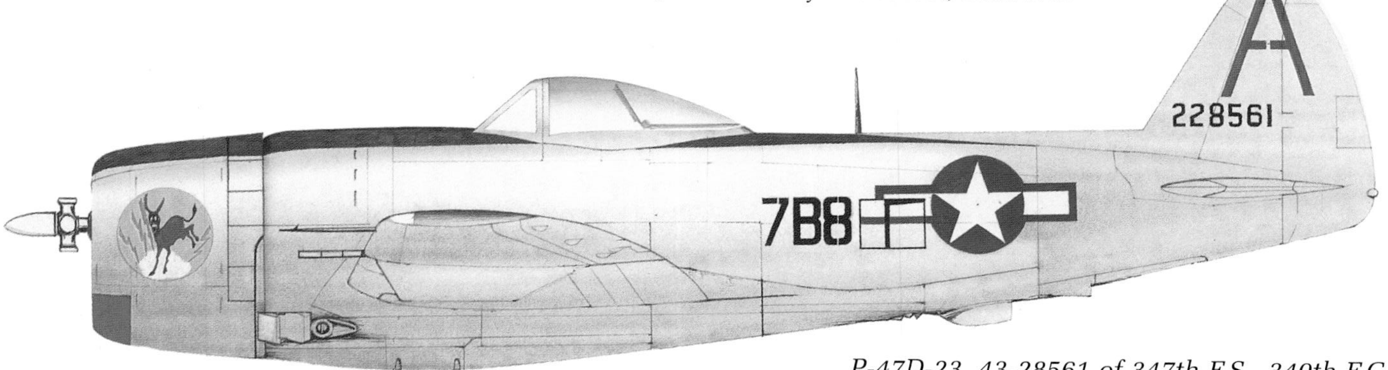

228561

788

P-47D-23, 43-28561 of 347th F.S., 340th F.G.

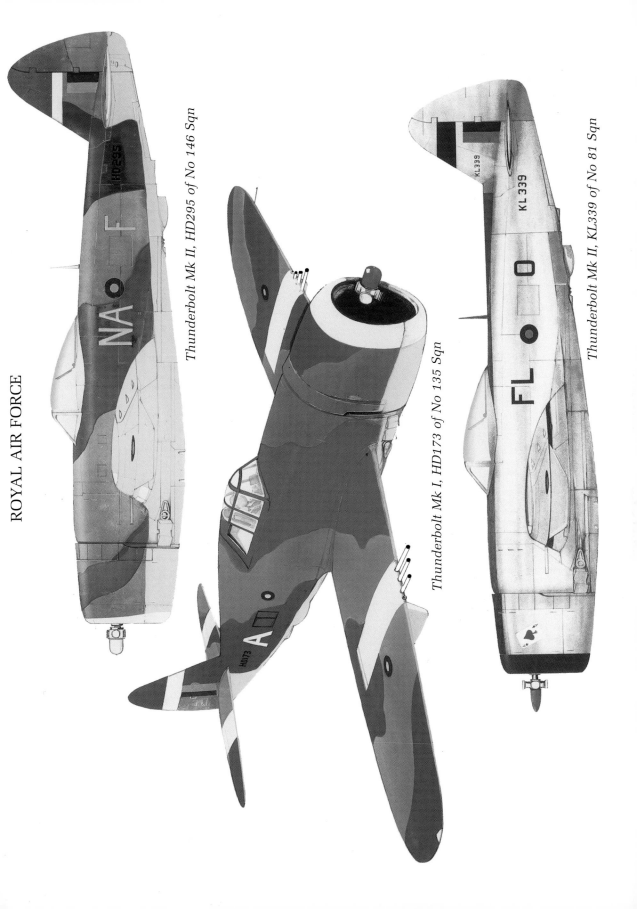

ROYAL AIR FORCE

*Thunderbolt Mk II, HD295 of No 146 Sqn*

*Thunderbolt Mk I, HD173 of No 135 Sqn*

*Thunderbolt Mk II, KL339 of No 81 Sqn*

ALLIED AIR FORCES

*P-47D-28, 42-28986 of 1 Grupo de Caca, Brazilian Air Force*

*P-47D-27, 42-27295 of G.C. II/5 La Fayette, Armée de l'Air*

*P-47D-30, 44-33722 of 201 Esc, Mexican Air Force*

the pilots were handing out to the enemy in perspective and although these were not expectionally high, every loss was felt. At the time, nobody could be sure that a pilot downed by ground fire had escaped, as numerous P-47 crashes, observed only briefly by other pilots on the mission, appeared from the air, at least, to give the pilot a fighting chance of survival. A gratifying number of pilots did make it to become prisoners while others evaded the Germans and eventually returned to the fold.

Ground attack was always a grim business, especially when the job involved strafing. Pilots were close enough to targets to observe the results of the machine-gun fire and many were sickened when horse-drawn vehicles came into their sights. The Germans used many horses during their retreat from France and, in some places, the slaughter among these hapless creatures was terrible to witness.

With the troops pushing inland from the Normandy coast, the U.S.A.A.F. and R.A.F. commands (the latter's 83 and 84 Groups) sent out sorties by their own tactical fighters and bombers to avoid duplication of effort, to ensure the maximum amount of damage being done to the defences fronting the beaches and to minimise risks to friendly airmen through collision in very crowded skies. Pilots flying across the Channel were comforted by the knowledge that everybody was supposed to have been briefed in Allied aircraft recognition. And the black and white 'invasion stripes' applied to all tactical aircraft helped minimise some of the risks from trigger-happy gunners on the same side.

D-Day was the first time that most of the Allied squadrons had actually supported their own troops in the field and it quickly became evident that fighter-bombers were a vital element – probably the vital element – in providing effective support. By destroying relatively small targets – single pillboxes and machine-gun nests, troop and vehicle concentrations – the single-engined and twin-engined fighters offered a quick and reasonably safe way to neutralise an obstacle. With troops advancing, heavy and medium bombing, intended to soften up targets, had misfired. Only pinpoint target identification and destruction enabled ground gains to be made in the critical first hours of *Overlord*.

Conventional bombing, particularly by the Eighth's heavies, could only add to the defenders' woes but as far as total destruction of, for example, heavy and light gun positions was concerned, a rain of high explosive from high to medium altitude could often hinder rather than assist friendly troops. Medium bombers were much better in this respect but there were still problems for the men on the ground. Bomb sizes were really too small to knock out very strong structures and explosions invariably created rubble which gave the Germans excellent cover.

With a fluid front line, aerial weaponry had to be carefully selected for fear of causing casualties to friendly forces; A.A.F. fighters tended to use only guns and bombs on sorties during the early stages and not until 9 July was the first use of M10 triple-tube rocket-launchers authorised for Thunderbolt groups.

P-47s also flew sorties in conjunction with the R.A.F. although such combined efforts were relatively rare due to the adequate number of aircraft available to each force. But some targets absorbed a considerable amount of ordnance before being neutralised, one being the defences ringing the port of Cherbourg. From 22 June, Thunderbolts added their bombs to the rain of high explosive released by P-38s, Typhoons and R.A.F. Mustangs.

As the Normandy beachhead became established, some of the first men ashore were engineers with the task of preparing Advanced Landing Grounds for fighter-bombers. Fortunately the weather held long enough for many of these French fields and meadows to be selected, inspected and prepared without delay. These makeshift airfields were vital to close-support operations but the Germans were fully aware of the danger they posed and some of the A.L.G.s were shelled and mortared during the immediate post-invasion period.

On 19 June, the first Advanced Landing Ground on the continent, A3 at Cardonville, was occupied by the P-47s of the 395th F.S., 368th Group. Construction work on the strip lasted until the 23rd by which time Deux Jumeaux (A4) was nearing completion, as were five other A.L.G.s. In July, the 404th Fighter Group crossed to France to operate from Chapelle, the 36th Group went to Brucheville and on the 19th the 373rd occupied Tour-en-Bessin which was then little more than a rural airstrip bordered by an orchard.

Commanded by Col William H. Schwartz jr, the 373rd's assigned duty was tactical support operations for the U.S. Third Army. The group had moved into the A.L.G. located at Woodchurch in Kent in April and gone operational on 8 May. To give some idea of the intensity of the tactical air effort during the invasion period, by 23 August the 373rd's three squadrons had flown 4650 sorties, dropped 788 tons of bombs and fired about 500,000 rounds of ammunition.

A typical mission for the 373rd during July was to help break the defences of the port of Brest; of twelve P-47Ds (both razorbacks and bubble-top models then being on strength) sent out, eight were each armed with two 500 lb bombs and four remained in 'clean' condition to act as fighter cover. Take off was completed in 2.5 minutes.

Formed up into a broad 'V' the P-47s aimed to arrive over Brest at 10,000 feet with the fighter cover 2000 feet above. The fighter-bombers dropped to 7000 feet and turned away from the port area for 5 minutes while precise orders were passed to each pilot by radio. They then turned and in pairs carried out a bombing run, diving on the target at the operationally proven 60° angle. Using the standard gunsight, bomb release was found to be accurate enough, provided that individual aircraft were not allowed to skid or slip at the release point. If they did, bombs would then tend to straddle the target. Bomb release was made when the nose of the Thunderbolt covered the target, at about 2000 feet, A.S.I. 350 mph.

As each pilot climbed away, he made a tight turn to observe the results of his bombing before forming up with the top cover at 12,000 ft to fly home. While the 373rd Group used 500 lb bombs during the Brest strikes, loads were varied according to the type of target being attacked. Limited use was made of the P-47's full load of 2000 lb (1000-pounder under each wing), two 500-pounders being found to be adequate for most ground support operations. The majority of A.A.F. bombing sorties in Normandy utilised only 250 lb and 500 lb bombs.

Army support sorties were often at the behest of Air Liaison Officers riding in the leading vehicles of armoured columns. These individuals, who were more often than not flyers themselves, briefed the pilots as to the latest situation – this information in turn being largely supplied by aerial reconnaissance. After each mission, the bombing results observed by pilots were passed to Army headquarters to be put with a mass of ground reports to build a comprehensive picture of enemy disposition and defence capability.

While it was at Tour-en-Bessin, the 373rd's groundcrews performed both minor servicing and major overhauls of the P-47s. The latter included full engine changes, repair of superchargers and minor or extensive airframe repair as necessary. Complete wing changes were made, often by cannibalisation of other airframes. All tasks were immeasurably assisted by an adequate supply of good quality tools, jacks and workstands, American units being renowned for the Army's generous issue of the means to service aeroplanes under almost any conditions.

Engine changes were made after 200 hours, with removal and installation being completed by the side of the strip in about three hours. Two hours were generally taken on testing and to properly 'run in' a new engine, the book stated that it had to be low-run in the air for 10 hours at not more than 2000 rpm. Whether or not front line combat groups were always able to comply with these neat and tidy regulations is, however, open to conjecture.

If any particularly tricky problems arose with the P-47s, the group servicing personnel could call on civilian representatives from Republic, Pratt & Whitney, Curtiss, and Hamilton. During its early period in Normandy, the 373rd had the services of Republic rep Charles J. Jacobie and he, like the others, travelled with a comprehensive tool kit which included some not issued to Army Air Force groups as standard items. Field representatives also had the authority to take major decisions concerning aircraft safety and availability for combat operations.

By August 1944, the 373rd had seen some combat with the *Luftwaffe* despite its modest time in the E.T.O. Lt-Col Michael J. Ingelido, D.F.C, 412th Squadron commander, had by 18 July claimed seven and a half enemy aircraft, more than enough to make him an ace. This score, even with one half claim added later, was later downgraded by the U.S.A.A.F. Victory Credits Board to an overall four and a half. Ingelido's total therefore fell just short of

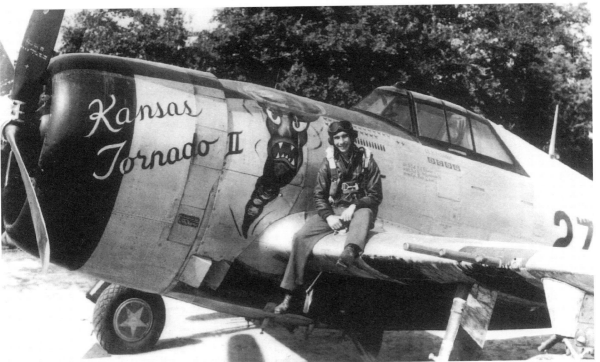

*Top: Gasolene and oil were the other vital commodities to sustain a front-line air force, which was what the Ninth became in mid-1944. While bowsers plied the flightline keeping the Thunderbolts topped up, men were kept busy filling the jerrycans from bowsers. (U.S.A.F.)*

*Above: Dozens of Ninth P-47s piled up 'scores' consisting of aircraft, trains, trucks, barges and bridges – and a stencil symbol was made for all of them. Updating the scoreboards took time and the rate of destruction in Normandy was so high that such things sometimes had to wait. A lull would enable the decoration to be completed, as on this blue-nosed P-47D of the 510th F.S., 406th F.G. (Campbell Archives)*

the magic five and he does not figure as an ace in postwar listings. 'Positive publicity' and press coverage of aces in wartime helped morale and it was only later, when *Luftwaffe* loss records could be checked, that anomalies emerged. On the other hand, Capt S. Scalzi swore not to have even seen an enemy aircraft at all during his first fifty missions. In total, the 373rd was credited with 107 aerial victories up to its last mission on 6 May 1945, with one pilot, Capt Edward B. Edwards of the 411th Squadron, becoming the group's sole ace with a score of five and a half.

Even though its groups were flying daily combat sorties, the Ninth Air Force was extremely accommodating to journalists and photographers, group P.R.O.s often going out of their way to publicise what the U.S.A.A.F. was doing to help the war effort. This extended to taking some of the war's greatest photographs and Col Schwartz himself helped to put the 373rd on the map by piloting a Piper Cub to shoot film of a 410th Fighter Squadron P-47D (42-25845/R3-G) over the historic Mont-St-Michel fortress.

The German situation became increasingly untenable as the Allies poured vast quantities of men, vehicles and equipment into the bridgehead at Normandy. Air cover was virtually absolute and although resistance on the ground was often stubborn, the enemy was gradually worn down.

Immediately after the landings, the fighter-bombers attacked a variety of targets but, in the first few days, bridges over the Seine and marshalling yards predominated. Fighter-bombers, which came under IX T.A.C. control as soon as they were able to operate from the continent, had the immediate priority of isolating the Germans in the Normandy area and cutting off all their escape routes out of France. The interdiction campaign against all forms of transportation and communications links, begun before the invasion, was continued.

During June, IX T.A.C. aircraft co-ordinated air strikes with those of IX Bomber Command mediums to knock out six Seine bridges, the P-47s and P-38s attacking other, less well built structures which could later take on increasing importance if all the primary bridges were destroyed. Fifteen marshalling yards were also hit by fighter-bombers in this early period and numerous locomotives and rolling stock were denied to the enemy as a

result. Many rail lines were also cut. Enemy vehicles of all kinds, from substantial road convoys to single trucks and horse-drawn wagons, were strafed and bombed.

Third Army landed in France on 6 July, whereupon XIX T.A.C. followed suit to provide close air support. Bad weather intervened early in July and on the 11th the P-47s of the 366th Group were forced to keep low, under 1000 feet on three rain-soaked missions to knock out tanks at St-Lô and prevent a German counterattack.

St-Lô became a bottleneck well defended by strong German forces and in an attempt to break it the Allies carpet-bombed the area. P-47s were part of a huge force totalling more than 2600 heavies, mediums and fighters that poured explosives into an area one mile deep and five miles long. Inevitably some bombs fell wide and 102 U.S. soldiers were killed. But the deluge of fire broke the German defence and the advance, previously held up by the notorious natural barriers of bocage, was able to proceed and make all speed for Avranches. Flying combat missions over St-Lô slightly delayed the move of the Raiders (406th F.G.) to France, the group becoming another occupant of Tour-en-Bessin on 5 August.

After the controversial carpet-bombing mission, IX T.A.C. issued a report stating that fighter-bombers were consistently showing better results in terms of bombing accuracy compared to the mediums and heavies. While this may have appeared quite obvious, the report recommended that distances from friendly troops to the bomb line be much more carefully estimated if any similar missions were flown – and that applied equally to the fighter-bombers. But there was no doubt that forward troops preferred fighter-bombers, exemplified in many sectors solely by P-47s, to take out enemy strong points immediately ahead of them, as bombers could never guarantee quite the accuracy required.

During the last week of July, the contribution made by A.A.F. fighters, the majority of them P-47s, was no less than 9185 sorties, during which the enemy was denied an estimated 384 tanks, 2287 motor vehicles and seventy-one gun emplacements as well as troops, locomotives and bridges. T.A.C. lost seventy-eight fighters, only ten of them to air action.

With *Overlord* a reality, the *Luftwaffe* reacted where it could although the battle area was little short of a vast killing ground for any German fighters if they ran into Allied aircraft or ground fire. The 404th F.G. clashed with the *Jagdwaffe* on 30 July while the group was conducting a 48-hour round of sorties against armour located between Granville and Avranches. A 507th Squadron flight ran into twenty Bf 109s which were largely dissuaded from tangling with the Thunderbolts. Capt Thomas L. Weller caught two of them. One German pilot put his machine into a violent snap roll before baling out, as did his colleague, but only after Weller's burst of fire had hit his aircraft.

In a busy day, a flight from the group's 506th F. S. clashed with nine FW 190s as the P-47s were making bombing runs. Lt Max W. Conn turned inside one of the enemy fighters, latched on to its tail and promptly blew it up with a short burst of fire. He damaged a second 190 and was himself jumped by a third which was chased off by Lt Earl Fisher, Jr who had himself just destroyed two. Lieutenants Charles R. Hansen and Eugene J. McClosky, respectively flying as wingmen to Fisher and Conn, scored one each.

Seven down was highly respectable but there was more action to come later in the day. Around eight in the evening, a 507th flight chased off a flock of eighteen Bf 109s. Then two more were spotted by the flight leader, Capt George C. Hughes and his wingman Lt John J. Rogers. Both pilots positioned their P-47s behind the unsuspecting German

fighters and in a classic one-two punch, shot them both down. Lt. John C. Ross added another to bring the 404th's tally of aerial victories to fifteen. Before the action the group's total score had been a modest five.

Isolating the Normandy battlefield was a task of systematic, relentless destruction. Creating such carnage held some unexpected horrors for fighter-bomber pilots, including 'target fixation'. Capt Wallace H. Cameron of the 48th Group's 493rd F.S. experienced his fair share and recalled vividly diving on a tank that was in the act of levelling its 88mm gun at an unsuspecting American infantry column. Leading his flight down, Cameron watched his 0.50-in calibre rounds bouncing harmlessly off the tank armour in a mesmerising, multicoloured display. It was almost too magnetic. At the very last moment, he stopped firing, stamped on both rudder pedals and pulled the stick back hard. The Thunderbolt shot up through the cloud, carrying a young American pilot wondering what he could possibly have been thinking about to risk his neck in such a fashion.

Another mission brought home to Wallace Cameron the sheer density of Allied air power over a given sector of the front. He was in the process of carrying out a text-book strafing attack on a troop train stopped in a forest clearing. The Thunderbolt flight leader carefully shot up the locomotive, the next pilot put his rounds in the coal tender and the P-47s then

*Meanwhile, back in England . . . the 56th had received new P-47Ds with the bubble-top canopy, these being used on operations alongside the razorback models. In natural metal finish, Shack Rat was a 63rd Squadron P-47D-28.*

worked their fire down the carriages. Cameron made one last pass and was about to thumb the firing button when the entire train blew up in his face, exploding all along its length. With no chance of avoiding the debris, Cameron flew through it, amazed at emerging unscathed.

It transpired that a group of B-26 Marauders had chosen just that moment to unload their bombs through the overcast, their bombardiers unware that P-47s were under them. The mediums were, nevertheless, deadly accurate, as their bombs destroyed not only the train but the lines and all the troops who had sought refuge behind an embankment when the Thunderbolts first attacked. What worried Cameron was that two seconds later he would have been directly in line with the falling bombs.

German *Panzertruppen* and lesser mortals tasked wth driving soft-skinned supply vehicles reached what became known as the Falaise Pocket in August – and there many of them would lay down their lives. Following the First U.S. Army breakout from St-Lô at the end of July in Operation *Cobra*, the Germans launched a counterattack at Mortain. It failed and the subsequent German retreat developed into an Allied envelopment of the exposed German Army. This was the Falaise Pocket in which a major part of the German Army was trapped and destroyed. The destruction was largely due to overwhelming Allied air power; bomb- and rocket-carrying Typhoons were instrumental in the victory.

The A.A.F. bemoaned the fact that it had not been able to field a true anti-tank aircraft, for German tanks outgunned most A.F.V.s on the Allied side. While it was true that most anti-tank aircraft used in the Second World War were the result of expedient modifications, the P-47 probably destroyed more tanks than any other U.S. tactical aircraft in the inventory without resort to any special weapons.

Although cannon were mounted on the wing racks for a series of operational tests, the Thunderbolt never carried into action these or any other large calibre guns as favoured by the *Luftwaffe* (and indeed by the R.A.F. to some extent), nor was the P-47D wing stressed to carry more than three-launcher tubes for rockets until later in the conflict. The 0.50-in machine-gun round remained such a good midway compromise between the 20mm cannon shell and the lighter 0.30-in machine-gun bullet that there was little reason to change, especially

as the 0.50-in Browning demonstrated outstanding reliability. So effective was the weight of fire that could be brought to bear by a single P-47 that many otherwise resilient targets succumbed. And the combat groups devised their own techniques to exploit this advantage. The 358th Group was one that regularly carried out target strafing with four P-47s attacking in line abreast formation – thirty-two guns blasting away at once usually did the trick.

Well-concentrated bursts of 0.50-in machine-gun rounds, high velocity aircraft rockets (H.V.A.R.s), napalm, general purpose and armour-piercing bombs were all effective in at least badly damaging or disabling even a Panther or Tiger tank. So much depended on skill – not to say cool nerve – of the pilot pressing in close enough to make his ordnance count. In the teeth of determined flak, it was never easy.

The triple-tube M10 launcher for 4.5-in rockets, widely adopted for various P-47 models, did little to improve airflow under the wings. Many pilots, on first acquaintance with the 'stovepipe' projectiles, felt the rockets themselves to be widely inaccurate. Practice and a good eye improved things and four Eighth Air Force groups, the 56th 78th, 353rd and 356th, were issued with sets of tubes and sixty rockets in August 1944. A number of attacks were made into September, after which the launch points were generally removed from the P-47s. Thunderbolts of the Ninth, Twelfth and the Pacific air forces used the M10 to good effect but it did little for the P-47's handling qualities. The pilots who flew the Eighth's operational rocket tests were actually comforted by the fact that these early model launchers were jettisonable in an emergency.

Gunfire could be used effectively against A.F.V.s if the pilot could aim his rounds at exactly the right spot adjacent to a tank from which the rounds richochetted up into its underside where it was not heavily armoured. Again, the wide margin for error can be appreciated. Many A.A.F. fighter pilots tended to lump all enemy armour under the heading of 'tanks' when in fact the *Wehrmacht* fielded a variety of self-propelled guns, tank destroyers and assault guns, all with varying degrees of protection against air attack. Many an American fighter-bomber pilot flew home confident in the knowledge that his accurate bursts of machine-gun fire had crippled a tank or two despite flames and especially smoke quickly obscuring the scene. Many tanks

Ole' Cock III *the mount of the Wolfpack's Donavon Smith, was one of many unusually camouflaged P-47Ds used by the group and this pilot's third Thunderbolt, a P-47D-26-RA, No. 42-28322, was coded HV-S. Note the long streamer from the pitot tube, affixed to prevent anyone walking into it. (U.S.A.F.)*

and other A.F.V.s survived such assaults – as indeed they had been designed to do.

Well-aimed armour-piercing bombs were probably the most effective weapon against tanks, provided that they hit with enough velocity in vulnerable areas, particularly the engine compartment, any hull section which had louvres for ventilation purposes and the wheel bogey system, particularly the track guide sprocket wheels. Tracks and individual wheels could be knocked off but, if field maintenance crews were on hand, the vehicle would not be out of action for long.

Thunderbolt groups also became adept at delivering a deadly addition to conventional high explosive bombs on a variety of targets. A P-47 could, in addition to carrying a 500 lb bomb containing various compositions including RDX, M17 or M76 incendiaries on the belly and wing racks, and accommodate multiple M41 fragmentation bombs. These small, 20 lb weapons were attached, usually in clusters of six, to a simple 'A' frame rack that straddled the main G.P. bomb, for a total weight of 128 lb. Up to twenty-four could be carried on the centreline rack of a P-47, although the clusters usually comprised a maximum of twenty bombs to hang from two lugs on a standard 500 lb bomb station. Deadly to ground personnel, 'frags' as they became universally

known, were widely used in all war theatres.

One drawback with fragmentation bombs was their unpredictability, particularly if the aircraft was hit and they 'hung up' for some reason. If the bombs could not be jettisoned they invariably exploded on touch down and destroyed the aircraft.

To put the bombs where they would have the most effect, forward air controllers (usually pilots on rotational duty) riding with the ground armies, directed the fighter-bombers. These 'airtank teams' as they became known, had the authority to switch briefed targets to airborne units if the front-line situation warranted more urgent attention. Alternatively, pilots would be directed to another sector of the front to receive an in-flight briefing for another target. This flexibility enabled numerous enemy strong points, fixed or mobile, to be attacked at very short notice.

By utilising the combined weaponry of different aircraft types and the special expertise of the pilots flying them, the Allies were able at Falaise and elsewhere, to cause terrible destruction to the retreating Panzer columns. Tanks on the battlefield do not necessarily have to be destroyed to render them useless. And by doing their best to ensure that German tanks ran out of ammunition and fuel by laying waste their columns of supply trucks, which were highly vulnerable to aerial assault, the Allied Expeditionary Air Force effectively starved the tank crews to death.

When the remnants of the *Wehrmacht* reached the Seine, the widespread destruction of the bridges by tactical bombers obliged the use of barges to ferry vehicles, supplies and men across. River traffic consequently began to figure prominently in Allied fighter-bomber briefings and further destruction was meted out to the Germans. Above all, being forced on to waterways and roads that were already heavily interdicted took precious time – time the Germans could ill afford.

Most P-47 targets in support of the Allied drive across France were on land but occasionally the Ninth Air Force groups were called upon to fly sorties against German naval units which were quite active around the French coast. A series of anti-shipping missions took place during the first two weeks of August, the 371st Group based at Beuzeville (A6) being one of the P-47 units involved in attacks on German minesweepers. These vessels, although small, could be formidable adversaries for fighter-bombers, as Eric Doorly found out. The pilots were briefed to use fragmentation bombs against the ships but most of these missed, probably because they were released too high, at 15,000 feet. The pilots went down to strafe in a 485 mph dive and pulled up very low – no more than 10 feet according to Doorly – around 1000 yards from the ships.

The German flak opened up and the 371st aircraft flew through a solid wall of bursts that were green in colour. Doorly's aircraft took hits in the left wing and an 11-inch section was shot out of the windscreen. Nevertheless, an explosion was seen aboard the minesweeper he had attacked, one of twelve such ships the enemy lost during the period. The 371st's Thunderbolts almost certainly sank the M370, the last to go down off Royen on 12 August.

## NEW COMMANDS

As the Allied advance continued across France, ground forces inevitably thinned out in some sectors and in general the armies had to cope with ever-lengthening supply lines. Tactical air power was, if anything, even more of an asset than before in that it could hit the Germans hard in rear areas well beyond the battlefields. American fighter-bombers, mediums and attack

bombers – B-26 Marauders and A-20 Havocs – R.A.F. mediums – Bostons and Mitchells – plus Typhoons, Mustangs, Spitfires and Mosquitoes, all focussed their main support effort on preventing *Wehrmacht* counterattacks interfering with the push to the German border. Operating both from bases in England and the liberated areas of continental Europe, they achieved a level of air superiority that was never lost.

From October, deteriorating weather conditions forced a slow-down in the advance although Allied air power coped well enough with low temperatures, a solid cloud base, fog and, ultimately, heavy snowfalls. But pilots still needed worthwhile targets and these became scarcer as the enemy appeared to go to ground under an all-enveloping blanket of winter. Air reconnaissance began reporting little of military value as the Allied armies, now spread thinly from northern Holland to southern France, prepared to sit it out and await some improvement in the weather.

The hectic pace of the push out of Normandy had taken a heavy toll in men and machines alike; many air units were understrength and not receiving new model replacement aircraft. In the tactical P-47 groups many razorback examples were not replaced by D-25s and later production models with bubble canopies until the end of the war. Some pilots preferred to stay with the older model which, apart from the cockpit blind spot (not so much of a problem with few enemy aircraft about) and some less automated systems, retained the good flying characteristics inherent in the early model P-47s.

To offset the vision problem, some razorback P-47s had their original 'greenhouse' style cockpit canopy replaced by a clear-view Malcolm hood. Designed and manufactured in England, this item was much sought after by individual American fighter pilots. Output was unfortunately unable to match high demand. Malcolm hoods were fitted to R.A.F. Mustang IIIs, A.A.F. P-51Bs and Cs and P-47s, in that order. The Thunderbolt appeared to come a poor third in this respect but the bubbletop D model solved the problem completely, at least for those groups that continued to fly the type. Fighter units generally anticipated the delivery of Mustang, the type that would largely replace the Thunderbolt as a fighter *per se* in most war theatres although the tactical groups would generally stay with the Jug.

# 7
# New Fronts

Having absorbed most of the American fighter groups sent to Europe in the autumn of 1942, the Twelfth Air Force in North Afica was marginally better placed to escort its bombers than the Eighth could escort its heavies. Attrition was high among the P-38 squadrons although the warmer conditions were somewhat kinder to the Lockheed fighter's systems. Otherwise, the Twelfth deployed primarily P-39s, Spitfires and P-40s in the fighter and fighter-bomber roles until the end of the campaign in North Africa. Following the surrender of Italy in September 1943, the Allied air war could be substantially expanded by moving forces up from North Africa to use airfields on the Italian mainland.

On 1 November 1943, the A.A.F. command structure in the Middle East was revised, primarily to create a new strategic bomber arm, the Fifteenth Air Force. Up to that point, the Ninth Air Force had flown both tactical and strategic sorties using B-17s and B-24s in company with the mainly tactical Twelfth which had controlled all U.S. air units earmarked for the Mediterranean Theatre of Operations to support Operation *Torch* in November 1942, and which it continued to do.

With the creation of the Fifteenth Air Force, P-38s, flown by the 1st, 14th and 82nd Fighter Groups, were retained as a bomber escort force, while P-40s remained with the 325th Group, the 'Checkertails'. This latter unit, comprising the 317th, 318th and 319th Squadrons, was listed to be the first group in the Mediterranean to receive P-47s. Led by the exuberant Lt-Col Robert L. Baseler, the Checkertails had gone through the P-47 transition training programme organised by the A.A.F., Republic and technical equipment representatives during late September 1943. Everyone went back to school to learn about the mighty P-47, the first example of which arrived in time-honoured fashion on 11 October when Bob Baseler buzzed the group's

*A black scorpion emblem and the low number identify this P-47D-10 (42-75713) as belonging to the 57th Fighter Group's 64th Fighter Squadron, probably photographed at Alto, Corsica. (J. Campbell)*

home airfield which was then Mateur in Tunisia. Wet weather forced a move to a drier part of the country at Soliman on 4 November, where pilots found paved runways, something of a luxury for the 'Clan' during its time in Africa. Ironically, Soliman was to be the group's last base in that part of the world.

Having latterly operated as part of North-West African Stategic Air Force (N.A.S.A.F.), the Checkertails had conducted what amounted to almost a private war against Axis airfields on Sardina before changing over to the P-47. The P-40 era had produced four aces, including Baseler. Duty for the group under the Fifteenth would be primarily bomber escort; the new home was Foggia Main in Italy. Transfer of the entire group to Italy had not been completed by the time the first P-47 mission was flown, a bomber escort to targets in Greece on 14 December. Five 'milk runs' followed. And then on Christmas Day the group lost three P-47s to weather-related causes.

These Thunderbolts were by no means the last Allied aircraft to succumb to the Allied planners' mistaken belief that 'sunny Italy' might enable bomber and fighter operations to be less disrupted by unfavourable weather conditions than those from England. A two-pronged bomber offensive against Germany was indeed achieved but such operations could not be as frequent nor as coordinated with those of the Eighth as smoothly as A.A.F. plans had foreseen.

The giant Foggia plain complex of airfields rapidly filled up with Allied air units and the 325th soon moved out to Celone, better known as Foggia No. 1, a move completed on 30 December.

When the Checkertails changed their P-47s for Mustangs, some of their aircraft were passed to the 332nd Group (manned exclusively by African Americans), pending the latter's re-equipment, also with Mustangs, for long-range escort duty. It was with some relief to the 332nd that this occurred, for the alternative type considered for the black pilots was the P-63 Kingcobra. Instead, the yellow and black checkers of the 325th were painted over with the unit's new all-red tail colour and the 100th, 301st and 302nd Fighter Squadrons returned to the war. Not all the handed-down Thunderbolts, some complete with their Checkertails identification numbers, were repainted as there

was precious little time. The 332nd flew its first Fifteenth A.F. mission as part of the 306th Fighter Wing, on 7 June 1944.

Flying a B-24 escort in the Udine area on 9 June, pilots of the 302nd Squadron shot down three Bf 109s, while 2nd Lt Frederick Funderburg of the 301st came home with two Messerschmitt victories from this mission. First Lieutenant Wendell O. Pruitt, who scored a wartime total of three victories with the 332nd, watched his Bf 109 explode under the impact of eight fifties after he had 'firewalled everything; to catch the enemy aircraft. This turned out to be the only aerial-scoring mission the unit flew in the P-47, but not the last time that the Thunderbolts used their guns. Something out of the ordinary occurred on 25 June.

Flying over Trieste harbour, Capt Joseph Elsberry was leading four other group P-47s when the pilots spotted an enemy warship which they identified as a destroyer, (although it was almost certainly of a smaller class). The ship's crew had clearly recognised the Thunderbolts as enemy aircraft and began throwing up an impressive flak barrage. Undaunted by the fact that they carried no ordnance suitable for sinking a warship, the 332nd attacked with Wendell Pruitt setting the scene by strafing the vessel and immediately starting fires. Lt Pierson's guns then set off a spectacular explosion.

Back at Ramitelli, the group's base, Fifteenth A.F. Headquarters was unconvinced of the success of the shipping strike until the pilots' combat film was processed. They were duly credited with sinking the ship, a fitting enough finale to the 332nd's brief association with the P-47, which ended in late June with the arrival of the first P-51Cs. The detached 99th F.S. returned to the group on 3 July and the 332nd thereafter achieved an exemplary record flying the P-51.

**TACTICAL CHANGES**
Along with the creation of a second U.S.A.A.F. strategic bomber force, the Twelfth also underwent re-equipment of its component groups. The first to receive P-47s was the 57th Fighter Group (comprising the 64th 'Black Scorpions', 65th 'Fighting Cocks' and 66th 'Exterminators' Squadrons) led by Col Arthur G. Salisbury. Then based at Alto, Corsica, the

*Checkertail Thunderbolt unmistakably identifies the 325th Fighter Group, one of the Twelfth Air Force's crack units. The Jenny A (No. 78) was flown by Lt William Carswell who named his aircraft after a Republic worker. (R.L. Ward)*

group took delivery of its first Thunderbolts on 28 November. The change-over from Warhawks (examples of which remained with the group until January 1944) found the 57th with a hard-won reputation for low-level bombing and strafing missions, roles for which the P-47 was highly suited.

Enemy aircraft, which had been reduced in number through combat, attrition and the voracious needs of the defence of Germany which took on increasing importance, could still be found and the 57th had claimed 189 destroyed at the end of its P-40 era. The group moved to Italy and flew its first P-47 mission from Amendola on 5 December, giving the 57th the honour of flying the first Mediterranean Theatre of Operations P-47 sorties slightly ahead of the Checkertails.

Having 'got its eye in' with the new fighter, the 57th destroyed several enemy aircraft over Yugoslavia on the 16th without loss. The 57th had, for some weeks, been flying sorties mainly against ground targets located in Yugoslavia, the pilots appropriately nicknaming the P-47s 'Thunderbombers'. Dive attacks, using guns, bombs and M10 rocket tubes, were made on a variety of targets including German tanks attempting to

reinforce the Adolf Hitler Line in northern Italy. Shortly before the 79th Fighter Group could celebrate a year of overseas combat duty, it too changed its Warhawks for P-47s. The group, comprising the 85th 'Flying Skulls', the 86th 'Comanches' and 87th 'Skeeters' Squadrons, checked out its first two examples at Capodichino, the group's Italian base, on 13 February 1944.

A mixed reaction to the P-47 similar to that experienced by many other new recipients, came from the 79th; while it now had an enviable reputation as a versatile, effective combat aircraft, its size still impressed even though it was one of the worst kept secrets in the Army Air Forces that Republic had 'built big'. Someone referred to the P-47 coming from 'the Republic Locomotive Works and Iron Foundry' which really said it all. While it was transitioning to the P-47, the 79th Group continued to patrol the beach-head at Anzio where the invading Allied armies had missed an early chance to push inland and had then been pinned down by strong German counterattacks spearheaded by armour in considerable strength.

For weeks, the outcome hung in the balance while the air above Anzio was the scene of intense air combat, fighter-bomber strikes by

*An armament specialist loads a single round into an M10 rocket-launcher under the wing of 44-19611, a P-47D-28. The bomb will have its tail and fuse added last, just before take-off. Note the aileron/flap plate. (P. Jarrett)*

both sides, artillery duels and tank versus tank skirmishes. Monte Cassino, bombed and blasted far too effectively by Allied air power, had become a virtually impregnable fortress for die-hard German defenders who took every advantage of the piles of excellent cover created every time a wave of bombers pounded the ancient monastery – in short, the drive to clear the Germans from Italy had ground to a halt.

The 79th put eight P-47Ds over Anzio for the group's first mission in the new type on 9 March; the Comanches drew the honour with the Skulls following suit six days later while the Skeeters flew a mix of P-40s and P-47s into April. One year overseas for the 79th came on 14 March, a sort of celebration interrupted by six fighter-bomber missions flown that day. On the 15th, the group flew as part of a massive Twelfth Air Force assault on Cassino and put up four beachhead patrols. One Skull flight Thunderbolt took a direct hit from a British 25-pounder shell which promptly tore one wing right off the aircraft

flown by Lt George Bolte who had little choice but to 'hit the silk'. He made a hard landing after the chute deployed low at 200 ft. British troops picked up Bolte, who survived the experience and enjoyed the mugfuls of spiked tea plied by his rescuers.

Another record came for the 79th on 16 March when Capt Carl Stewart shot down a Bf 109, one of a gaggle carrying out dive-bombing sorties. Charles DeFoor also got a Bf 109 while Earl Maxwell damaged a third. These were the group's first victories with the Thunderbolt and the participants in the combat were reportedly well impressed by the Jug's speed and firepower.

On 19 March, the day Operation *Strangle* began, Mount Vesuvius stole some of the air planners' thunder by violently erupting. Volcanic ash boiled 20,000 feet into the air and, as a safety precaution to prevent its P-47s being damaged, the 57th Group was among those units which made a timely move to an airfield north of Cercola beyond nature's wrath. The Group then moved out to Alto, Corsica.

Col Archie J. Knight took over command of

the 57th on 23 April and operations, begun with the wide-ranging *Strangle* target list in the spring, continued with few breaks. *Strangle* was literally that – an ambitious plan to throttle all north-south links and deny the Germans their vital supplies by destroying whatever means of transportation they could use as they retreated progressively further north.

As a precaution against *Luftwaffe* interference, 18 March had seen the 57th mounting a massive strike on enemy airfields at the head of the Adriatic which all but neutralised much of the enemy fighter force remaining in Italy. The Germans retained a presence until the Italian *Aeronautica Nazionale Repubblicana* largely took over the air defence of the country. But Allied pilots would henceforth encounter relatively small numbers of interceptors to threaten heavy bomber strikes and challenge the tactical fighter and bomber sorties that were the crux of *Strangle*. Many were Bf 109s with Italian pilots at the controls and Allied aircrews were to encounter numerous Macchi C.202s and C.205s plus Fiat G.55s in the ensuing months.

The 79th Group also flew escort missions to heavy and medium bomber operations, as did the other P-47 groups in the M.T.O./E.T.O. and the now increasingly infrequent clashes with the *Luftwaffe* still exacted casualties on both sides. On 30 March, the 79th drew a B-25 escort and the 86th F.S. had along a number of French pilots to gain P-47 experience. Lt Pierre Gouachon shot down an FW 190, a useful morale booster to his brother pilots. Carl Stewart's fire flamed another 190 for his fourth victory.

As front-line tuition for French airmen continued, so on 31 March the 79th bade farewell to the black pilots of the 99th F.S. who had received enthusiastic help in transitioning to the P-47 from their white colleagues. The 99th had an already generally high degree of readiness through its P-40 combat experience and some excellent pilots but few men had flown any other aircraft type. Colonel Earl Bates had done much to make the black pilots welcome and to provide a fair assessment of individual capability before they joined the 332nd Group and the 306th Fighter Wing. This also had the P-38 groups as well as the 31st, 52nd and 325th Groups with single-seaters.

Fighter-bomber operations continued under *Strangle* directives, the P-47-equipped units maintaining the pressure on a daily basis. The 79th drew a target list typical of the theatre and the tactical situation – the pilots dive-bombed, rocketed and strafed marshalling yards, bridges and railway rolling stock. And on 28 April, the group attacked harbour installations at San Stefano. This absorbed ninety-eight sorties, some ordnance being shared with the marshalling yards at Orbetellow.

On 15 April, the 79th hung record loads on three Comanche aircraft, a 1,000-pounder on each wing rack and a 500-pounder under the belly. Local trials confirmed A.A.F. directives that the P-47D could cope well enough with 2500 lb of ordnance, but this was the first time that the full load was carried in action in the M.T.O. The Thunderbolt trio dropped its load in the Cassino area without any mishap.

### NEW MODELS

On 1 July, the 66th F.S., the 'Exterminators', encountered the increasingly elusive enemy in the air and shot down six Bf 109s without loss. Having flown all its early P-47 sorties with razorback models, the 57th took delivery of the first examples fitted with the bubble canopy during the month. By then some of the squadron aircraft were looking decidedly the worse for wear, due both to the continual need to have the maximum number on the line for operations and the often spartan, dust-laden airfields that often prevailed in the M.T.O. and which did little to enhance paintwork.

While the 57th was based at Alto, film director William Wyler moved in to shoot the movie *Thunderbolt*, a superb visual record of one A.A.F. group's contribution to the tactical air war over Italy. Recorded during several weeks' operations, the film remains one of the best wartime documentaries and one of the few to really capture the M.T.O. All the 'actors' were the pilots, groundcrews and P-47s of the 57th Group.

Targets for the ordnance of Thunderbolts of the Flying Circus soon included German positions in southern France. Pilots eagerly anticipated the invasion, which took place on 15 August. The 57th's Thunderbolts were ordered to patrol the beaches and five flights from each squadron were up by 07.30. As the invasion forces pushed inland, the 57th remained on Corsica, much to everyone's disgust but on 9 September it was confirmed that the group's new location would be Italy. The group duly moved to the mainland and wound up at Grosseto which had better drainage than the quagmire conditions experienced after every heavy rainfall at its allocated base at Ombrone.

With the Germans all but impregnable within their Gothic Line defences, the Allies relied on air power to isolate the battlefield by cutting road and rail links bringing reinforcements through the Brenner Pass from Austria. From Alto, the 57th had had to fly east for 60 miles to make landfall on the coast of Italy. A new northerly heading would then position the fighter-bombers anything from 150 miles to 200 miles behind the German lines.

Operation *Bingo*, designed to stop all enemy traffic using the Brenner Pass, began on 6 November. It was *Strangle* over again but now the enemy's notorious ability to defend vital targets with anti-aircraft guns reached new proportions. It was estimated that the Germans had nearly 1000 guns, more than half of them heavy 88 mm and 105 mm pieces, guarding the 160-mile stretch from Verona to Innsbruck. 'Little black flowers that grow in the sky' was the airmen's poetic comments on the deadly flak bursts that relentlessly greeted them during the Battle of the Brenner. Turbulence that built up over the Alps also bounced heavily laden Thunderbolts about, making accurate bombing even more difficult. Pilots experienced wind speeds of up to 60 mph in the vicinity of mountains reaching up 7000 feet to 10,000 feet.

Rail bridges were the toughest targets of all, requiring a high degree of precision bombing by fighter-bombers with relatively small loads while the Germans used any ruse to disguise the effects of the air interdicton, particularly smoke to blanket transport movement. Natural shadow from mountain crags also made the pilots' task that much more difficult. Where possible, the Germans circumvented rail cuts by utilising road haulage but this took much more time and roads were relatively easy targets for interdiction by Allied *Jabos*. But despite adverse natural hazards, weather conditions and the flak, the A.A.F. Thunderbolt groups ensured that the main rail line was cut on an almost daily basis,

medium-bomber strikes backing up those by the fighter-bombers.

Such was the pace of operations during the winter of 1944-5 that the 57th flew its 3000th sortie on 21 December. Fittingly, Col Knight led the milestone sortie at the head of the 66th Squadron. Normal attrition and enemy action took their toll particularly of those young, inexperienced men who had inevitably been thrown in at the deep end; of one new group of sixteen replacement pilots assigned to the 57th in November 1944, nine had been lost on combat flights or in accidents by 4 February 1945.

On a 7 February mission, the 36th for replacement pilot Ken Lewis, the P-47 flown by his flight leader was hit by flak. A fuselage fire burned through the control cables to the tailplane, leaving the pilot only ailerons and trim tabs. A small explosion apparently extinguished the fire but the Thunderbolt was a cripple, impossible to land. The pilot baled out.

Ground attacks were always dangerous, as the pilots of a two-ship flight of the 57th found out on 9 February while attacking a train. Such was the speed at which the attacks were made that fighters invariably had difficulty in avoiding resulting explosions. On this occasion, a direct bomb hit caused a giant explosion which engulfed the lead P-47 and set it ablaze. The pilot pulled up and baled out, his wingman later reporting that he was being fired at while his parachute drifted earthwards. The 57th kept up the pace.

## ENTER THE 86th

Having moved to Capodichino airfield near Naples in January 1944 as one of the two original A-36 M.T.O. dive-bomber units, the 86th Group with its 525th, 526th and 527th Squadrons, continued to fly P-40s in support of the Anzio landings and received its first razorback P-47s in March. Operations continued much as before; *Strangle* sorties were interspersed with attacking German Fourteenth Army positions around Anzio where the Allies had been pinned down. Escort to medium bombers attempting to break the deadlock and get the Allies moving on the road to Rome maintained the group's hectic sortie rate.

Working further north where the German Tenth army was strung out across Italy, the 86th was subject to attack by Axis fighters. It soon became a deadly gamble to see if the enemy

*Top: Dispersed P-47Ds of the 86th Fighter Group at Pisa, Italy in 1944. The aircraft on the left was from the 526th F.S., that on the right from the 527th. Both had the group red-and-white striped tail marking. (P. Jarrett)*

*Above: Remembered as the only natural-metal finish P-47D in the 325th Group, the second mount of Checkertail Clan pilot Lt Warren Penny was similarly named* Topper *after a camouflaged machine assigned to him. The slight crash damage in evidence here was repaired. (J. Campbell)*

pilots were seriously bent on dogfighting the Thunderbolts or were merely making a feint to make the American pilots jettison their bombs. If the Americans did so and the German and Italian fighters then sought the nearest cloud, the fighter-bomber mission was a failure. The 86th's aircraft began keeping their bombs firmly attached until the enemy's intentions were known and some pilots even took on the enemy aircraft and manoeuvred with their ordnance aboard. Apart from the weight, unfused bombs did not represent as much of a handling restriction as they might have seemed, even in a hectic dogfight.

Rail targets also offered the pilots the deadly challenge of trying to block tunnels. For these 'guts' missions the P-47s needed a steep dive angle with ample room to pull up as the sheer rock face loomed ever nearer. On occasions pilots had the unnerving experience of their bombs missing a tiny tunnel entrance, hitting the rock wall and ricochetting upwards. Actually seeing your own bombs pass the aircraft as it clawed for altitude was a far from happy feeling. Fused or not, the pilots always mistrusted rogue bombs, although there were no instances of aircraft being lost to this cause.

The 86th joined the rest of the 12th's fighter-bomber groups in Corsica, its home airfield at Serragia being shared with the P-47s of the 79th, the latter having arrived on 11 June. Along with the 57th at Grosseto, these three P-47 groups formed the 87th Wing, XII T.A.C.

A similar history attended the fortunes of the original A-36 dive-bomber unit in the M.T.O., the 27th Fighter-Bomber Group (522nd, 523rd and 524th Squadrons), which more or less ran out of replacement aircraft after North American terminated the production run of 500 aircraft. There was little choice but for the Group's pilots to keep their hand in by flying some quite 'war weary' P-40s which they did from January 1944, pending the delivery of P-47s. These arrived in May while the group was based in Italy under the command of Col E. Newton.

More P-47 muscle would be added to the Twelfth Air Force during May 1944 when the 324th Group with its 314th, 315th and 316th 'Hell's Belles' Squadrons operating out of Pignataro Maggiore, Italy also turned in its P-40s. But it would be July before full conversion was completed and the Anzio and Cassino areas of the Italian front gave the group more than enough to think about.

Similar operations had been flown by the 350th Fighter Group with the difference that its original aircraft in the Twelfth had been the P-39 Airacobra with some 'export' P-400s making up the numbers. At the end of the Tunisian campaign, the 350th's component squadrons, the 345th 'Devil Hawk', 346th 'Checkerboard' and 347th 'Screaming Red Ass', had also received a number of P-38s to maintain mission require-ments, the supply of P-39s and their spares having inevitably deteriorated during some fifteen months of combat over North Africa. The unit was based on Corsica for much of 1944 and did not move to Italy until the autumn.

The M.T.O. Thunderbolt groups had three main targets areas: south of Florence, north of the Apennines to the Po Valley, and southern France. Operating from Corsica, all these locations had involved long and sometimes dangerous overwater flights and dangerous target approaches where well-sited enemy guns could hazard the low flying fighter-bombers without even hitting them. Shots into the water ahead of the formation created deadly geysers of water which were peppered with shrapnel. Low-trajectory shells fused for air-burst could be equally lethal.

Italian bases were therefore far more practical, with target ranges significantly shortened – which in turn enabled more ordnance to be carried by the P-47s for some missions. The Italian weather left much to be desired and although an intensive sortie rate was generally maintained, some revisions had to be made when loaded fighter-bombers became bogged down on waterlogged dispersals.

From being a little unreliable at first, the supply of new P-47s to the M.T.O. had picked up well by August 1944, so much so that a pilot could be virtually sure that a new aircraft would be awaiting him, should he have cause to abandon one during a mission or wreck one during a crash-landing. Nevertheless, not all the P-47s groups could report an abundance of fighters and some had to carefully marshal resources so that the ever-ingenious and hard-working groundcrews could keep them flying.

As the M.T.O.-based U.S.A.A.F. fighter-bomber units continued to pound away at the enemy, progress by the ground armies was definitely being made by the spring of 1944. The German position in Italy grew increasingly difficult and isolated and by April Operation *Diadem*, which was to last through to May, finally secured Cassino and forced a breach in the Gustav Line. The road to Rome finally lay open. The Eternal City welcomed the first Allied troops on 4 June 1944, the capital formally surrendering the following day.

Afterwards, the southern front was overshadowed by events in Normandy and other fronts, yet the Italian campaign was to grind on; there were thousands of German troops equipped to withstand Allied pressure and the country was politically fragmenting into numerous partisan groups. Little wonder that predictions for the war to be over by Christmas were heard far less. In the fighter and bomber group mess halls, men who flew daily against the German defences were all too well aware that despite Allied air superiority, the enemy could, if he chose, probably hold out for months. Optimism about winning the war quickly could, as had been shown before, be stifled by events.

## SLOW-DOWN IN THE WEST

By the autumn of 1944, Allied progress in the West and in Italy had stalled; the Rhine had not been crossed and northward progress on the Italian peninsula was proving far tougher than anyone had imagined. Fortified German lines of resistance had hampered many Allied plans and wrecked timetables aimed at ending the conflict by the end of 1944. And winter was looming.

In an attempt to break the deadlock and make a decisive crossing into Germany, Operation *Market Garden*, a British and American assault with airborne and ground forces intended to take the bridges at Eindhoven, Nijmegen and Arnhem, was launched on 17 September. The air support effort for the main force assault involved about 350 of the Eighth Air Force's fighters from fourteen groups which bombed and strafed German positions in the Nijmegen and Arnhem areas.

From the 17th to the 19th, one of the groups heavily in action over Holland was the 356th Group from Martlesham Heath. The P-47s were briefed to patrol the battle area at 2500 feet to draw fire. Having thus identified as many flak batteries as possible prior to the arrival of the troop-carrying transports over their drop zones, fighter pilots were to strafe and bomb as many as possible.

Initially, the Germans made the location of their guns relatively easy by the use of tracer – but they quickly refrained from doing this after the first attacks. More than eighty gun positions, ranging from pill-boxes to light machine-gun nests (this figure later being reduced to thirty-nine positions) were claimed to have been destroyed but as the group records candidly noted, 'it would be difficult to determine how successful the group was in silencing flak batteries, but there can be no doubt about its success in drawing enemy fire'.

The 356th lost five Thunderbolts during this three-day period but its work was recognised by the award of a Distinguished Unit Citation. One FW 190 was shot down by the 360th's John P. Tucker who was himself killed later when his aircraft went down after attacking a gun position near Nijmegen. Three of the five downed pilots survived.

Few pilots had quite the experience of Lt John W. Crump of the 360th, who, apart from having to take violent evasive action to avoid German ground fire, had his vision temporarily impaired by a levitating coyote. Very few men ever carried a passenger in the cockpit of a P-47, but to Wild Bill Crump this was routine. Combat flying would not be the same without his coyote copilot-cum live mascot, 'Jeep'.

Taking the legendary U.S. pilots' regard for pets to the extreme, early in 1944 Crump had christened a coyote cub after the animal in the Popeye cartoons of the time. Smuggled across the Atlantic in the *Queen Elizabeth* when the 356th sailed to England, Bill Crump continued Jeep's training and regularly flew combat missions with the animal ensconced on the floor of the P-47, apparently unperturbed by the machinations of human conflict, as most missions were below oxygen height. Both occupants survived the Arnhem incident without harm but the coyote was later run over, ironically, by a Jeep.

That the P-47 had grown into a formidable fighting machine was hardly in doubt by late 1944, even though its role had undergone considerable change. The 356th was one of the groups that retained the type somewhat longer than its contemporary groups in the Eighth, which had or were in the process of switching over to the P-51 by that time.

## JUGS VERSUS JETS

Escort missions by P-47s in 1944 occasionally brought first-hand reports of German advances in warplane design that were to spell the death knell for aircraft powered by reciprocating engines, however efficient they had become. The new fighter powerplant was the turbojet and its most practical application had, by the autumn of 1943, been achieved by the Germans in the Me 262 interceptor fighter and Arado Ar 234 bomber.

In addition, the *Luftwaffe* had taken delivery of the rocket-powered Me 163 and it was this type, in a number of early, brief encounters, that gave P-47 pilots a chance to witness this 'wave of the future' in action if not to readily appreciate its advantages. Indeed, the first two Thunderbolts, from an unknown group, intercepted by an Me 163 on 13 May were flown by pilots who were apparently unaware that a tiny, 30 mm cannon armed, 550 mph plus fighter was about to open fire on them. Flown by none other than Wolfgang Späte, commander of JG 400, the rocket fighter was almost within range when

Spate was obliged to break off due to loss of control which prevented him from firing. The Thunderbolts flew on.

An encounter with the Me 262 on 28 August saw the 78th Group which flew P-47s until December, credited with the first jet victory in history. Maj Joe Myers and his wingman were flying at 11,000 feet as top cover for an afternoon group train-busting mission when what was taken for a B-26 was seen heading low, west of Brussels. Myers dived to investigate and found an Me 262 at 5000 feet.

After executing some evasive turns, the Me 262 pilot bellied into a field. Myers immediately strafed the enemy machine while it was still moving, hoping to claim an 'airborne' as against 'ground' kill, the pilot making a rapid exit from the shattered cockpit. He was lucky not to be hit when Lt Manfred Croy, Myers's wingman, made a strafing pass. Myers was duly credited with one Me 262 destroyed.

Three October interceptions of Me 262s resulted in further victories for the 78th, the last month that the pilots of this particular unit would meet the 'jet threat' in action. On the 2nd, the Ninth Air Force's 365th Group was responsible for the destruction of another Me 262 although the pilot involved, Capt Valmore J. Beaurault, did not actually fire at it. After a brief combat in which the P-47s evaded the aggressive jet pilot, the enemy aircraft dived, side-slipping to zero feet with Beaurault hot on his heels. The German misjudged his height and the Me 262 touched the ground with a wing and exploded. Although he received no official credit for the kill, Beaurault was awarded the D.F.C. for his trouble.

An escort to Kassel on 7 October followed by strafing was the order of the day and *en route* in, the 361st Squadron led by Capt Don Strait, who would be the 356th Group's top ace at the end of the war, broke up an intended attack on the bombers by four Me 262s. There was little action that merited the term air combat and no American claims. German jet pilots had orders to concentrate on shooting down bombers and avoid combat with the U.S.A.A.F. escort if at all possible and on 7 October the 356th was probably felt to be merely in the way. But the day's action was not over for Lt Harold Whitmore who damaged a couple of Bf 110s before having to put his P-47 down safely in a field at Arras, low on fuel. Whitmore spent three days 'rounding up some gas', got his aircraft started and flew back to England.

A half credit for the first Me 262 to fall to the 56th Group came on 1 November when the group was flying a mission with the 20th and 352nd Groups. Walt Grioce was the pilot who shared the kill. Only one other encounter with the 262 was recorded by the Wolfpack, that being on 14 March 1945, but it did clash with Ar 234s that same month.

That the Me 262 had the edge on all fighters like the P-47 was starkly demonstrated on 8 November when the 356th was in the process of converting to Mustangs but still flying both types on operations. During an escort to Merseburg, Green Flight was bounced and Lt Charles C. McKelvy had his P-47 badly shot up by the German jet's cannon. Lt Edward G. Rudd turned and fired at the fleeing Messerschmitt. Moments later, the jet pilot reversed and came back on McKelvy's tail, 30 mm fire also putting enough holes in Flight Leader Lt William L. Hoffert's Thunderbolt to oblige him to bale out.

McKelvy, meanwhile, still had control, eluded the jets and headed for Brussels, only to be set upon by nine Bf 109s which chased him to the deck. With few options left open to him, McKelvy bellied the Jug and was captured. This was the last time in 1944 that Thunderbolt pilots reported combat with the German jets, no Me 163s or Ar 234s having been observed thus far.

A few more missions in P-47s were flown by the 356th for the P-51s were proving a little temperamental and a substantial number were awaiting repair as a result of accidents. The Thunderbolt was therefore in time to participate in the group's best day of the war in terms of aerial victories, on 26 November.

Paderborn was the target area for the bombers the group was due to escort, and about 20 miles northwest of Dümmer Lake, the *Luftwaffe* appeared. Group C.O. Don Baccus took the 360th and 361st Squadrons to counter the bounce while the 359th maintained close station on the bombers. The end result of the individual combats that inevitably developed was twenty-four destroyed and twelve damaged claimed without loss by the Martlesham group.

*Any shelter seemingly beat the frigid outdoors during the winter of 1944-45. A P-47D of the 387th F.S., 365th Group gets some attention in a well air-conditioned former Luftwaffe hanger. Note the blister cockpit side panel which improved rear and downwards vision from the razorback P-47D's 'greenhouse' canopy. (U.S.A.F.)*

## WOLFPACK LOYALTY

As is well known, the 56th Fighter Group was allowed to retain the P-47 throughout hostilities and was not unduly pressured by commanders wishing to standardise all the Eighth's fighter groups to convert to the P-51. Having flown most of the razorback and bubble top models, the Wolfpack began, in late 1944, to receive examples of a new subtype, the P-47M.

Early January 1945 saw the group experimenting with formation bombing under the direction of the microwave early warning (M.E.W.) radar system. In a few sorties reminiscent of the days of Bill Kepner's Buzz Boys, when Hub Zemke tried the bomb-on-signal technique using a B-24, radar control was theoretically far more reliable. Weather generally intervened to prevent accurate analysis of the results of a tight diamond formation of P-47s dropping their bomb load on radar signal, such a mission being flown on 5 January.

Despite the participating pilots, led by Dave Schilling, flying close enough to create a diamond 450 yards long, 250 yards wide and 300 yards deep, and the M.E.W. station (alias 'Nuthouse' its radio call-sign) passing coordinates for the bomb release point, the conditions were too overcast for the results to be observed. The target was a factory at Siegen and each P-47D carried a pair of 250 lb G.P. bombs.

On arrival over the 'socked in' target, the radar operator sent the group round again to bring the pilots back on track, and the bombs were released on the second attempt. Results unfortunately could not be observed and on this, and a few subsequent missions, disappointing results were about all the group had to show for its efforts.

Meanwhile, much attention was given to the first P-47Ms to arrive at Debden, for this was rumoured to be the fastest, most powerful P-47 model yet. The claims for the outstanding performance of the P-47M were true enough as its C series powerplant gave up to 2800 hp with water injection compared to 2300 hp for the P-47D. But as far as the 56th was concerned, the aircraft lacked one vital attribute – reliability.

Throughout that bitter winter of 1944-5, the 56th Group's engineering sections slaved to get the P-47M's engine to run smoothly. It was frustratingly difficult to cure a list of problems with the R-2800-57, these appearing similar to those associated with P-47s during the early days of Eighth Air Force operations. Most people concerned might have assumed that the P-47M was merely duplicating those and showing a marked reluctance to run in damp English weather conditions. But it was worse than that.

About 20 mph faster than the P-47D-30 at low altitude, with a better ceiling and rate of climb, the P-47M-1 issued to the 56th had more electrical equipment than before and this appeared to cause many problems. Engine failures in the air prevented the group from sending the new Thunderbolts on their first mission for many weeks.

Work was also needed on the linkage between the throttle and supercharger so that the Pratt & Whitney would deliver its rated power continuously. Engine warm-up was also erratic, this leading to uneven airflow around the cylinder heads. The result was that some cylinders grew very hot while others stayed at lower than normal temperatures, a sure recipe for a rough-running engine. Locally-produced baffles, which rerouted the air that reached the cylinders, partially solved the P-47M's problems but others manifested themselves.

Nevertheless, the Wolfpack pilots, proud in the knowledge that the 'hot' P-47M had been exclusively issued to their group, persevered as far as they could with a potentially excellent aircraft. Developing and fostering a degree of individualism, the 56th sidestepped standard U.S.A.A.F. camouflage edicts and proceeded to paint the P-47Ms in a variety of snazzy, individualistic schemes, going to war in them for the first time on 14 February. The 61st Squadron favoured some camouflage uniformity but only insofar as the shade chosen for its P-47Ms was black.

On this occasion, there was no aerial action as the 'A' and 'B' groups covered Liberators bombing Magdeburg and Gifhorn respectively, although two German jets were seen. Bad weather continued to disrupt mission schedules and, when the group

did fly, the *Luftwaffe* often failed to show up, for much the same reason. Overcast skies affected each side. And the new Thunderbolts were still proving to be troublesome.

A grounding order on 18 February was enforced after the cause of a crash-landing of a P-47M was traced to cracked electrical leads in the ignition harness. Changing these partially solved the problem and when the Wolfpack went out again on 21 February a number of P-47Ms were included. But seven had to abort the escort to Nürnberg and four more put down on the continent. On 23 February, the P-47Ms were grounded again.

Most of the Wolfpack reverted to flying P-47Ds on scheduled missions during this difficult period during which the engineers worked though a labyrinth of suspect areas which included cracked carburettor diaphragms, too high a grade of fuel, and burned pistons. Finally, someone found that the P-47M's engine problems really stemmed from (quite simply) insufficient protection against corrosion having been applied prior to shipment from the U.S. All engines that had been run for less than 50 hours were changed and the 56th was soon back in business. By then, spring was well on the way and on 5 March the group was able to fly as a three-squadron unit for the first time in four weeks or so. Other uneventful escort sorties followed until the 10th when the 56th was detailed to protect the Remagen Bridge over the Rhine, which had just been crossed by the Allies. The Wolfpack came up against Bf 109s and FW 190s doing their best to destroy the intact spans of the one bridge overlooked by the Germans in their otherwise complete demolition of all the others. The Thunderbolts persuaded the enemy fighters to jettison their bombs and one of each type was shot down for the only victories claimed by the entire Eighth Air Force that day.

A series of milk-run missions for the 56th preceeded action with Ar 234s on 14 March. The heavy bomber targets were a mix of oil installations, rail links and factory sites in Germany, VIII B.C. sending out 1200 aircraft. The 56th sent 'A' (the 62nd and 63rd Squadrons) and 'B' (the 61st F.S.) Groups and it was the former that encountered the jet bombers. Flying back from Frankfurt, Capt Williamson's Blue Flight spotted two flights of Arados and immediately attacked them. Lt Sandborn Ball and his wingman, Lt Warren Lear, nailed the first one and shared the kill. Red Three, alias 1st Lt Norman Gould, systematically shot out an Ar 234's starboard engine, pulled back and hit the port side B.M.W. turbojet. The aircraft spun in for Gould's fourth and last kill.

More mundane fare fell to 1st Lt Sherman Pruitt who made a firm claim for a Bf 109, the pilot having baled out. Four Jugs were lost. Three machines were forced down by mechanical failure, one being Pruitt's. He was obliged to telephone Boxted to report his kill. One P-47 ditched in the Channel after its engine quit, 2nd Lt Earl Townsend being killed when his parachute failed to open.

A nine-day stand-down for the group ended with a mission to support Operation *Varsity*, the huge parachute crossing of the Rhine on 24 March. Frustrated this time by good weather in which the bombers they were guarding plastered German aerodromes so well that nothing rose to challenge the raid, the Wolfpack had to mark this one down as another boring milk-run.

Major George Bostwick had a skirmish with Me 262s on 25 March. Having alerted 2nd Lt Edwin Crosthwait to get one of the jets, which he duly did, Bostwick gunned his personal P-47M in pursuit of a second machine which led him over an aerodrome. He found four more jets in the circuit. One of the Me 262s made too tight a turn to get out of the charging Thunderbolt's way, dug in a wing and cartwheeled. Bostwick fired at another 262 and claimed a 'damaged'.

By now, the P-47Ms were flying well enough to stave off the groundcrews' apparent dread of having to work on Merlin engines in the P-51s — 'Spam Cans' in their parlance — that had been delivered to Boxted. These were on hand as a precaution in case the newest Thunderbolt could not be made reliable. The groundcrew worked almost round the clock to achieve that state. They at least wanted to stay on piston engines. And most of the Wolfpack pilots believed that the P-47M was 'the finest propeller-driven aircraft in the world'.

There were fewer chances to prove this expansive claim in terms of air combat although the 56th made the most of a series of strafing missions. Unusual aircraft such as Ju 88/fighter *Mistel* combinations and flying boats were shot up along with the more common bombers and fighters, the American pilots ranging over Germany almost with impunity by April. Not that the *Luftwaffe* was quite beaten. There were

always the jets to contend with and these, at least, had the potential to give the Wolfpack a run for its money. All too often there was no combat as such, the Me 262 pilots frequently making mistakes and failing to take on the American fighters in contests that they should have won with ease. Flak, too, had not given up the ghost. On April 10, a mission that otherwise brought widespread strafing claims, saw thirteen P-47s damaged by A.A. fire, and two were lost.

That date also recorded one of the last Wolfpack encounters with jets. Two pilots, Lt Walter Sharbo and Capt Walter Wilkinson, claimed the destruction of one Me 262 each, Sharbo's victim being the result of cooperation with Lt Donald Healey. Both the P-47s chased the Me 262 for some distance before they clobbered it. Wilkinson's jet kill was his one and only of the war but he made sure by diving on the jet from 22,000 feet and shooting it down near the ground.

There followed a few more ground-attack missions when the Eighth Air Force fighter groups, the 56th included, shot up hundreds of German aircraft abandoned on various aerodromes. Few of the bases had been abandoned by *Luftwaffe* flak personnel, however, and on 13 April the Wolfpack lost Lt William Hoffman over Eggebeck. Despite the 63rd Squadron shooting up the defending guns, Hoffman's aircraft was crippled. Attempting to bale out, he was killed when his chute failed to open. The 63rd was then using T-44 0.50 calibre ammunition with improved incendiary capability and a higher muzzle velocity than previous ammunition; pilots rated it as very effective.

April 21 was the last operational foray over Europe for the Wolfpack — and it was quiet. Ranging out to Austria, the Thunderbolts found nothing of value to the Germans worth their time and they all returned without opening fire, a 'no strafing' order having been imposed by the Allies by that time. For one of the most famous exponents of the P-47, the war was over.

As things transpired, the P-47M was used in combat only by the 56th Group. Almost the entire production run of 130 aircraft was shipped to England and by the end of the war the Wolfpack had used up a considerable proportion of the total through experiencing an artificially high attrition rate. But when its engine problems were finally cured, the P-47M was indeed one of the finest piston-engined fighters ever built.

# 8
# Eastern Juggernaut

As a result of the urgent priority given to establishing a strong force of escort fighters in England to support the bomber offensive against Germany, the P-47 was a comparative latecomer to other theatres of war. The line was held in the Mediterranean, in China and the Pacific by the P-39, P-40 and P-38, the latter type particularly possessing the substantial range that was increasingly required of fighters as the A.A.F. embarked on a long campaign to win back all territory that had been lost to the Japanese.

In the Navy-dominated Pacific war it was the capture of island bases that made the deployment of the medium range P-47 an economical proposition, for no other fighter in the A.A.F. – or Navy – inventory then had similar hitting power or could match its ruggedness in carrying out ground attacks. Yet the first group to fly combat with the Fifth Air Force, the 348th, was something of a disappointment – in terms of the aircraft it flew – to commanding General George C. Kenney. He wanted Lightnings and more Lightnings, not the P-47. Range was of paramount importance to Kenney who was in the process of fighting his way up the coast of New Guinea. And while Japanese troops were on the same land mass as U.S. airfields, most targets lay at the limit of the range of the early P-47D-2 and D-4 models issued to the first Thunderbolt groups to go to the Pacific.

In order to utilise the P-47 at all, Kenney required drop tanks and by July 1943 enough of these had been delivered to the 348th Group at Port Moresby in time for its combat debut. The razorback aircraft it flew would largely remain the standard Thunderbolt model throughout the Pacific theatre until almost the end of the war.

Drop tanks for the P-47 were supplied from both U.S. and Australian sources and in the early days Fifth Air Force and group engineering sections devised a makeshift rack for a 110-gal P-39/P-40-type tank so that it could be attached to the belly shackles of the P-47D. This was subsequently replaced by a 'flat' tank developed and produced in Brisbane and holding 200 gallons, which proved highly successful in operational use.

Fortunately, the 348th Group had the redoubtable Lt-Col Neel Kearby at the helm. He was very positive about the P-47's capabilities and with his pilots set out to build on the Thunderbolt's reputation for ruggedness that augered well for Pacific combat. Kearby faced quite a task, for New Guinea was a challenge in more ways than one. In particular, the Japanese fighters his and other groups would invariably encounter in combat had superb manoeuvrability and dogfighting them in a much heavier (but better protected) Allied fighter was to be avoided if possible. Similar 'dive, fire and away' tactics, as previously adopted by the lower performance P-40, were utilised by the Thunderbolts to reduce any disadvantage they may have had compared with such Japanese Army fighters as the Ki-43, Ki-84 and Ki-61 and the Navy's A6M at heights below 15,000 feet.

Kearby soon realised, however, that nothing could touch a P-47 in a power dive and zoom climb and he urged his pilots to capitalise on this. Constant practise flights also developed the 348th's skill in observation – seeing the enemy first was a maxim the pilots followed to good effect in combat.

**SINGLE SQUADRON**
Only one squadron of the 8th Fighter Group flew Thunderbolts. While the 35th and 80th Squadrons respectively retained the P-38 and

*Top: All P-47Ds of the three squadrons of the 318th Group were launched safely from two escort carriers off the Marianas, as much a relief to the Army pilots as the Navy handlers. This bold operation put Thunderbolts right in the front line as the Japanese still contested their airfield on Saipan. Both camouflaged and natural-metal finish razorback P-47Ds were used by the 318th, the latter by the 333rd F.S. (U.S.A.F.)*

*Above: When the 318th had installed itself on Saipan, a P-47 repair facility was established away from the landing strip, a wise precaution until the enemy was wiped out. Aircraft from the 73rd F.S. are receiving attention. (P. Jarrett)*

P-40, the 36th F.S., the 'Flying Fiends', traded its P-39s for P-47Ds during October and November while the group was based at Moresby. This gave the 8th the distinction of flying three different fighter types at the same time. The mix was not untypical in the Fifth Air Force which did not always have first call on new aircraft and rarely in the numbers George Kenney required.

Despite any limitations imposed on the P-47, Kearby himself found no difficulty in running up an impressive score of aerial victories, including a mission on 11 October 1943. Leading a flight of P-47s over Wewak at 28,000 ft, he destroyed an enemy aircraft seen taxying on Boram airstrip. A single A6M then fell into the sea in flames when Kearby attacked at 15,000 feet altitude. The Japanese pilot took no evasive action. Then the 348th encountered thirty plus fighters escorting twelve bombers and the P-47s waded in. One 'Zeke' succumbed to combined fire from the charging Thunderbolts and then Kearby selected another, the pilot of which, again, appeared not to have noticed the danger. Kearby's guns turned the 'Zeke' into a flaming wreck. A second Zeke fell to him soon afterwards.

With the Japanese finally alerted to the presence of their attackers, the 348th's small force climbed to 20,000 feet and headed for home. But the enemy fighters offered further combat and Kearby shot two Ki-61s off the tail of a colleague before the fight was finally over. He had downed six, a feat that brought him the Medal of Honor, the first to be awarded to an A.A.F. fighter pilot in the Second World War.

Razorback P-47Ds were also the new equipment of the 35th Group, commanded by Col Edwin A. Doss; from November, when the group was based at Nadzab, all three squadrons, the 39th, 40th and 41st, received Thunderbolts.

Neel Kearby had been attached to Fifth Air Force headquarters from March 1943 and was seconded to assist the 9th Fighter Squadron, the 'Flying Knights', of the 49th Group in making a smooth transition to the P-47 to make up a shortfall in the delivery of P-38s. Kearby went to Gusap where the squadron was based from 20 November 1943 and flew a few shakedown missions before returning to Wewak. As with the 8th, the 49th had only one squadron flying the P-47, an association that did not last long.

Combat with the Japanese air forces demonstrated once again that the P-47D was an excellent gun platform; eight 0.50-in guns were generally more than enough to destroy the nimble but generally unarmoured J.A.A.F. and J.N.A.F. fighters. Most importantly, using lightweight, incendiary ammunition in their guns, the American pilots found that they could often shoot down Japanese aircraft at double the range that was generally required against the better-protected *Luftwaffe* fighters over Europe.

The Army Air Forces' build-up in most theatres of war during 1943 brought many changes. Not the least of these was reassignment of combat groups to theatres other than those the 'scuttlebutt' assured everyone they were definitely bound for, although the whole process was supposed to be secret. Arrival in a theatre often saw groups being issued with a different aircraft type to those used for training in the U.S. Thus the 80th Fighter Group, which had in 1942 been the second unit to fly the P-47 when it took over the B models left behind by the 56th at Farmingdale, arrived in India to be equipped with the P-40. It would later receive P-47s. The 358th Group had, on the other hand, originally been destined to go to England.

By December 1943, about 300 P-47s were on hand in Australia and New Guinea, enough to re-equip the 35th F.G., already in theatre and flying P-39s, and the 58th, newly arrived from the States with its 69th, 310th and 311th Squadrons. This gave General Kenney eleven squadrons of P-47s, a useful enough force to harry the Japanese troops remaining in New Guinea.

## CAPE GLOUCESTER

During the invasion of Cape Gloucester, New Britain on 26 December, P-47s flew a total of 117 sorties as part of a large-scale air effort to soften up the landing area and cover the Marine ground forces. Swift Japanese Navy reaction from Rabaul brought twenty-five Aichi D3As escorted by fifty A6Ms into the invasion area. This force was intercepted by sixteen P-47s of the 35th Group and 36th Squadron, plus sixteen P-40s and forty-nine P-38s. The result was twenty-two 'Vals' and twenty-five 'Zeros' shot down for the loss of two P-47s and two P-38s.

A follow-up effort saw fifteen torpedo-carrying 'Bettys' attempt to attack the

*1st Lt Ralph Wandrey in the cockpit of his P-47D of the 9th F.S., 49th Group, with his ace status marked up. As the 9th F.S. C.O., Wandrey soon achieved a sixth kill and was one of the few pilots who did so while flying the P-47, which the 9th's pilots did not really take to.*

American ships. This was largely foiled by twenty-six P-47s of the 341st and 342nd Squadrons, pilots of which claimed fourteen bombers despite the heavy fighter escort. Two Japanese fighters were also downed, and one P-47 was lost to Allied naval gunfire.

Cape Gloucester airfield was secured on 30 December although fighting on New Britain would continue into 1944; Distinguished Unit Citations went to four units, including the 35th Group and the 36th Squadron for attacking a formation of seventy-five enemy aircraft on 26 December; the 348th was similarly cited for an outstanding record of seventy-nine enemy aircraft destroyed between 16 – 23 December for the loss of just two Thunderbolts.

Amphibious operations along the coast of New Guinea early in 1944 secured an airfield on Saidor and on 16 January 1944 P-47 pilots of the 35th F.G., many of whom had little combat experience, were out covering a convoy. Suddenly, the vessels were attacked by escorted Aichi D3As, plunging out of low cloud and mist. They reckoned without the P-47s and paid the price of eighteen of their number lost. So aggressive were the Thunderbolt pilots that the attack on the supply convoy was foiled.

Such unfavourable odds in air combat became grimly typical for the Japanese who generally flew agile but lethal firetraps. If hit in vital areas by American machine-gun rounds, most Army and Navy types burned terribly quickly, making some combats appear incredibly one-sided. Numerically and qualitatively overtaken in the air, the Japanese began to wage a war increasingly hallmarked by defeat and retreat. But there was no shortage of courage among the Japanese fighter pilots – indeed they were aggressive to the point of foolhardiness on occasion and their A.A.F. counterparts often noted the soundness of their tactics in combat. There was rarely any room for complacency.

Declared operational in February 1944, the 58th Fighter Group, commanded by Col Gwen G. Atkinson, moved from Australia to Dobodura, New Guinea with camouflaged razorback Thunderbolts. Early combat flying involved protection patrols over U.S. bases and escorting transports – vital, but tedious work for the pilots. Some bomber escorts were also flown while the group embarked on its main ground-attack role, supporting the final drive to secure all of New Guinea from the Japanese.

With U.S. air and naval forces continually hammering their bases, the Japanese were obliged to make a partial tactical withdrawal to reorganise and re-equip. This became particularly urgent for the J.N.A.F., which had lost so many of its aircrews at Midway and in numerous smaller-scale actions since. Almost every time that they clashed with the Americans, the Imperial Navy's formations were whittled down and pilots and aircrews died.

The gradual movement northwards in New Guinea secured new bases to put U.S. air groups within range of hitherto secure Japanese airfields, supply dumps and transportation. A general enemy pull-back to Truk enabled Allied forces to secure Finschhafen on the tip of the peninsula overlooking Huon Gulf. With the important Japanese airfield at Lae secured, targets on New Britain, which lay across the Solomon Sea could be more easily attacked.

Virtually all the P-47s of the 348th Group, forty-six aircraft in total, covered the landings during the daylight hours, patrols being maintained with Lightnings for 36 hours. When not intercepting Japanese bombers, the Thunderbolt pilots escorted their own heavies and mediums.

On 21 December, the 342nd Squadron led by Capt William D. Dunham was patrolling over Arawe when an 'in the clear' radio message came through, telling the fighters to fly east. Suspicious, Dunham knew that any Japanese attack on friendly shipping would come from the west. A radio call to surface units confirmed that the enemy had indeed sent the first message. Dunham split his flight and took his own formation of three fighters down to the deck, under deteriorating weather. The high cover of four P-47s found their quarry – a formation of 'Vals' were at 20,000 feet and about to dive-bomb Allied ships. The P-47s attacked and shot down eight of them, three falling to Dunham and two each to Lieutenants Robert Gibband and Randall Hilbig.

When the Marines stormed Cape Gloucester on 26 December, P-47s of the 348th were part of the air umbrella. The 342nd Squadron had elements at 12,000 feet and 18,000 feet, ideally placed to intercept enemy reaction to the landings. Sure enough, fifteen 'Bettys' and a small fighter escort were sighted. The outcome was another one-sided affair – the American pilots claimed fourteen bombers downed before the enemy could even get near the fleet and, to make it almost total, two Japanese fighters were also destroyed. Lt Lawrence F. O'Neil came just short of becoming an ace-in-a-day when he dispatched four 'Bettys'. Thunderbolt firepower was demonstrably even more effective against the Mitsubishi G4M than other enemy aircraft types; it was not for nothing that the Americans nicknamed the 'Betty' the 'Flying Lighter'.

The 36th was also in action over the cape. Engaged with Japanese fighters and dive-bombers, the squadron claimed five for the loss of two P-47s, one of the downed pilots subsequently being recovered. Keeping the air clear of enemy dive-bombers and level bombers involved P-38s and P-40s as well as the P-47s, the P-40s taking on the bombers while the Lightnings kept the fighter escort busy. The U.S. pilots' personal victory tallies spiralled during this time and on 27 December the 340th and 341st Squadrons got eight 'Vals', seven 'Zekes' and a 'Tony' without loss to themselves, Lt Myron getting three.

The last air battle over the area was on 31

December when the 348th again took on an enemy formation over Arawe. The cost to the Japanese Navy was again high, eight more 'Vals' falling, along with four of their escort.

The early weeks of 1944 were marked by further Allied gains to which the enemy reacted only sporadically. The Fifth Air Force then turned its attention to supporting landings on Hollandia and the Admiralty Islands. Attacks on Rabaul which would not be invaded but allowed to 'wither on the vine' continued as required. Again the degree of air combat varied, the enemy choosing to intercept only a certain number of U.S.A.A.F. sorties. Heavy bombers were always a fighter magnet and on 3 February the 340th F.S. put up sixteen P-47s on a B-24 escort.

A mixed force of different fighter types, numbered at about forty, bounced the P-47s at 25,000 ft and obliged them to drop to 20,000 ft. But seemingly having gained an inital advantage, things did not go entirely to plan for the Japanese. A Ki-61 pilot met his match when Capt Michael Dikovitsky split-essed after the 'Tony' dived under his Thunderbolt. When he fired, the 'Tony' suddenly exploded. Dikovitsky then shot down a 'Zeke' and the P-47s added a further quartet to their tally before breaking off.

By March 1944, there were more P-38s on hand in New Guinea and the 9th F.S. gave up its P-47s for Lightnings. As in other war theatres, the A.A.F. strove to achieve standardisation of aircraft in the Pacific and, while Kenney preferred the P-38, his fighter groups continued for various reasons to fly all types in the inventory.

In May 1944, tragedy struck the Fifth Air Force. Every fighter pilot, squadron and group commander on up to Kenney himself was shocked at the news that Neel Kearby had been killed in combat with enemy fighters on the 5th of the month. Only years later with the discovery of the remains of the ace's Thunderbolt in March 1946 did the details emerge. That day, Kearby had been flying P-47D-4 (42-22668) when he came in contact with Ki-43s. The serial number was clearly visible on the burned-out wreckage. At that time, Kearby seemed almost obsessive about making his victory tally better than Dick Bong's and colleagues reckon that this drove him just that bit too hard to stay ahead.

The full details of how Neel Kearby met his end will probably never be known for certain but there is no doubt about the general events of the 5 March combat. Having taken off from Saidor with William Dunham and Sam Blair comprising his flight, Kearby spotted a formation of three Ki-48 'Lily' bombers. He dived fast and attacked one which caught fire and went down quickly. Dunham and Blair quickly dealt with the remaining two. After his kill, Kearby had made a 360° turn and by so doing lost flying speed. He began a slow climb back to altitude.

At that moment it appears that a Ki-43 pilot of the crack 77th *Sentai* bored in and fired from close range. The Japanese pilot was not alone and his colleagues were aggressive. Blair and Dunham headed for cloud cover and home, Kearby's aircraft barely being seen before it plunged into the jungle. The ace managed to bale out and but reports suggest that he was either shot at after getting out or had been hit by machine-gun fire beforehand. Either way, he was apparently dead by the time the Japanese found him, suspended from tree branches by his parachute lines.

The 348th Group was taken over by Col Robert Rowland after Kearby's death and he was to lead it almost until the end of hostilities. This and the other P-47 groups were to find plenty of air combat, for the Fifth Air Force had a gruelling campaign ahead of it. Pacific strategy had determined that, if humanly possible, the Japanese would be prevented from any further territorial gains. Every convoy, every army unit, every airfield would be bombed and strafed repeatedly until the enemy was either destroyed or forced to withdraw.

As the U.S. Navy, revitalised and overwhelmingly strong, prepared to secure strategically vital island bases for long-range bomber attacks on Japan, some enemy garrisons would be bypassed. Some like Rabaul on New Britain would be attacked regularly by Fifth Air Force and Marine Corps bomber and fighter units to prevent them building any sizeable force to constitute a threat to Allied plans in the southwest Pacific area. This policy of neutralisation applied particularly to the enemy's air strength which would be relentlessly whittled down. Not that the Japanese were expected to take this punishment lying down. They would react, and react viciously. But Kenney had the confidence to take up the challenge, and he believed that his forces could deal with any move the enemy might make.

## THE PHILIPPINES

By December 1944, the Fifth Air Force had ably supported the drive across the Pacific which culminated in the invasion of Leyte in the Philippines in October. The 460th F. S. was a fourth 348th Group squadron and was the first P-47 unit to move north to assist the liberation. Covering B-25s *en route*, William Dunham led his pilots in a strafing attack on enemy shipping. The Japanese gunners immediately switched their sights to the fighters from the B-25s, at which point the Thunderbolts headed for their new base on Tacloban.

The order of the day was bombing and strafing of land and seaborne targets. The squadron became adept at sinking Japanese shipping at a steady rate. On 24 November, Dunham led the 460th against a convoy of three transports and a gunboat, the P-47s sinking all of them.

The rest of the 348th moved to the Philippines in December, along with the 58th Group, which went to Mindoro. An urgent message on the 24th revealed that a Japanese task force was inbound for the islands to attack U.S. transports unloading supplies for Mindoro.

Taking off on the night of 26/27 December without any bombs on their racks – ordnance stocks having not arrived at that time – the twenty-eight P-47s of the 58th did not, on the face of it, constitute a major threat to two cruisers and six destroyers. But the Thunderbolt pilots, in company with P-40s, P-38s and B-25s, attacked all the ships at least once. The night's effort achieved a good deal more than was hoped for, including one destroyer sunk. The 58th lost thirteen aircraft but despite the enemy warships opening fire on the beachhead anchorage, their appallingly inaccurate gunnery sank but one U.S. vessel – neither did simultaneous Japanese air attacks achieve anything. This poor showing was attributed to the strafing by Army aircraft, which not only knocked out even main batteries and killed some of the key gun crews but thoroughly unnerved the Japanese.

While the majority of Thunderbolt models used by Fifth Air Force squadrons were razorbacks, the 348th Group took delivery of some P-47D-25s and later models in time for a last round of combat in the Philippines. Other units were converted to P-38s and P-51s before the end of the war, so newer model P-47s were consequently not required in great numbers.

To the nations that declared war on the Axis powers and sent their nationals to fight as airmen was added Mexico, the last Allied country to enter combat. Equipped with P-47Ds, a single fighter squadron, the *Escuadron Aereo de Pelea* 201 of the Mexican Expeditionary Air Force (M.E.A.F.) undertook training at Randolph and Majors Fields in Texas. The induction course began with a P-47 checkout at Farmingdale in July 1944 and all flying tuition was completed by late March 1945, two pilot fatalities having occurred during training.

The M.E.A.F. shipped out on 27 March bound for the Philippines and arrived in Manila Bay on 30 April. Assigned to the Fifth Air Force, the Mexican unit was established at Porac Field, part of the giant Clark Field complex of airfields, and joined the 58th Fighter Group, then under the command of Maj Edward F. Roddy. *Escuadron* 201 would become a fourth squadron of the U.S. group, the Mexicans starting pre-combat training on 7 May.

Despite Mexico being a recipient of combat aircraft under Lend-Lease arrangements, *Esc.* 201 initially flew 'secondhand' Thunderbolts, a pool of eighteen razorback and bubble-top models formerly operated by the 35th and 348th Groups being made available. Both the U.S.A.A.F. groups had by that time converted to P-51s. Theatre training continued and three more aircraft were lost in accidents before the Mexican pilots flew their first combat mission on 4 June.

To support the American advance into northern Luzon, the Mexicans flew five ground-support missions, using bombs and guns, that first day. They joined U.S. pilots in bombing enemy troops, gun positions and a concentration of Japanese tanks; five more similar missions followed on the 5th and seven on the 6th. In difficult terrain, mainly in the vicinity of Infanta, the pilots continued to harass the Japanese and on 12 June the P-47s were given target marking help by a Stinson L-5. Two Mexican aircraft were damaged by ground fire on 16 June but throughout the month the pilots maintained the pressure without undue attention by the enemy. Weather posed its usual challenge to low-flying aircraft and not all sorties went ahead as briefed.

Also, the good progress being made on the ground by the army meant that some targets no longer needed to be attacked and the Mexicans accordingly jettisoned their bombs in the sea on a few missions where the rendezvous with the L-5 airborne controller could not be made. Few risks were taken with the lives of the U.S. troops all but hidden from the pilots' view under the jungle canopy.

Up to 4 July, *Escuadron* 201 pilots flew forty support missions as an integral part of the 58th Group, there being no need to make any distinction between American and Mexican pilots. That in itself was a source of pride to the Latin American nationals. P-47s allocated to Mexico arrived in New Guinea during July and these were ferried to the Philippines by *Escuadron* 201 pilots, three of whom were lost *en route*. No more missions were flown in July but in August the Mexicans made one attack on targets in Formosa and carried out a convoy escort, to bring a grand total of forty-two wartime missions.

## CENTRAL PACIFIC

When the Marianas Islands were secured during June-July 1944, plans were executed to ship the Seventh Air Force's 318th Fighter Group and its complement of 111 P-47Ds to Micronesia to provide the earliest possible *in situ* air support force to the invading troops. Aircraft of the 19th and 73rd Fighter Squadrons were accordingly loaded aboard the escort carriers *Manila Bay* and *Natoma Bay*. There was no land base in range of the P-47, so to get the group near enough to the action, initially seventy-three Army Thunderbolts were catapulted off, the first time that the big fighters had been sent into action this way. Over a period of days beginning on 20 June, all aircraft were catapulted without mishap.

Japanese reaction to the convoy was a dive-bombing attack by four Aichi 'Vals' which dropped two bombs each some distance from each of the carriers. No more enemy aircraft were sighted. As it left the carrier deck, each P-47 headed for Saipan's Aslito airfield. All were in place at Aslito on 24 June, pilots flying missions immediately their aircraft were

fuelled and armed. Sorties were a constant round of bombing, strafing and rocket attacks on the nearby enemy, the pilots having to run the gauntlet of continual small-arms fire.

Sweating out the loss of most of their tools on the beach, the 318th's groundcrews performed their usual miracles using abandoned enemy equipment and Yankee know-how. Disturbed by 'Bed Check Charlies' which dropped anti-personnel bombs in their area and enemy snipers, the 318th settled into its rugged new home. Only once did the enemy succeed in getting close enough to the P-47s on the ground; despite a massive effort by 300 Japanese troops early on 26 June, the 318th Group 'infantry' successfully defended their airfield. A Molotov cocktail-type weapon destroyed one P-47D and the groundcrews taxyed other Thunderbolts to safety while the attack was beaten off.

Tenaciously holding the south coast of Saipan, the enemy had fire support from numerous bunkers and gun positions located on nearby Tinian which were exceedingly difficult to spot, let alone destroy from the air. But the average 18 minutes taken to fly from Aslito to Tinian was so short that officially pilots flying these sorties received a half rather than a full mission credit. Needless to say, nobody thought much of that idea.

So frequent were these operations that by 17 July the two 318th squadrons had flown more than 2500 sorties. The following day, the group's third squadron, the 333rd F.S., was launched from the carrier *Sargent Bay*. No enemy aircraft were seen during the period but three pilots and P-47s were lost.

One Thunderbolt was the victim of a landmine on 27 June when the 19th F.S. was sent to make a rocket attack on artillery positions on Gurguan Point, Tinian. As Lt Wayne F. Kobler made his run, the enemy detonated the mine directly under the charging Thunderbolt. It crashed almost immediately, giving the pilot no chance to get out. When a second landing strip at Aslito was established, it was named Kobler Field in the pilot's honour.

The Seventh Air Force's premier fighter group also assisted the ground troops complete the invasions of Guam and Tinian, the Marianas chain being declared secure by 1 August. Before that, the 318th had initiated the use of napalm in this particular campaign and become one of the first groups to use the weapon. On 23 July with the pre-invasion air strikes on Tinian reaching a ferocious climax, the P-47s used this deadly weapon in the form of drop tanks filled with a mixture called goop which included gelled fuel (napalm) and powdered magnesium and ignited by a genade detonator. They were very effective against hitherto difficult, well dug in enemy positions. The demoralising effect on the Japanese was also evident.

When the war moved on from the Marianas, the 318th remained, flying ground-attack sorties to nearby Pagan Island and occasionally escorting B-24 Liberators on raids on Marcus, Yap, Truk and other garrisons held by the Japanese but bypassed by the main U.S. Navy thrust across the Pacific. Not all the group's ageing P-47Ds had the range to reach out far into the vast Pacific but the pilots were well aware that the small numbers of heavy bombers the Seventh was able to send on missions could be vulnerable to prowling enemy fighters.

Then in October 1944 there came the invasion of the Volcano Islands. On the 21st of the month, the 318th mounted an escort mission to protect the bomber force, comprising thirty-two B-24s. Utilising every drop of fuel carried in three drop tanks apiece, sixteen P-47Ds successfully flew the 1400-mile round trip to Iwo Jima and although they failed to stir up a hornet's nest of the enemy they did shoot down a lone Ki-45 'Nick' which was attacking the bombers. Capt Charlie Tennent of the 19th F.S. inflicted the first damage but five other pilots queued up to make passes, despite four A6Ms loitering in the distance. They cleared off when their pilots recognised American fighters, leaving the *Nick* to its fate. Back home at Saipan, the weary pilots entered a mission lasting 6 hours 38 minutes in their logbooks, an historic achievement.

Recognising that such extreme-range missions would become normal procedure as the war edged ever closer to Japan, A.A.F. planners moved to re-equip the 318th Group. As a temporary measure, the group broke with single-engined tradition in November 1944 when P-38s arrived to replace the P-47Ds but it would not be too long before the group's pilots were back in a Republic saddle.

## CHINA-BURMA-INDIA

The U.S.-designated C.B.I. (China-Burma-India) theatre of war had at one extreme China with Burma at the other. Both were at the end of extremely long supply lines from the U.S. and in view of American commitments to help Generalissimo Chiang Kai-shek contain the Japanese armies, primarily through the provision of air power, China took on a greater perceived strategic importance in Washington. Liberating Burma from Japanese control was primarily a British responsibility although both nations were pledged to assist in defeating the common enemy by whatever means. Fighter and medium and heavy bomber units were active in both theatres, the fighter groups generally opening combat operations during 1942-3 flying P-40s pending re-equipment with newer, more capable types – the P-47 included – in 1944.

Sustaining the Chinese in their struggle was far from easy. Even though in only two out of the three countries in the designated region were Allied and Japanese armed forces in contact, with Nepal and the Himalayan mountains jutting between the two war zones, the 'front' stretched for thousands of miles. And therein lay the problem in operating a fighter such as the P-47. Always a heavy consumer of fuel, the Jug was looked upon as something of a liability in China, where every gallon had to be hauled across the Himalayas – the 'Hump' – to keep aircraft flying.

Army Air Force operations over Burma generally came under the direction of the Tenth Air Force which had been activated on 4 February 1942. This air force also undertook responsibility for China until the formation of the Fourteenth Air Force to more closely direct combat operations over that continent from 10 March 1943. The P-47 made its debut in the theatre in the hands of the 33rd Fighter Group (58th, 59th and 60th Squadrons) commanded by Col Loring F. Stetson. Having transferred from the Mediterranean along with the 81st Fighter Group (91st, 92nd and 93rd Squadrons) to join the 10th in Burma in March 1944, both these groups had previously flown their early combat missions in P-40s against the Germans and Italians.

The 33rd personnel felt they were really living up to the group's adopted nickname 'Fighting Nomads'. In the C.B.I. the group was

*A P-47D-11 assigned to the 1st Air Commando Group at Fenni, India in 1944. The aircraft has blue S.E.A.C. identification bands on the nose, wings, tailplane and fin/rudder but lacks the five diagonal commando fuselage stripes.*

not untypically shuttled between China (when it came under Fourteenth Air Force jurisdiction), Burma and India (when it was part of the Tenth Air Force). Camouflaged razorback P-47 models equipped the unit upon arrival in Asia, where all aircraft had to have a D/F loop aerial installed behind the cockpit in place of the standard radio mast for local G.C.A. over China, a general requirement for most fighter types. The 33rd was non-operational before the pilots began ferrying their aircraft across India to China to join the Fourteenth Air Force, a move that took place in April 1944.

Combat patrols were carried out over China for some six months until the squadrons of the 33rd pointed the noses of their Thunderbolts back towards India during September. Little action with the Japanese air forces had been found, and one of the P-47s had the dubious distinction of being the first of that type to be lost in China when the 33rd's base at Liengshan was bombed. The high fuel consumption of the P-47 did not endear the type to the 33rd and some pilots opted to remain with the P-40 which was much more economical. This rather unsatisfactory state of affairs was solved when Thunderbolts were given up by the Nomads entirely in favour of

the P-38 in November 1944.

Combat operations for Col Philip B. Klein's 81st F.G. which arrived in China in May 1944 equipped with P-47Ds, were similar to those of the 33rd but only two of its squadrons, the 91st and 92nd, remained in that country until the end of hostilities. These went operational at Kwanghan and Fungwanshan respectively in June, with the 93rd Squadron following suit, also based at Kwanghan, in August. In September, the 93rd transferred to India to serve as an operational training and replacement unit, flying out of Gushkara.

The two squadrons in China saw relatively little action before January 1945, with occasional B-25 and B-24 escort missions interspersed with routine patrols. The group, despite being without one of its squadrons, returned to full combat status in January 1945, whereupon it aided Chinese ground forces by attacking enemy lines of communication, troop concentrations and storage dumps.

Another Tenth Air Force P-40 outfit, the 80th Fighter Group, brought its three squadrons, the 88th, 89th and 90th, plus the administratively attached but otherwise independent P-38-equipped 459th, to India in May 1943. Beginning operations that

September from Nagaghuli under the command of Col I.W. McElroy, the group received razorback P-47s in 1944. During the year the 80th moved south to operate over Burma and was based at Tingkawk Sakan from 29 August 1944 by which time command had passed to Col Albert Evans.

Interspersed with an intensive round of ground-attack sorties, the 80th Group's aircraft flew defensive patrols over the transport routes across the Hump and, at the end of 1944, took on the Japanese in the air. This now rare occurrence, which took place on 14 December was more than welcomed by the pilots of the 90th F.S. who shot down four enemy aircraft. The lion's share fell to the guns of Lt Samuel E. Hammer whose victory over three of them made him the squadron's only ace.

On 20 January 1945, a further move was made, the 80th Group's uncamouflaged P-47Ds of all three squadrons operating from Myitkyina in Burma. The unit had flown its Thunderbolts from there on a temporary detachment basis for several periods beforehand.

### AIR COMMANDOS

The reorganisation of the 1st Air Commando Group, formed to support General Orde Wingate's Chindit guerrillas operating behind enemy lines in Burma during the spring of 1944, saw the fighter secton originally equipped with P-51As replaced by two squadrons flying razorback P-47Ds. Both were activated in the C.B.I.

First to reach operational status was the 5th Fighter (Commando) Squadron led by Capt Roland Lynn, at Asanhol, India on 1 September 1944. From 15 to 21 October a detachment was

*A pair of 1st Air Commando P-47s, both with the familiar fuselage stripes, taking off from Comilla on 21 December 1944. At left is P-47D-23 (42-28149/78) while the machine in the background has no serial marked and is identified only by the number '0'.*

*1st Air Commando Group P-47D-23 (42-28163) from the final production batch of razorback models making a clearly demanding downwind landing at Comilla, India on 8 November 1944. The Air Commando C-47 Skytrain on the right may have been awaiting a P-47 escort before another flight over the 'Hump'.*

operating out of Cox's Bazaar. The 6th F.S. (Commando) under the command of Capt Olin B. Carter was activated in India on 30 September. Aircraft of both squadrons were given the distinctive Air Commando fuselage stripes which had first appeared on Commando P-51As and other types, plus S.E.A.C. dark blue bands which served as a visual link to Eastern Air Command's 224 Group, R.A.F. under whose control the commando units operated for a time.

The commando P-47s undertook a variety of missions, mainly ground attack and bomber escort. The fighter element of the force was combined for a short time to form a third squadron of the group which also had the 1st and 2nd Commando Squadrons equipped with P-51Ds. About fifty P-47Ds were available for operations and, having been activated just as the 14th Army's IV Corps was about to start its bid to capture Meiktila and its vital airfield, the 1st A.C.G. flew support sorties for this force beginning on 14 February 1945 with the crossing of the Irrawaddy.

Sorties rapidly piled up to pass the 500 mark during the advance to Meiktila and by early March 1945 this had been all but achieved. The commando units were returned to the control of 224 Group R.A.F. on the 6th of the month, thereafter to hunt down the remnants of the Japanese air forces in Burma. This move brought back more autonomy to the squadrons – Air Commando units being unique in the U.S.A.A.F. – and on 9 March the 5th and 6th Squadrons sent thirty-six P-47s and thirty-two Mustangs to escort Liberators bombing Rangoon. There was no Japanese aerial reaction on this occasion, nor on the 11th when the bombers hit the same target.

The last stages of the Burma campaign were marked by a very low level of activity by the emaciated enemy air forces, which were reduced to flying routine patrols and the occasional aggresive sortie from sanctuaries in Thailand. The air war in Burma, as least as far as aerial skirmishes were concerned, faded away as the 14th Army increasingly proved to be a tenacious and successful as had the Japanese in 1941 – only this time the latter were to lose far more than a series of battles.

# 9
# Thunderbolts with the R.A.F.

In line with standard practice, the R.A.F. identified its P-47s by the adopted name, the razorback models being known as Thunderbolt Mk Is and bubble-tops as Mk IIs. The R.A.F.'s direct association with the P-47 in South-East Asia Command did not occur until 15 May 1944 when the first examples of an initial batch of 240 mixed Mk Is and IIs arrived in India. British forces were then conducting operations in the Arakan peninsula with the ultimate objective of destroying all Japanese forces occupying Burma. This offensive had started in late 1943 and followed a first attempt to inflict a heavy defeat on the invaders but this had stalled during the monsoon period. At the same time, the Japanese themselves were preparing a final thrust into Assam, with their ultimate goal a breakthrough to India.

Although never exactly overburdened with air power, the R.A.F. and U.S.A.A.F. presence in Burma was gradually reinforced and the number and type of aircraft in the theatre increased. By early 1944, better aircraft enabled more effective long-range interdiction sorties to be flown to deny the Japanese vital troop reinforcements, to disrupt their supplies and render untenable the airfields likely to support fighters that could threaten Allied air transport flights. These would be the key to success in Burma; if the

*Razorback Thunderbolt Mk I of No. 146 Sqn in typical S.E.A.C. markings. Some R.A.F. machines in the theatre were quite well decorated with mission markers and personal emblems, as shown by the shamrock and fifteen bomb symbols under the cockpit. (Peter Cope)*

supply flights could be maintained, the army would press a limited offensive throughout the monsoon period, which had previously curtailed military operations.

The plan was to continually push back the Japanese however slowly the job would undoubtedly be at times. General Sir William Slim's 14th Army had a momumental task ahead of it but the Japanese Army in Burma commanded by General Kimura was not of the same calibre as the force that has been so successful in combat in 1941-2.

South-East Asia Command had been formed in November 1943 to rationalise Allied air forces in the area, with Eastern Air Command being created to control the U.S. Tenth Air Force and R.A.F. units based in Bengal, Assam and Burma. E.A.C. had the Third Tactical Air Force which controlled two R.A.F. groups, 224 and 221, which directed operations on the Arakan and Imphal fronts. It was proposed by Air H.Q. India to convert eight existing Hurricane squadrons to Thunderbolts. Strangely, considering its very widespread use by American groups, the Air Ministry harboured some reservations about the suitability of the Thunderbolt for ground-attack operations. These doubts were quelled by evaluation at the Aeroplane and Armament Experimental Establishment, Boscombe Down and P-47Ds in seven different production models were eventually used operationally by the R.A.F.

Production delays at Republic resulted in the first two P-47D-15s (FL731 and FL732) not being delivered to 301 Maintenance Unit at Marachi for evaluation until February 1944. Thereafter, P-47D-21s and D-22s served as the operational Mk Is, with P-47D-25s, D-27s, D-28s, D-30s and D-40s being known as Mk IIs. The R.A.F. decided to deploy the Thunderbolt exclusively on combat operations in the Far East, although 73 O.T.U. had earlier been established at Fayid in Egypt to extensively test the type's operational suitability and provide a pool of trained pilots.

The Thunderbolt would be another U.S. type unique to Burma as far as the R.A.F. was concerned, following deployment of the Curtiss P-36 Mohawk and the Vultee Vengeance dive-bomber. The versatility offered by the Thunderbolt was in the tradition of the Beaufighter which had already seen extensive service in the region in the ground-attack role. The war had, however, proven without any shadow of a doubt that a single-engined fighter with a good range and weapons-carrying capability was ideal for the fairly broadly interpreted role of fighter-bomber.

While the Thunderbolt had the advantage over types powered by liquid-cooled engines in that overheating due to the prevailing hot weather was not a major factor, there were some spectacular crashes as pilots fought to master the heaviest fighter most of them had ever flown — and that included some twins. A

*Thunderbolt Is of No. 146 Sqn including FL831/NA-N, fully bombed up with 'round fin' British 500-pounders. (Peter Cope)*

*Emblems galore! Thunderbolt Mk Is of No. 79 Sqn lining the strip at Meiktila Main in the summer of 1945 including KJ295/NV-N, second from right. (A. Thomas)*

different technique to that of the lighter Hurricane was required but few pilots experienced any real problems.

What pilots always appreciated about the 'T-bolt' was its tremendous versatility. It could climb higher than virtually any other aircraft apart from a heavy bomber, due to its turbocharger and could remain in the cool, clear air without 'running out of steam' as other aircraft might. Down low it always felt very tough and safe but the most lasting impression for many R.A.F. pilots was the terrible destructive power of the eight guns. Enemy aircraft could be taken on with impunity, and most fixed ground targets, which mostly consisted of locally built huts, even if they were substantial structures, simply disappeared under the rain of bullets. Supply dumps and river traffic could also be dealt with easily. Eight Brownings simply sawed them to bits.

Thunderbolt conversion training had commenced in May and been carried through to June 1944, a duty primarily handled by Nos 146 (commanded by Sqn Ldr L. M. O'Leary) and 261 (Sqn Ldr R. E. A. Mason) Squadrons at Yelahanka and by No. 135 Squadron at Minneriya in Ceylon, led by Sqn Ldr L. C. C. Hawkins.

Deliveries of P-47D-22s to India were followed by D-25s in late June and, while it appeared desirable to issue Mk Is and Mk IIs to separate squadrons, the differences between

them from a servicing viewpoint were minimal. Consequently, most R.A.F. units invariably flew a mix of both razorback and bubble-top models.

The first six R.A.F. Thunderbolt squadrons to go operational left Yelahanka in August 1944, by which time Slim's forces had retaken Imphal and were advancing towards the River Chindwin. Operations *Capital* and *Dracula* were intended to secure the land routes between India and China and ultimately liberate Rangoon. In the face of appalling weather, R.A.F. Thunderbolts began operations, escorting transports and attacking enemy ground targets along the Chindwin.

The honour of flying the first R.A.F. Thunderbolt sorties fell to No. 261 Squadron which carried out an armed reconnaissance over the Chindwin on 14 September 1944. With the monsoon rains and accompanying low cloud waning, No. 30 Squadron (Sqn Ldr T.A. Stevens) moved up to Chittagong to operate as part of 90 Wing which included No. 135 Squadron's Thunderbolts plus those of Nos 146 and 261 Squadrons, both of which operated briefly from Cox's Bazaar as a composite fighter unit alongside the P-47Ds of the 80th Fighter Groups, the 5th and 6th Air Commando Squadrons and the P-38s of the 459th F.S.

From Cox's Bazaar the P-47 units were ideally placed to carry out strafing attacks on enemy airfields and these began on 18 October. R.A.F. pilots attacked Zayatkwin, with A.A.F. aircraft going to Mingaladon. Two days later, the target locations were reversed, with the American fighters additionally strafing Honawki. No. 261 Squadron stirred up the resident Ki-43s and Ki-44s at Mingaladon, pilots seeing many Japanese fighters circling high above the base. Hope as they might that the enemy would be tempted to come down and fight, it was not to be. Everyone wanted to emulate the Thunderbolt victory recorded earlier that day by W O Carter who shot down an 'Oscar'. No other air combat claims were filed as a result of this operation, although another pilot did fire at a group of 'Oscars' that formed a defensive circle, without any results.

American P-47s in the theatre, otherwise identified by fuselage numbers, received similar blue tail bands in line with S.E.A.C. directives for R.A.F. Thunderbolts. This marking also applied to the Air Commando P-47s, which retained their bold fuselage stripes and later had identification numbers painted in the blue tail band.

One P-47D in these markings was flown extensively by the American liaison officer to the British Army, one Colonel Schmidt. Based at Monywa, Burma, he ably assisted the army in selecting targets, particularly for the Mitchells of the 12th Bomb Group which became an integral part of S.E.A.C. operations in Burma.

Schmidt flew his P-47 with great elan, seeking out likely Japanese targets and often taking them on himself if the threat was dire enough.

By 2 November, 902 Wing was operating from Cox's Bazaar and operations from there included airfield strikes and escort to Eastern Air Command Liberators. On 4 November, thirty-one Thunderbolt IIs of No. 30 Sqn were escorting Liberators. *En route* to their target, over Taikkyi, a Ki-44 'Tojo' attempting to attack the bombers was shot down in flames by Flt Lts Whidborne and Fulford. In addition, an 'Oscar' was claimed destroyed on the ground during a strafing attack on Zayatkwin.

Clashes with the enemy in the air were mostly inconclusive and frustrating for the R.A.F. pilots, for the Thunderbolt could be evaded by Japanese pilots of some ability due to the extreme agility and lightness of the types they flew. It was clear that without a good deal of luck, few fighter pilots were going to become high scorers on Thunderbolts over Burma.

For some British and commonwealth pilots, the Thunderbolt remained a demanding aircraft and a number were lost in accidents, some of them fatal. But once the characteristics of the aircraft were understood, its rugged qualities were highly appreciated, particularly in a theatre that could be terribly hard on aircraft structures and finishes.

*In April 1945, No. 113 Sqn at Ondaw flew some Mk Is passed on by No. 146 Sqn, AQ-R (serial no. unknown) being one example. (R.L. Ward)*

Fighter sweeps against airfields were generally most productive in terms of men, fighter aircraft, material and transport denied to the enemy, the Thunderbolt having lost none of its reputation as a ground strafer *par excellence*.

Aerial retaliation by the Japanese was sporadic and generally on a very small scale in terms of the aircraft involved but on 25 November a little more damage than usual was inflicted when two aircraft attacked Myitkyina South. They dived from 6000-7000 feet and dropped mainly 100 lb fragmentation bombs. These found their mark and destroyed one Thunderbolt, a drop tank storage area and a truck carrying napalm tanks. No less than eighteen aircraft 'scrambled' to catch the intruders, without any luck.

With successful British crossings of the Upper Chindwin having been completed by December 1944, the Japanese regrouped to form a defensive line Lashio-Mandalay-Yenangyaung to Kangaw on the Arakan coast. This would effectively deny the Allies access to the Burmese oilfields and rice-growing area of the Irrawaddy delta. The Allied advance, Operation *Capital*, began on 4 December.

Finding the enemy in strength south of Mandalay, 909 Wing attacked areas in the southeast to secure airfields for supply of the ground troops by air while 910 Wing comprising three Thunderbolt squadrons, Nos 79 (Sqn Ldr R.D. 'Gaddy' May), 146 and 261, formed on 1 December and occupied Wangjing near Imphal. On 10 December, F/O R.A. Crayner was part of a nine-aircraft element of No. 79 Sqn that attacked Meiktila airfield. Spotting a taxying 'Oscar', Crayner opened fire and blew it up. A second parked fighter was damaged by F/O E.C. Reed.

Although the squadrons followed slightly different procedure, No. 79's deployment of the Thunderbolt was representative of the others, as were the conditions with which they coped. The squadron invariably sent off its total strength of twelve aircraft, even though only two flights of four or eight were usually required to attack the target. The average duration of a sorties was 2.5-3 hours with, in No. 79's case, the Thunderbolts arriving over the target area in echelon formation at about 8000 feet. Standard load for the majority of operations was two 500 lb bombs with instantaneous fusing, carried on the wing pylons and aimed by using the reflector sight.

The Meiktila airfields now became prime targets and a number of Japanese aircraft were destroyed in the execution of these strikes. On

*Thunderbolt Mk II KJ225 of No. 261 Sqn taxying out at Wangjing early in 1945. (A. Thomas)*

*Part of a batch of P-47D-28s, HD267 was, like all Thunderbolts earmarked for the R.A.F., originally painted at the U.S. factory which built it. Repainting was subsequently carried out in India when S.E.A.C. markings were applied. (M.A.P.)*

7 December, 905 Wing comprising Nos 134 (Sqn Ldr D.K. McDonald) and 258 (Sqn Ldr Neil Cameron) Squadrons began airfield sweeps at Magwe on the Lower Irrawaddy before turning their guns on enemy positions on the Arakan coast in company with Nos 30 and 135 Squadrons which were part of 904 Wing. By 18 December, 905 Wing had the Thunderbolts of Nos 5 and 123 (Sqn Ldr A. J. McGregor) Squadrons added to its strength.

By that time, the number of Thunderbolt Mk Is was dwindling, supplies of P-47D-28s and D-30s having been taken on charge by the squadrons as replacements. The latter model's electric bomb release made it the first R.A.F. Thunderbolt model ideally suited to ground-attack work, the earlier aircraft having been fitted with a manual release.

The pressure was maintained on the Japanese, the Allies working up to implement Operation *Dracula* by first neutralising the island of Akyab. Thunderbolts maintained an effective air umbrella over the troops, while Nos 5 and 123 Squadrons flew escort to vital Dakota supply flights and No. 79 worked over the enemy airfields at Heho, Meiktila and Kangaung, a task they were soon sharing with

aircraft of 910 Wing. The last momentus months of 1944 saw the Allies firmly on the offensive in Burma, the once 'invincible' Japanese Army being steadily pushed back. On 2 January, Akyab island was found to have been abandoned, the town, port and airfield offering a valuable base complex. No. 258 Squadron soon moved in.

Commando landings at Myebon had the advantage of close air support – cab rank – patrols by fighter-bombers directed by visual control posts. With the slight drawback that Thunderbolts had to fly standing patrols and burn up a considerable amount of fuel while waiting to be called in, cab ranks were highly successful and a huge boost to troop morale. Pilots refined their skills to rain devastation on the Japanese as near as 30 yards from friendly forces.

On 10 January, Thunderbolts added their bombs to an *Earthquake* strike by heavies near Gangaw – and so totally smothered the area in front of advancing troops that the last flights had no need to release their loads. An *Earthquake* strike was a combined operation led by bombers – a 'Major' if they were Liberators and 'Minor' when B-25s led the force in. Fighter-bombers would attack last, to bomb and strafe anything left.

Although more airfields were captured at this time, 14th Army supply lines were lengthening and Operation *Extended Capital* was aimed at bridging the Irrawaddy north and west of Mandalay and if possible capturing Meiktila, thereby forcing the Japanese to commit their reserves. By mid-January, the southward drive, well supported by No. 79 Sqn which attacked the Meiktila airfields, had gained momentum; small pockets of enemy resistance were dealt with and the Thunderbolt squadrons flew escort to Liberators bombing beach defences at Ramree Island and airfields in the area.

To secure Ramree as a jumping-off point for *Dracula*, Thunderbolts of 224 Group joined F.A.A. Hellcats, R.A.F. Liberators and 12th B.G. B-25s (appropriately nicknamed 'The Earthquakers') to pound an area that was one of the most heavily defended by the enemy. Close support operations occupied the Thunderbolts for some weeks, one machine being lost when it suddenly burst into flames for no apparent reason and crashed. Two other such incidents had been logged and tests were run to determine the cause. It had been suspected that petrol vapour from leaking fuel lines compressed in the lower fuselage by negative *g* had been ignited by exhaust flames. Ground tests seemed to confirm that fuel drain pipes venting near the exhaust outlet was the true cause and although some modifications were made, further in-flight fires were experienced by R.A.F. Thunderbolts during the remainder of their service. Fortunately, these were infrequent and not considered serious enough to interfere with operations.

As with other war theatres, Allied air units now found the Japanese far less able – or inclined – to indulge in air combat, although heavy bombers were often perceived as the greatest threat by the enemy and some effort was made to intercept them. On 29 January, a single Ki-43 made a half-hearted attempt to attack A.A.F. B-24s well covered by No. 123 Sqn's Thunderbolts, with those of No. 5 flying medium altitude cover and P-38s of the 459th F.S. acting as top cover. Little came of the enemy's attempt to intercept this formidable force, Flt Lt Aris of No. 123 Squadron quickly persuading the 'Oscar' pilot that, on this occasion, discretion was the better part of valour.

Napalm was a relatively new weapon to the Burmese theatre and No. 135 Squadron's Thunderbolts carried it on 29 January, with No. 5 and other units soon following suit. The limited effectiveness of the weapon resulted in future use (and then only an occasional basis) only by Thunderbolts of Nos 135 and 30 Squadrons. While the fire effect was spectacular, napalm burnt out quickly if it had nothing to ignite. If released manually, napalm tanks could also hang up in the same way as bombs, resulting in the aircraft yawing off target. A fix in the form of a bar that linked each separate toggle helped overcome the problem to some extent but the release cables could become stretched, another cause of hang-ups.

It was in the nature of things that half-attached ordnance invariably needed the shock of the aircraft touching down to fully release – the spectacular, highly dangerous results being another reason why pilots were not totally sold on the merits of napalm over G.P. bombs. In lieu of an electric release gear on the P-47D-30, R.A.F. groundcrews obtained parts from Liberators (on which nearly everything was electrically operated) and wired them into the circuits of the earlier model Thunderbolts.

Relatively few Thunderbolts had been shot down by Japanese A.A. fire, but one such incident occurred on 1 February when No. 261 Sqn lost a Mk II while attacking Meiktila Main airfield. The Japanese were observed to be using considerable quantities of light Bofors-type A.A. guns to defend key points, particularly artillery positions, and in those instances where aircraft were hit, the rugged construction of the Thunderbolt again came into its own. But strafing airfields was always a risky business and pilots rarely had the chance to confirm the destruction of enemy aircraft, many of which were well protected by revetments. One pass with a good dive angle to place some of the bullets into the revetments, preferably maintaining air speed at 500 mph plus, was the chosen method. Follow-up strafing runs were hardly ever risked. Bombs and napalm were used on a variety of targets throughout February.

Most of the front-line Thunderbolts were now Mk IIs and 'offensive patrols' became the order of the day, the forward troops using the

*Top: A early Thunderbolt Mk I used for conversion training at Yelahanka in July 1944, HD118 was on the strength of No. 146 Sqn. Numerous Mk Is survived the rigours of combat flying over Burma and many pilots appreciated their rock-steady flying characteristics. (P. Jarrett)*

*Above: No. 42 Squadron Thunderbolt Mk II KJ358 flying north-east of Meiktila in 1945. (A. Thomas)*

*At Alipore about December 1945, a Mk II of No. 5 Sqn coded 'X' shows typical beat-up finish as result of long exposure to the elements. Note that the S.E.A.C. bands are not carried over the tail flying surfaces as per regulations – a practice not always followed. (A. Thomas)*

services of ten air support signals units and visual control posts. These pinpointed the targets that had to be hit and the fighter-bombers obliged to help maintain the momentum of the advance.

British aircraft introduced to combat in Burma in the last months of the war included the Mosquito. On 8 February, an *Earthquake* mission saw Mosquitoes, B-25s and Thunderbolts joining forces to pound the enemy north of Singu. Most of the Thunderbolt squadrons were in action on succeeding days and on 11 February Sqn Ldr Cameron, C.O. of No. 258 Sqn, nailed one of six Ki-44s attacking Liberators *en route* to Rangoon. Cameron's fire obliged the enemy pilot to bale out when his aircraft was hit.

Troops of the 14th Army then faced the Irrawaddy along a 200-mile front with the Japanese contained on the right bank at Sagaing. Nos 123 and 134's Thunderbolts helped blunt strong enemy counterattacks as the army moved across the river, adding fuel to the Japanese

belief that the ultimate Allied objective was Mandalay, which was not the case.

Early in January 1945, the Allies captured Akyab and on the 7th it was announced that the vital Ledo Road, linking the railhead at Ledo in Assam with Myitkyina and Bhamo, with a branch running into China, had finally been completed. Heavy fighting, meanwhile, continued for control of the communications centre at Meiktila.

February brought a hazard far worse than anything the enemy could do to curtail air operations: torrential rain all but washed away 910 Wing's fair-weather strip at Wangjing. In Bengal, 904 Wing also had to abandon waterlogged forward strips and pull back to Cox's Bazaar – in effect all the Thunderbolt squadrons were grounded by the weather. American air support was used in the meantime but on the 18th No. 261 bombed a supply dump at Taugledaw, one Thunderbolt being brought down by the effects of exploding munitions. Sgt Kay got out of his machine and was captured – until he made a run for it. Evading his pursuers, Kay was back with his unit within four days, a feat which brought him the Military Medal.

Enemy dumps were now frequent targets, the largest yet discovered, at Yinmabin, going up in flames under attack by No 258 Sqn aircraft on 21 February. Nos 134 and 258 followed through the next day and pilots observed the explosions from 50 miles away with smoke reaching to 10,000 ft. The attendant hazard of debris to low-flying aircraft was experienced the hard way by a No. 134 Sqn Thunderbolt pilot whose machine was badly damaged. Instructions went out to pilots carrying out shallow bombing or dive-bombing attacks to break away from the target at 150 yards instead of the usual 50 yards.

Much of the fighter-bomber support for the army was indirect, i.e. some distance from the fighting. 'Remote' support included knocking out all Burmese road and rail bridges which could be of use to the enemy and the Thunderbolts did their share in 'busting' them to disrupt Japanese supplies. One such operation was mounted by No. 123 Sqn on the rail bridge at Toungoo on 25 February; No. 79 skip-bombed others before flying a 740-mile round-trip sortie to Pyinmana on the 27th.

On the ground, the enemy was kept guessing as to Slim's main intention, the confusion serving to divide his forces to meet threats from different sectors. Allied air superiority was now virtually absolute in the battle area but the Japanese showed no sign of giving up. Thunderbolt strikes could be called in within minutes.

With numerous Thunderbolt Mk IIs in storage it was decided to equip two more R.A.F. squadrons and on 6 March, No. 34 Squadron's 'B' Flight, embarked upon the 910 Wing conversion course at Wangjing. Led by Wg Cdr J.A. Bushbridge, No. 34 had

*Pleasing view of Mk II KL308 of No. 30 Sqn., probably snapped from the waist window of a Liberator. The white spot in the blue S.E.A.C. fin band is the squadron badge. (R.L. Ward)*

previously flown Hurricanes. Conversion took only a matter of days and the squadron was back in the line by mid-month. No. 146, which had been flying Thunderbolt Mk Is since May 1944, received new Mk IIs, 'B' Flight being detached to Wangjing while 'A' Flight went to Sinthe for the same purpose, there to join No. 134 Sqn which used the strip to fly cab-rank sorties over Meiktila for three days during March.

By 5 March, Meiktila airfield was in Allied hands – at least during the hours of daylight – and by that time advance motorised elements of the 19th Division had reached the outskirts of Mandalay. No. 79 Sqn gave air support to the occupation of the lower part of Mandalay Hill. The city was all but cleared of Japanese troops during March although No. 134 Sqn's help was needed to break enemy resistance at Fort Dufferin, the citadel guarded by giant brick and earth fortified walls, not to mention a moat. No. 258 Squadron's Thunderbolts also attacked the Fort on 13 March.

Sqn Ldr McGregor, meanwhile, led four Thunderbolts of No. 123 to clear Meiktila airfield which came under Japanese artillery fire and continued to be partially occupied by the enemy each night. The R.A.F. Regiment dealt with the incursions during the day, allowing Dakotas to land with supplies; No. 123's attack was made against enemy batteries which bombarded the airfield at every opportunity.

No. 34 Squadron's 'B' Flight returned to operations on 20 March. Sorties included an *Earthquake Minor* against the Japanese guns shelling Meiktila Main, which apparently achieved little on that occasion. And hauling more bombs to the fortifications of Fort Dufferin made a less than spectacular impression. It would be ground troops who finally secured the fort towards the end of March when 2nd Division crossed the Irrawaddy and marched on Mandalay. They found few enemy soldiers.

Now came a race to Rangoon and a need for 14th Army to inflict a decisive defeat on the Japanese before the start of the monsoon season. Bitter fighting ensued while the enemy tried to hold on to the vital airfields used by air-supply Dakotas. A major prize for the Allies was the capture of the port of Myingen into which supplies could be fed down the

Chindwin from depots further north.

During this period, 910 Wing undertook another *Earthquake Minor*, hitting a variety of enemy positions but concentrating on artillery. Now the Japanese army was finally broken as a cohesive fighting force and reduced to small pockets, it retreated into the Shan Hills, all but isolated from all vital supplies, including food, medicines, fuel and ammunition.

An *Earthquake* on 1 April included No. 146 Sqn 'B' Flight, the squadron's 'A' Flight returning to Sinthe in exchange for 'A' Flight of No. 261, which began a week of standing patrols. After the 6th, the unit went back to close-support sorties, the pilots helping to reduce the threat from a strong enemy force ensconsed on the slopes of Mt Popa.

On 5 April, No. 113 Sqn, part of 906 Wing and commanded by Sqn Ldr J. Rose, relinquished its Hurricanes for Thunderbolts at Wangjing and thereafter joined No. 34 Sqn at Ondaw, bringing the number of 221 Group Thunderbolt squadrons to five. Meanwhile, it became clear that the enemy intended to hold a line from Yenangyaung on the Irrawaddy to Thaze, east of Meiktila until the monsoon broke and halted Slim's forces.

Another worry for Slim was that the U.S.A.A.F. would withdraw the bulk of its C-47 units by June. The U.S. transport force was committed to Burma only until such time as land routes between China and India had been secured. With this objective achieved, most of the cargo capacity available to 14th Army would disappear. A combination of these factors could stop Slim's offensive in its tracks and perhaps wreck *Dracula*. Airfields needed to be secured near Prome or Toungoo to cover the planned parachute landing at Rangoon scheduled for 1 May. It was clear that *Dracula* must go ahead earlier than intended, before the end of April. A seaborne assault from the Rangoon river would link up with army columns using available land routes and forces using the Irrawaddy. Slim had about five weeks.

To support the *Dracula* landings, 905 Wing was disbanded and its four Thunderbolt squadrons, Nos 5 (Sqn Ldr L. H. Dawes), 123 (Sqn Ldr A. J. McGregor), 134 (Sqn Ldr D.K. McDonald) and 258, passed to the control of 904 Wing. Nos 79 (Sqn Ldr C. G. Ford), 146 (Sqn Ldr R.A.E. Weir) and 261 (Sqn Ldr R.H. Fletcher) Squadrons moved to bases in the south before the end of April. No. 30 Sqn, meanwhile, remained in the Arakan region where it was the only unit flying Thunderbolts in the area and supported Operation *Turret*, the landing at Letpan. This was followed up with a drive to Taungap to threaten an enemy supply line along the Irrawaddy valley. No. 5 Sqn, based at Nair, but invariably operating from forward strips at Sadaung and Sinthe, joined 910 Wing in support of the ground forces heavily engaged around Meiktila and Mandalay.

But increasing success now attended Slim's advance; on 10 April Kywebe, 30 miles south of Toungoo, was captured. A southern push began immediately. Rangoon was 300 miles away. An *Earthquake* on 11 April with No. 146 Sqn Thunderbolts escorting B-25s of the 12th B.G. persuaded the Japanese that holding Yamethin and its airstrip was futile. The strip was in Allied hands later that same day.

Such was the pace of operations that the R.A.F. did not immediately repair damaged aircraft but saved valuable time by using replacements. Fortunately, the Thunderbolt squadrons flew an aircraft well able to stand up to the rigours of combat over Burma. Forward airstrips were quickly made available by specialist Royal Engineers airfield construction units which travelled with the forward ground forces so that little of the momentum achieved by close-support aircraft was lost. Fortunately pilot and aircraft casualties remained well within limits, although No. 261 Squadron's detachment at Sinthe lost three aircraft during April while supporting the drive on Meiktila.

Pilot fatigue, in operating conditions that never even approached the ideal, was a greater cause for concern than aircraft attrition. Aircraft of 910 Wing in support of the pre-*Dracula*

*Thunderbolts could easily survive damage that would have written off flimsier aircraft. Mk II KJ165/0 of No. 5 Sqn at Meiktila on 28 July 1945 had previously had an argument with a brick wall – the wall came off worst! Repairable though they were, there was little need at that stage of the war to carry out the necessary work on numerous aircraft. (Peter Cope)*

phase, had to fly half the length of Burma to reach their targets, their base at Wangjing being about 380 miles away from the front lines. And while shorter-ranged Spitfires and Hurricanes could operate from strips nearer to the fighting, neither type could deliver the ordnance regularly lifted by the Thunderbolt.

But it was not simply a matter of moving these squadrons forward to any available strip. The impending monsoon, plus the substantial pounding that dirt runways received every time a Thunderbolt touched down, could soon render some strips unsuitable for any aircraft. Such occurred at Myingen North when 910 Wing moved in on 19 April. Storms quickly rendered the base untenable. A move was then made to Meiktila on the 23rd with No. 261's Sinthe detachment arriving the following day. On the 20th, 906 Wing occupied Kwetnge south of Meiktila, although No. 34 Squadron found the strip far from ideal for its Mk II Thunderbolts. Older model P-47s were still going strong, No.113 Sqn flying a mix of Mk Is and IIs. A stand-down gave 906 Wing's six Thunderbolt squadrons a brief respite on 20 April, pending a move southwards.

Aircraft of 904 Wing flew daily sorties in support of an army now frantically advancing to beat the worst of the monsoon. Pockets of enemy resistance were bypassed where possible, the race becoming a dual one – to beat the monsoon and secure airfields in the forward area. On 17 April, Sqn Ldr M.W. Hubble, commanding officer of No. 146 Sqn for less than a month, was lost when his Thunderbolt was seen by other pilots to dive into the ground in flames. Hubble was replaced by Sqn Ldr W.M. Souter.

The Japanese Army Air Force made a rare appearance on the 22nd when some Ki-43s strafed Lewe airfield but they failed to detect a number of Dakotas which were inbound to the strip. No. 146 Squadron's own strafing was more effective on 24 April, enemy troops also being bombed at Pegu. The cost of these operations was one Thunderbolt which flew too low and hit a tree. Nos 34 and 113 Sqns turned their attention to cab-rank patrols that same day, their firepower assisting IV Corps which was then advancing on Nyaunglebin.

Japanese plans now had a more practical purpose than pointless sacrifice against heavy odds. If the decision was made to withdraw

troops from Rangoon rather than defend the city to the last man, General Kimura reasoned that he must hold Pegu until the monsoon had broken. Then he would have a chance to withdraw across the Sittang where he could anticipate less aerial action against his forces.

## RANGOON SURPRISE

Allied convoys for the Rangoon operation sailed from Ramree and while the ships were *en route* it was vital to capture the airfields at Toungoo to put the Thunderbolts in range of the city. During this period the squadrons moved base; Nos 5, 123 and 134 flew south to Kyaukpu on the 28th, No. 258 arriving the next day to operate under 902 Wing. On the 29th, 903 Wing welcomed Nos 30 and 135 to Akyab Main. That day, 902 Wing stood down pending a move to Kyungon, north of Toungoo, on the 30th.

Thunderbolt squadrons of 224 Group and 910 Wing sortied early on 1 May to cover parachute landings at Elephant Point on the Rangoon estuary to capture coastal batteries that could threaten the *Dracula* beach-heads. Having to contend with storms along the Arakan coast, the Thunderbolt pilots nevertheless bombed and strafed Japanese positions. A massive storm stretching some 60 miles off the coast did deter No. 135 Sqn but No. 5's pilots, finding marginally better conditions, successfully attacked enemy bunkers along the river. Some of the targets were only lightly held and as the landing parties arrived it became clear that the Japanese had all but abandoned Rangoon. Thunderbolts nevertheless found some 'trade' in the form of manned gun positions at Thilawa, No. 261 Sqn dealing with these.

Now the full fury of the monsoon broke and operational flying became extremely hazardous. Kyungon had to be temporarily abandoned on 3 May but No. 79's fighters were able to use the strip for close-support sorties on the following two days. A move to Myingen North was made in the next 48 hours, enabling 910 Wing to continue operations.

## FOCUS CHANGE

With seasonal weather conditions having all but halted ground operations, the planning proceeded for Operation *Zipper*, the landings in Malaya. A new threat emerged when intelligence estimated possible interference by Japanese naval forces which could attack supply covoys. Accordingly, Thunderbolts of No. 261 Sqn prepared to operate against warships using 500 lb semi-armour-piercing bombs, in company with No. 146. In the event they were not needed, the main Japanese Navy force being sunk before it could get anywhere near vulnerable Allied freighters.

Although tactical air operations continued, this was a relatively quiet period for the fighter-bomber units and a number of base moves were made in deference to the appalling weather. Gradually the Thunderbolt squadrons began to be withdrawn to India, in some cases to be equipped with other types of aircraft, primarily Spitfires. With the war winding down and many men completing their tours, personnel repatriation was already causing some difficulty in maintaining a full complement of pilots, although replacements were drawn from the pools established by 73 O.T.U. at Fayid and 8 R.F.U. at Yelahanka. The run-down caused the formerly Spitfire-equipped Nos 81, 131 and 615 Sqns to be disbanded on 10 June, their aircraft having been passed to the Royal Indian Air Force.

These squadron numbers were transferred to Thunderbolt units: No. 134 became No. 131, No. 135 became No. 615, and by 25 June No. 123 was renumbered No. 81 Squadron, with Sqn Ldr P. A. Kennedy commanding. The last 'new' R.A.F. Thunderbolt squadron was No. 60, previously equipped with Hurricanes, which received its Republic fighters in mid-July. The C.O. was Sqn Ldr J.B. Wales.

*Zipper*, meanwhile, had still to be undertaken and in addition to the foregoing units, 905 Wing with Nos 5, 30, 81 and 615 Sqns was working up for the operation in India. Action was still going on in Burma with 221 Group battling the weather more than the Japanese. More enforced base moves had to be made, Nos 79 and 146 Sqns using Meiktila Main from 8 June while No. 261 at Myingen ceased operations on the 18th and moved to India. No. 113 finally re-equipped with Thunderbolt Mk IIs and although on 24 June No. 146 became No. 42 Squadron it remained under the command of Sqn Ldr Souter. Both this unit and No. 79 continued to bomb and strafe the enemy in the Sittang Valley area, a duty it shared with 910 Wing's Nos 113 and 34 Sqns by 1 July.

Fighting flared again on 3 July, the Japanese making an attempt at Waw to cut 12th Army's lines of communication with Rangoon (14th Army had been renumbered) and secure sections of the main roads. No. 34 Sqn was in the thick of the counterattack, losing one Thunderbolt on 9 July, the aircraft, like others before it, spinning into the ground. This attack was broken but the enemy continued to mount small, potentially dangerous thrusts for almost another month. But by early August, the heavy losses inflicted by both Allied troops and tactical air power finally broke the remnants of the Japanese Army in Burma.

On 6 August, the atomic bombing of Hiroshima brought hope that the war would quickly end; *Zipper* preparations continued however and fighter-bomber operations were still being flown in Burma. Nagasaki was hit by the second atomic bomb on 9 August and Japan sued for peace, the surrender announcement coming on the 14th.

Nos. 42 and 79 Sqns flew the final R.A.F. Thunderbolt operations of the war when they attacked enemy positions at Sittang. Thereafter until 30 August, Nos 34 and 113 Sqns dropped more bombs — but now these were packed not with high explosive but with leaflets informing Japanese prison camp guards and inmates alike that the war was over. Although the fighting had ceased, Thunderbolt attrition remained a factor, No. 34 Squadron losing two aircraft on three long-range humanitarian sorties. Operation *Zipper* went ahead on 9 September, a peaceful reoccupation of Penang, Singapore and all areas previously in Japanese hands.

For the R.A.F. in South-East Asia, the wind down of forces continued, although a number of Thunderbolt-equipped units remained operational. No. 5 Squadron, still flying Mk Is, returned to Burma in September. Scheduled to transfer to Sumatra, it was based at Zayatkin near Rangoon before moving to Biagachi near Calcutta in February 1946. There the unit bade farewell to its venerable razorbacks, some personnel still perhaps wondering why their long service had apparently not merited the squadron being issued with newer Mk II T-bolts. Pilots familiar with the latter would have stressed however that No. 5 had an aircraft that was just as capable as the later models and, in the opinion of many, usually

*Engine trouble forced Mk II KL882 of No. 60 Sqn to divert to Don Muang in Siam while en route to take part in Operation Tiderace, the occupation of Singapore in mid-1945. The Thunderbolt units stood by just in case the defeated enemy offered any resistance but there was none. (L. Manwaring)*

possessed superior flying characteristics. Instances of instability were indeed rare in the earlier models and although there remained the slight drawback of restricted vision to the rear, this was largely overcome with the use of mirrors and the pilots, through experience, simply allowing for it. In any event, poor rearwards vision was not the problem it might have been had the S.E.A.C. Thunderbolts been heavily involved in air combat.

To support *Zipper*, a re-formed 905 Wing comprising the Thunderbolts of Nos 60, 131 and 258 Sqns, used Kuala Lumpur as a base, while No. 81 Sqn occupied Port Swettenham. No. 615 was disbanded at Vizgapatam on 25 September, followed by No. 261 at Tanjore on the 26th. No. 113 at Kayatkwin ceased to exist on 15 October and No. 34 Sqn was disbanded at Palem on the 17th. No. 30 Squadron traded its Thunderbolts for Tempest IIs in December while based at Vizgapatam.

Despite the high utilisation of the Thunderbolt in Burma, the squadrons serving there lost a total of only seventeen aircraft to enemy action. This was a remarkable figure and even when combined with those lost in accidents and non-operational causes, the Republic fighter returned one of the lowest loss rates for any type the R.A.F. used in the Second World War. At least nine enemy aircraft were shot down by Thunderbolts during the course of operations, the highest scoring squadron being No. 261 with five. All victories were achieved by different pilots between October 1944 and February 1945.

Having served for well over a year on South-East Asian operations and endured some of the worst flying conditions on the face of the globe with remarkably light losses, the R.A.F. Thunderbolt squadrons could pride themselves on a fine record. It would be hard to envisage an alternative aircraft type, one available in sufficient numbers, that could have done a similar, outstanding job in Burma.

# 10
# Battle of the Bulge

Under a canopy of fog, freezing rain and heavy snow, sudden German movement on the stalemated Western Front on 16 December heralded one of the greatest frustrations for Allied air power since D-Day. On Hitler's orders, the spearheads of twenty-five divisions grouped in three armies commanded by General Gerd von Rundstedt, attacked weakly held Allied front line positions in the Ardennes region. In total secrecy, only hinted at by *Ultra* intercepts which gave no dates, Operation *Wacht am Rhein* crashed forward, taking many green U.S. troops completely by surprise. German tanks soon created an armoured salient that was virtually invisible from the air due to a perpetual overcast that would last for days. The Battle of the Bulge was on.

Early on the 16th, IX and XIX T.A.C. flew sorties elsewhere; the weather still curtailed operations to a significant degree but the 509th F.S. at St-Dizier was roused early, but only because a German paratroop assault on the airfield had been rumoured. As the news of the real German attack gradually filtered through to the air bases, leaves were cancelled, guards doubled and everyone lost precious sleep. It was pilots of the 356th F.G., the 'Hell Hawks' who first spotted unusual enemy activity on 16 December. A convoy 150 vehicles strong, observed from the cockpits of their Thunderbolts during a morning sortie against targets of opportunity, turned out to be part of the big offensive.

When the pilots called in the lucrative target, the group sent up reinforcements and the P-47s went to work. Maj John W. Motzenbecker led the strafing and bombing attack which followed up an initial bombing

*By mid-1944, Ninth Air Force P-47 units were spread out across Europe. The 371st Group was at Metz-Frescaty where its 404th F.S. (code 9Q) and 405th F.S. (code 8N) aircraft continued the pressure on the retreating German armies. (U.S.A.F.)*

by the earlier patrol. Although the German vehicles had scattered to seek cover under the trees, the Hell Hawks found many targets. German flak caught the Thunderbolt flown by 2nd Lt John D. McCarthy whose aircraft went straight into a hillside. Joined by other aircraft of the group, Motzenbecker's Blue Flight contributed significantly to the tally of 107 vehicles claimed destroyed. A second P-47, flown by Lt Herbert A. Sting, was shot down.

Weather conditions on the 17th improved marginally, enough for the *Luftwaffe* to step up its sorties; the task of the substantial German fighter force assembled to protect the ground forces was to ward off Allied fighter-bomber attacks and JG 27 was one of the units involved in a morning combat with the 404th Group. Reacting positively to being intercepted, the Thunderbolts turned the tables and shot down six Bf 109Gs.

For the first time in months, the opposing tactical air forces had a plethora of targets and the first of numerous large- and small-scale clashes took place as the German attack developed. More Bf 109s fell to the guns of the 404th before the day was finished, the German fighters making prudent use of ample cloud cover if their American adversaries proved too much of a handful. Inexperience plagued the *Jagdflieger* at that stage of the war although enough 'old hares' were flying to make the Allied task of blunting the ground advance a very difficult one on occasion.

At best, the Allied fighter-bomber units were thinly spread and unable for a time to coordinate retaliatory ground-attacks against this totally unexpected development. Neither could the theatre commanders get a cohesive picture of what the immediate situation was and which sector was under the greatest threat. Hampered by the appalling weather which persisted for days, the Allied air effort was at the mercy of the elements. Only air reconnaissance, which hardly paused throughout the Ardennes campaign, could clarify things. Pilots risked their lives to get photographs and reports back to headquarters, their Mustangs and Lightnings having at times to outrun Messerschmitts and Focke-Wulfs in order to do so.

The bad weather front extended to England where U.S.A.A.F. depots such as the giant B.A.D. No. 1 complex at Burtonwood began experiencing a huge backlog of new and repaired fighters and bombers that would normally have been dispatched straight to the front-line units. There was nothing to be done as the weather clamped down to hold up flights. P-47s were among the most numerous types ready to be ferried to France as soon as the conditions improved and, although the depot put through 231 P-47s in October 1944, 189 more were caught on the ground by bad weather during the month. It was to be January 1945 before the slightly more modest stockpile of 139 Thunderbolts began to be reduced. Burtonwood personnel, of course did not stop signing off new and rebuilt P-47s all through the winter – it was just that while the weather made flying too hazardous, they remained out on the airfield. The depot had to call on the services of thirty 1st T.A.C. fighter pilots to help ferry the fighters to France.

Allied reaction to a confused situation soon galvanised into enough action to bring fire and destruction down on the Germans; ground-air liaison enabled numerous pockets to be attacked to prevent, if only temporarily, Allied positions from being wiped out. Now the troops needed time, not to advance but to pull back. Many men were captured in the first few days' fighting.

Among the P-47 groups flying the early Bulge missions were the 366th, 368th, 405th and 367th. Most of the squadrons had P-47s shot down and a considerable number damaged by the bristling guns of the German armoured columns and supply convoys. Very low-flying aircraft could be nailed by guns of many calibres, even massed small-arms fire but once again the P-47 showed its propensity to survive quite extensive damage from ground fire and not uniquely, obstacles that the pilots could not always avoid flying into at zero feet.

Renowned Thunderbolt survivability was even appreciated by the 354th Group. Equipped with P-47s rather than P-51s since November, the pioneer Mustang unit made no secret of the fact that it remained fiercely loyal to the North American product. But it might have had higher losses had it not been flying Thunderbolts during that particular winter period of operations. On the 16th, the group attacked a German command post and blocked a railway tunnel, fortunately without taking any losses.

The scale of air combat that took place over

the Ardennes can be gauged by the fact that 1020 non-battlefield sorties, i.e. those flown directly to counter the *Luftwaffe*, took place on 17 December, the first day that Allied reaction approached a coordinated effort. German sorties ran into hundreds for the first time in months. Some Allied pilots had never seen the enemy at all and his potential strength now in evidence all over the Western front was quite awesome to behold.

On the 18th, fog hampered operations to such a degree that even reconnaissance was next to impossible. 'Pete' Quesada, IX T.A.C. commander, having had word that the Panzers were less than 15 miles from the H.Q. of General Hodges, First Army Commander, personally asked for volunteers to find an enemy column near Stavelot. The call was answered by two Mustang pilots but their efforts, even with radar guidance, were initially to no avail. Equal difficulty was faced by a flight of P-47s of the 365th Group, the follow-up strike force that flew through the 'soup' to attack the tanks and A.F.V.s that were being sought. The ceiling was less than 200 feet as the Thunderbolts threaded their way over, sometimes through, fog-filled valleys. Suddenly the German column – identified as the notorious *Kampfgruppe* Peiper – was seen and for once the weather sided with the Allied aircraft. Only at the last moment could the German gunners pick up the attacking Thunderbolts.

By hitting the column in relays throughout the rest of that day, the Jugs were able to ruin *SS-Obersturmbannführer* Joachim Peiper's plan to reach the River Meuse. Harried by strafing P-47s of the 356th, 366th and 404th Groups, the Panzers were slowed long enough for two bridges to be blasted before they could cross, the most important being that at Cheneux. The Panzers were not stopped but the delays affected by the American *Jabos* would ultimately cost them dear.

The pattern of attacks in the first 48 hours of the Battle of the Bulge were repeated many times in succeeding days, with the Germans taking a terrible pounding whenever the Allied fighter-bombers could locate their columns. Equally, flak remained a hazard to the pilots and to the inevitable losses was added a substantial number of aircraft damaged in such missions. Yet the fighter-bombers managed to turn the low overcast to their advantage by initiating a series of fast dive-and-climb attacks. By dodging back into cloud immediately after strafing or bombing, their losses to flak were minimised and they retained an element of surprise over the enemy ground forces. The weather remained bad until two days before Christmas. And when dawn broke on 23 December, the air commanders could hardly believe they were seeing the sun and deep blue skies. It was finally clear.

There followed an aerial assault incredible to behold. All day, fighters and medium bombers thundered off the aerodromes to fill the skies of Belgium and Luxembourg with an unforgettable display of air power. The weather was not good everywhere and some tactical groups could not participate in the day's action but *Luftwaffe* airfields were attacked by the 36th and 373rd, and the P-47s bombed and strafed numerous tanks, half-tracks and trucks; other Thunderbolts did their best to keep the German fighters away from B-26s which were out in force.

Groundcrews worked feverishly in terrible conditions to keep each operational P-47 armed and loaded with a constant supply of ordnance. Few undercover facilities were available on the fighter airfields, some of which had been badly bombed and most such replenishment work had to be done in the open.

When the American 10th Armoured and the 101st Airborne Divisions were surrounded in Bastogne, P-47 sorties helped to keep the Germans from overrunning the town. Dropping napalm, dive-bombing and strafing enemy transports seeking cover in surrounding woods, the Thunderbolts winkled out and neutralised many an armoured threat, but the fighting was bitter. The German positions were ringed by flak, making every sortie hazardous. Fortunately a ground-air radio net had been established to guide in the American fighter-bombers and the defenders were mighty glad to get supplies by air drop on the morning of the 23rd. A difficult escort mission was carried out by eighty-two P-47s of the 354th, 362nd, 405th and 406th Fighter Groups which shepherded 214 IX Troop Carrier Command C-47s over the American positions.

All participating pilots would remember the Ardennes for a long time to come. For many it was the most intense air action of the war, spiced as most sorties were by the appearance of enemy aircraft. Certainly few of the airmen were ever faced with so many targets in such a relatively small area of country.

Christmas Eve 1944 brought little sign of peace. On the contrary, the *Luftwaffe* made a supreme effort to rout some of the U.S.A.A.F. medium bomber sorties and casualties among the Marauder groups reached an all time high in one 24-hour period. For the fighter-bombers, the seemingly endless numbers of enemy vehicles and tanks required a constant shuttle service of high explosive between their airfields and the front line. Clear weather meant that von Rundstedt's offensive must eventually peter out, for significant progress could no longer be made in the teeth of such opposition. On the contrary, the Germans would soon be fighting for their very lives. But there was still a hard fight ahead.

Resorting to cunning camouflage ruses to hide a dwindling number of tanks still did not avail the Germans very much because the battlefield was constantly under aerial surveillance – P-47 pilots learned to take a close look at haystacks when the Germans began using them to disguise their tanks.

To reinforce the tactical groups fighting in the front line, VIII Fighter Command dispatched the Mustangs of the 361st and 352nd Groups to the continent. Not that the Eighth had been out of the Ardennes fighting for long. As soon as the conditions improved, the heavies were used to attack strong points in the battle area, the escort continuing the attrition of the *Jagdwaffe*. Trying to divide its *Jagdgeschwader* between interception of the heavies and maintaining a defensive over the Panzers was a nightmare for the German high command. Rarely did the fighters emerge unscathed from combat with the Allied tactical units – indeed their losses, although not always as high as the Americans claimed, included many instances when the German pilots suffered fatal injuries. This grim toll was in direct contrast to the experience of their U.S. opposite numbers, where the pilot mortality rate, even among fighter-bomber groups, was gratifyingly low.

General Nugent of XXIX T.A.C. reported on 26 December that most of his squadrons were down on numbers. A P-47 squadron with twelve operational aircraft rather than the usual twenty-five plus gave it parity with an R.A.F. squadron or a *Luftwaffe Jagdstaffel*. But tactically, it meant that unless replacement Thunderbolts were made available, the spiralling attrition as a result of continual ground-attack operations could curtail Nugent's ability to mount maximum-effort operations at short notice. Replacement pilots also unwittingly caused the front-line tactical groups problems. Although they were available in ample numbers, the newcomers could not immediately fill the shoes of those who had been shot down or had completed their tours and elected to return home. Men fresh from U.S. training schools, while they had had excellent tuition and considerable flying experience, had rarely had the chance to fire their guns, certainly not in anger.

Europe's present weather conditions – which could rarely be duplicated in the U.S. - were hardly conducive to calm theatre training flights and, through no fault of their own, freshman pilots were more of a liability than an asset until they had a few missions under their belt. Pete Quesada endorsed his colleague's view when he officially complained that by 1944 operational training should not have been the responsibility of the front-line groups. This turned out not to be the problem it might have been earlier in the war but the principle was sound enough.

## SURPRISE ATTACK

With the Ardennes offensive wrecked, largely as a result of Allied air activity and a shortage of fuel, the Germans had little choice but to abandon the *Wacht am Rhein* offensive. The *Luftwaffe*, which had fought the last of its major tactical air battles, had one more ace up its sleeve – if it can really be called that. On 1 January, Operation *Bodenplatte*, the mass strike on Allied air bases in Belgium and Holland, resulted in more losses to the attacking force in terms of irreplaceable pilots, than on the Allied side. Thunderbolt units generally escaped destruction of their aircraft on the ground when the *Luftwaffe* roared spectacularly over seventeen airfields with all guns blazing. Strafing runs, some with more enthusiasm than skill, achieved surprise at the majority of U.S.A.A.F. and R.A.F. bases. Numerous aircraft of all types were shot up on the ground at some while at others the attacks

*Initially horrified at changing its P-38s for Thunderbolts, the 367th Fighter Group soon found the Jug to be a formidable ground-attack aircraft. The 'Dynamite Gang' was at Jarny, west of Metz when orders came through to hit Kesselring's H.Q. Some of these 394th F.S. P-47s were on the surprise attack. (J. Campbell)*

were a total failure. And unfortunately for the *Jagdwaffe*, wherever ground defences or Allied fighters were able to react, a fearful toll of pilots was taken.

At Asch, the 366th Group, which was then sharing the airfield with the Mustangs of the 352nd, gave a good account of itself. The 391st Squadron missed the main German attack, due to having flown an early morning anti-tank mission to the Odenval area as part of the Allied reaction to the Ardennes offensive. *En route* back to Asch, the Thunderbolt pilots spotted two Bf 109s which were quickly shot down. In the meantime, the FW 190s and Bf 109s of JG 11 had come upon a far from passive target. P-47s of the 389th and 390th Squadrons had just taken off with full bomb loads when a radio message informed the pilots of the attack. The P-47s jettisoned their bombs and came barrelling in over Asch to witness the FW 190s and Bf 109s going in on their strafing runs. Doggedly the German pilots did their best to carry out their orders – but they were completely surprised by the 366th.

Lt Melvin Paisley had a particularly good

day by shooting down three enemy fighters. He claimed four in the mêlée that developed as the *Jagdflieger* were forced to defend themselves. Capt Lowell B. Smith and Lt Bob Brulle were among the other victors. Being so low, the Germans suffered badly if their aircraft were hit, the resulting high-speed crashes often killing pilots who would otherwise have been able to bale out. Twelve of them succumbed to the combined fire of the P-47s and the 352nd's Mustangs, which became an unbeatable duo in some engagements. Embroiled in a series of bloody dogfights, JG 11 was torn to pieces.

At other P-47 bases, the attack achieved more in terms of aircraft destroyed; at Metz, the Germans caught the 365th Hell Hawks on the ground and destroyed no less than twenty-two Thunderbolts and damaged eight more beyond economical repair. The score at St-Trond, then housing the 48th Group, was a more modest two P-47s and fourteen slightly damaged. The raiders, hampered by restrictive secrecy, poor navigation and pilot inexperience, missed some plumb targets. One was Le Culot. There the

*Jagdflieger* would have found over 100 P-47s of the 36th, 363rd and 373rd Groups, but this airfield was hardly touched.

For *Bodenplatte* to have had any lasting effect on their own future operations, the Germans really needed to inflict heavy casualties among Allied pilots, not aircraft. This was next to impossible to achieve but their own losses in human terms on 1 January were little short of catastrophic. The Allies could replace aircraft in a matter of days and their pilot losses – at all airfields attacked – were minimal. The *Luftwaffe*'s 'last throw' came to nothing and there was worse to come. With the weather easing, tactical missions could be stepped up and the ground advance moved into high gear to mount the final offensive that would end in inevitable German defeat.

As January waned, the P-47 groups tangled once more with the German jets. The Ninth Air Force groups got all the action in January and February, David Fox of the 391st Squadron, 366th Group recording the first contact with the Arado jet bomber on 22 February. Only three Ar 234 actions would come the way of Thunderbolt groups before the end of the war.

## FRANCO-AMERICAN FORCE

On 15 August 1944, operation *Dragoon* resulted in the seventh U.S. Army making a successful landing in southern France. Faced with depleted German forces, casualties were very light and beach-area defences had been, and continued to be, heavily pounded by fighter-bombers, mediums and heavies. Fighter-bomber sorties were controlled off-shore from U.S.S. *Catocin*, where personnel of the 2nd Air Combat Control Squadron (Amphibious) directed the fighters by voice link using data gathered by reconnaissance sorties and combat reports.

In a highly successful operation with which the *Luftwaffe* was hardly able to interfere, M.A.A.F. could afford to ignore German airfields and sent its fighters on counter-air patrols. On D+2 such operations claimed eighteen enemy aircraft destroyed, the participating groups including the P-47Ds of the French 4th Fighter-Bomber Group.

As part of the First French Air Force, six *Groupes de Chasse* converted to P-47s to operate as part of First Tactical Air Force

(Provisional), commanded by Brig-Gen Gordon Saville. The units were manned by French pilots and serviced by groundcrews who had formally been part of the Vichy French forces in North Africa. Materiel support and operational training was initially provided for the first two *Escadrilles* by U.S.A.A.F. tactical units although these were not permanently attached to the First Tactical Air Force. The American link with the famed 'Lafayette' unit went back to December 1942 when twenty-five P-40s were handed over to G.C. II/5 and the French unit embarked on operational training with the similarly equipped 33rd Fighter Group of the Twelfth Air Force.

Thunderbolts were delivered to France the following year, with two razorback models, the P-47D-4 and D-22, being the first of 446 to be delivered direct from the U.S. This allocation covered 470 aircraft but other examples were apparently passed to the French from U.S. depots in the Mediterranean during the conflict, bringing the total to 600 according to one source. Four bubble-top models were flown by the *Armée de l'Air*: the P-47D-25, -27, -28, and -30.

The U.S. connection was maintained in that American pilots assisted the Frenchmen to complete conversion training on the P-47 at Bone, Algeria. Personnel of G.C. II/3 *Dauphine* and II/5 were the first to complete the course, the former unit being first to be cleared for combat operations on 1 May. It was decided that the French pilots would make their operational debut with the U.S.A.A.F. in the Mediterranean theatre, in company with the 57th Fighter Group in Corsica.

On 1 May 1944, the Lafayette pilots flew thirty P-47Ds to Alto to join the 57th which had arrived on Corsica fifteen days earlier. The U.S. group conducted operational training for the French pilots, each man flying five sorties to complete the check-out process. The sixth sortie was a combat mission accompanied by aircraft of the 57th, French pilots first being included on mission rosters on 8 May.

Targets continued to be largely in Italy as part of the Operation *Strangle* list which Allied air forces had begun attacking in February – March 1944. Flak bristled around most *Strangle* targets to take its inevitable toll on fighter-bombers and G.C. II/5 had lost four pilots by 4 July. On the positive side, Lt Gouachon had endeared himself to his American colleagues by shooting down a Bf 109 that had approached the P-47 formation unseen. The German pilot was about to attack an element of the 57th when the Frenchman opened fire.

Although the early French – U.S. missions from Alto were coordinated, the American pilots did not count such sorties as part of the group's wartime mission total. The *Armée de l'Air* units were operating independently by mid-summer. On 14 August, G.C. II/5 prepared to fly its first combat sorties over France since 1940 – a poignant, historic occasion for many of the participating pilots. Briefed by General Rivals-Mazeres *Commandant* of G.C. II/5 at Alto, fifty-two pilots were briefed to carry out

*Top: As the autumn came in, Ninth Air Force groundcrews little realised how bad conditions were going to get but there was an inkling at Le Culot, Belgium, where the 36th Fighter Group was based. A P-47 of the 22nd F.S. is about to get what looks like a fairly major engine overhaul. (U.S.A.F.)*

*Above: In Italy, winter conditions were little better but the 86th Fighter Group helped maintain the pressure on the southern front. This aircraft, a tail-striped P-47D of the 526th F.S., has its serial number marked forward, a peculiarity of this group.*

*Top: Yellow lightning bolts adorned the blue tail of the 79th Fighter Group, another of the Twelfth Air Force's veteran P-47 units operating from Italian airfields by 1944. Pounding such choice targets as the Brenner Pass rail links kept the pilots on their toes. Rockets and bombs were used liberally in the drive to contain the Germans. (B. Parsley)*

*Above: At Luneville, France the 324th Fighter Group added its bombs and bullets to the offensive which had the Germans at least contained in northern Italy. Persuading them that their stand was hopeless was not too easy to do however. In this view, a P-47D-30 (44-20719) is being refuelled to carry on the persuasion. (R.L. Ward)*

the mission which was specifically to knock out German radar stations located between St-Tropez and Toulon.

With the southern France campaign proceeding with all speed, the two French units in Corsica prepared to move to France to become part of a newly constituted *Armée de l'Air*. Prior to this transfer on 13 June, G.C. II/5 vacated Alto for Folelli, some 10 miles south of Bastia. One reason for this was that G.C. II/3 had moved into Alto on 6 June and Col Archie Knight, C.O. of the 57th, was mindful that the base, which was usually hot, should not become too overcrowded. Pilots had to come to terms with the huge clouds of sand and dust kicked up after every take-off; the more aircraft there were, the worse this hazard became. Another drawback for the French aircrew and groundcrews in Corsica was American rations – the gastronomic merits of Spam, beans and Coca-Cola were not readily appreciated.

It was from French bases that G.C. I/4 'Navarre' and G.C. III/3 'Ardennes' flew their first P-47 ground-attack sorties, in September and October respectively, with G.C. I/5 'Champagne' just making its mark in 1944 by being announced combat ready on 31 December. Finally, G.C. III/6 'Roussilon' became the sixth and last wartime *Armée de l'Air* formation to take the P-47 into action, on 1 February 1945.

Under 1 T.A.C. control, the French P-47 units operating over France were grouped into two fighter-bomber groups – G.C. I/4, I/5 and III/6 became collectively the 3rd Fighter-Bomber Group and G.C. II/3, III/3 and II/5 as the 4th Group. G.C. II/3 having moved to Besancon in September 1944, was based at Amberieu at this time and tragically the C.O., *Commandant* Edmond Marin la Meslee, was killed while leading an attack on Neufbrisach bridge on 2 February.

A third group of Thunderbolt squadrons was contributed to First Tactical Air Force by the U.S.A.A.F. when the 27th, 86th and 324th Groups were attached to First Tactical Air Force, the 324th being the first in November 1944 with the other two groups following suit on 21 February 1945.

All the French P-47 units ended the war based on French soil as part of First Tactical Air Force, some moving into Germany after the surrender. The Americans presented the *Armée de l'Air* with the balance of 131 P-47Ds of all models that had survived the rigours of training and combat and these later formed the basis of a ground-attack force that would see further action in Algeria.

## BRAZIL

Next to Britain and France, Brazil was the country that made the largest Allied contribution in terms of flying the P-47 in combat during the Second World War. The country had declared war on the Axis powers on 22 August 1942 and, in addition to training at home, Brazilian nationals undertook pilot training in the U.S. A tactical fighter squadron was deemed to be the most practical way to demonstrate Brazil's willingness to take an active part in the war and following conversion to razorback P-47Ds at Suffolk A.A.B. on Long Island, 342 officers and men of the *Primeiro Grupo de Aviacao de Caca* (formed on 18 December 1943) set sail for the Italian port of Livorno. The Brazilians, forty-two of whom were pilots, then travelled by train to Tarquinia where they formed a fourth squadron of the 350th Fighter Group.

Two weeks were spent in settling into their spartan surroundings, test-flying P-47s as they arrived and conducting familiarisation flights. On 31 October, the Brazilians began flying missions in the M.T.O. under the command of Lt-Col Nero Moura.

With *Luftwaffe* activity in the area drastically reduced, the Latin American pilots, all of whom had been thoroughly trained in the whole spectrum of A.A.F. fighter and fighter-bomber operations, found themselves flying tactical ground-support missions, during which contact with the enemy in the air was frustratingly rare. Dive-bombing and strafing became the order of the day, the targets including bridges, gun positions, railways and ammunition depots behind enemy lines. Most sorties were against predetermined targets but the Brazilians also supported troops who directed them, via ground-air controllers or observation planes, to pinpointed local targets. Escort missions, mainly to M.A.A.F. mediums, were occasionally flown.

Ground fire and accidents took an early toll of the Brazilian pilots, one tragic accident claiming the lives of two who were aboard a C-47 which was airborne to film a section of

Thunderbolts for publicity purposes. All went well until the Skytrain inexplicably banked into the path of the P-47s and collided with the number two fighter before crashing in flames with no survivors. Four pilots had been killed even before the 1º *G.Av.Ca* was officially declared operational on 11 November 1944.

On 4 December, the Brazilians left the very wet conditions of Tarquinia and relocated to Pisa San Gilusto airfield along with the rest of the 350th Group. There the pilots and groundcrews integrated their operations with those of the American group. Missions during the winter of 1944-5 were mainly against fortified Axis positions in the northern reaches of the Apennines, the Gothic Line which represented a barrier to Allied advance into the strategically vital River Po valley. Numerous dive-bombing missions were carried out by 1º *Grupo de Aviacao de Caca*, - which took the nickname 'The Ostriches' after the cartoon bird depicted on the squadron badge – and the Brazilians quickly built up a fine reputation with the destruction of many enemy vehicles, strong points and trains to their credit. In total, the unit was to drop 991

U.S. tons of bombs using the P-47D exclusively, eighty-eight examples of which were eventually delivered. Only a proportion of this total was used on operations during the war, the survivors of combat, plus new machines, being shipped home to modernise the postwar Brazilian air force.

Continual pressure on the Italian transport system, particularly the rail bridges over the Po, were designed to further isolate the Gothic Line defenders from all sources of supply. Flak remained the greatest hazard to Allied air operations and the Brazilian fighter squadron was not alone in suffering most of its combat losses from this cause. Downed pilots ran the risk of capture or rescue by friendly partisans and both circumstances befell Brazilian Thunderbolt pilots.

In total, the 1º *G.Av.Ca.* lost sixteen Thunderbolts to ground fire plus four to non-combat causes; at least two of the latter were traced to the problem caused by airflow breaking away over the bubble-top Thunderbolt's slimmer rear fuselage profile. As mentioned before, this had been experienced by other groups in other theatres. A P-47D

*Brazil's contribution to the war in Italy was both appreciated by the Allies and a source of great pride to the participating pilots and groundcrews. The machine, flown by the commander 1º G.Av.Ca, was one of many Brazilian P-47s that recorded the constant ground attacks in bomb stencils stretching down the fuselage.*

*Bombs for the Thunderbolts were hauled by all kinds of transport, carts such as shown here at a French base used by the 324th F.G. being very handy. Mud, the groundcrews' constant companion at some airfields, appears to have been contained at this 316th Squadron dispersal. (R.L. Ward)*

Technical Bulletin issued on 18 October spelled it out, warning that under certain circumstances 'uncoordinated manoeuvres' using rudder and ailerons could cause the rudder to lock in the direction of application. In turn, this could induce a vicious, whipping roll that was virtually uncontrollable, followed by a spin.

The bulletin recommended (initially) the field installation of a dorsal fin from a factory-supplied kit, this being subsequently introduced on the production lines from the P-47D-40 on. Although the fin was widely fitted as a field modification, by no means all earlier-model P-47s with the bubble canopy actually received it. There were hundreds of unmodified examples in front-line service and although the work took only a few hours, such airframe changes would normally be carried out as part of a major overhaul. Some groups simply never got around to modifying all their aircraft and there were surely some pilots who were not slow to state that 'their' P-47 flew perfectly well without any changes being necessary.

In the meantime, the programme of standardising the Ninth Air Force tactical groups on the P-47 continued. In February 1945, the 367th F.G., 'The Dynamite Gang', became the last group to convert before the end of the war in Europe. Having flown Lightnings since its arrival in the E.T.O. in March 1944, the pilots howled at the thought of losing the twin-engined reliability inherent in their beloved P-38s. As had happened before though, when pilots actually flew the P-47, there were enough converts to convince the rest – almost. In any event, official policy could not be denied and there was little time, with the ground war then at the stage it was, for lengthy deliberation on the relative merits of the Republic and Lockheed products. Some individuals were reminded that a similar situation had occurred when the Gang was obliged to change its P-39s for P-38s (without admittedly having flown the Airacobra in combat) back in the spring of 1944. Then everyone wanted to stay with a single-engined fighter.

Commanded by Col Edwin S. Chickering, the 367th, with the 392nd, 393rd and 394th Squadrons assigned, flew its first P-47 mission from St-Dizier in February. Having received its first example for conversion training the

*When it was at Riems in 1945, the 373rd F.G. found itself sharing the airfied dispersals with complete, often flyable, examples of its main Luftwaffe adversaries. The 412th F.S. P-47D in the centre has a Bf 109G for company. (J.V. Crow)*

previous December, the 367th's pilots and crew chiefs awaited the next deliveries. Every pilot had to have a minimum of five hours' flying time before he was allowed to take a Thunderbolt into combat but the retraining phase was not helped by the conditions at 'St-Diz' which was wet and muddy all the time the Gang was based there. Missions consequently continued with P-38 sorties until 16 February, almost the group's final fling as a twin-engined fighter organisation. By then, although P-47 conversion had been completed by the pilots, missions were flown by both types for about two more weeks, each squadron having received only four P-47Ds up the 11th.

Some pilots hoped A.A.F. headquarters had had a change of heart and the P-38s would stay after all. The arrival of thirteen P-47s for the 392nd F.S. scotched that hope and in five days the first all-Thunderbolt mission was flown. The 394th got its full complement of aircraft on 16 February to begin operations on the 21st and the 393rd flew its debut P-47 mission on the 26th, its aircraft having arrived three days earlier.

Standardisation on the P-47 did not extend to delivery of identical subtypes to transitioning groups, as the 367th's crew chiefs found out. They were somewhat perplexed, considering a general lack of tools

and servicing manuals for the new type, to be presented with one P-47D-10, one D-21, three D-22s, nine D-28s and six D-30s in the space of five days, 12-16 February. Undaunted, the groundcrews performed yeoman service in checking out all aspects of the aircraft and readying them for combat, a task that including painting all of them in the Dynamite Gang's colours and identity markings.

Comparisons with the P-38 lingered and then quietly died away as the group got used to the P-47. In a few months, the 367th notched up an impressive number of Thunderbolt sorties as the Allied armies made the final push into Germany, the target list including on 19 March its most memorable mission of the period. This was long remembered because of its unusual nature.

The group's best pilots were briefed for a specific shot at none other than the German C.-in-C. West, Albert Kesselring. Allied Intelligence determined that the Germans planned a high-level conference in a castle at Ziegenburg, 150 miles west of the 367th's new base at Jarney near Metz, which had been occupied three days earlier. The group was then gearing up to support Third Army's crossing of the Rhine and the P-47s had been ranging freely across Germany's last natural barrier for some weeks.

Believing that Field Marshal von Rundstedt (who had recently been replaced) rather than Kesselring was in the castle made little difference to the carefully planned mission. Neither did the fact, unknown to the air planners, that Reich armaments minister Albert Speer would also be present. All three squadrons of the group contributed forty-eight of their most experienced pilots to fly the mission. Led by Lt Allen J. Diefendorf of the 392nd F.S., the group achieved complete surprise and hit the castle hard with 1000 lb G.P. bombs and napalm, which completely gutted the fortified headquarters, demolished the outbuildings and started enormous fires.

Only by reacting very quickly, even as the Thunderbolts' machine-gun fire dissolved the windows above their heads, did Kesselring and Speer escape the inferno. Both men reached the safety of an underground bunker and tunnel complex.

## ITALIAN FINALE

Casualties among fighter-bomber pilots were understandably heavy in most war theatres, the M.T.O. being no easy ride in this respect. The 79th and 86th Groups averaged losses of twenty-three per cent during two years of combat and relatively few pilots completed the required 200 missions without a high degree of careful planning, skill and that indefinable attribute that few military men would deny – luck. As their territory shrank, the Axis always seemed able to surround potential targets with a sufficient number of A.A. guns. These, compressed into small areas, positively bristled around vital bridges, marshalling yards, bottlenecks and airfields.

'Flak Suppression' a term more associated with postwar tactical air operations, was certainly carried out in the Second World War, but in general ground fire was treated as a hazard to be avoided rather than directly attacked and neutralised on a regular basis. Flak consequently accounted for most individual unit losses in the closing stages of the war, the 57th Group, for example, recording more than fifty P-47Ds downed during the last four months. Overall however, the group's ratio of aircraft losses to effective sorties was considered to be excellent.

The 79th was part of the massive all-out effort to finally break the Axis in northern Italy. On 9 April, more than 800 heavies set out on what enemy observers assumed was another strategic strike into Germany. But the bombers made a sharp turn to pound German positions along the River Senio with fragmentation bombs in order not to churn up the ground over which the Eighth Army was soon to cross. Then came an artillery barrage followed by fighter-bombers. The

*Strikingly marked P-47Ds of the 324th Fighter Group's 346th F.S. on a long-range mission over Italy. Lack of bombs suggests a strafing attack when the aircraft reach the target, where the P-47's battery of guns would have been quite able to destroy a range of vehicles, aircraft and installations useful to the enemy. (U.S.A.F.)*

*Brazil's substantial inventory of P-47s both during and after the war made it the largest user in Latin America. This example, (42-26773) the last of 385 P-47D-25s built, was shot down on 22 April 1945 and the pilot taken prisoner. (M.A.P.)*

Thunderbolts carried their standard variety of ordnance and hit anything that made a worthwhile target. Right behind this came Allied tanks. Rarely had the Germans experienced such a deluge of fire and they began to give ground. When night fell, the medium bombers were over dropping their loads nearer to friendly troops than ever before. Morning brought the heavy bombers back over the line and the fighter-bombers. So effective had the ground-air liaison system become that a card index of photos could be used by the controllers riding in tanks to identify specific targets for the pilots.

By 11 April, the breakthrough had begun and by the 19th the German position was dire. A retreat to the Po was the only hope but this was vetoed by Berlin. When a belated attempt to disengage was made on the 20th it was too late. Now the fighter-bombers had more targets – river transport, pontoon bridges and transport of all kinds south of the Po were devastated; all permanent Po bridges had been destroyed and even those Germans who managed to swim to the northern bank had little equipment with which to build more defence lines. Many were made prisoner.

Verona was in Allied hands by 26 April and skirting Lake Garda, the Allies' task was now to fan out across the upper Po valley to block the Brenner Pass and the remaining escape routes into Austria. Interdiction missions in Italy continued virtually until hostilities ceased. For the 350th Group at Pisa, 24-25 April brought orders for further ground-attack sorties, despite a shortage of aircraft at that time. Lt Raymond Knight of the 346th Squadron consequently volunteered to fly three hazardous, small-scale sorties against Italian aerodromes in this 48-hour period.

Despite the generally low level of enemy sorties at that time, most active airfields were known to be well defended by flak. On the 24th, Knight led two other P-47s against Ghedi. Knight went down to reconnoitre the target while his two colleagues remained high. He spotted aircraft dispersed under trees, called down the other pair of P-47s and led them into the attack. Seven enemy machines were claimed destroyed, five by Lt Knight. Later that day, he led a flight of three P-47s against Bergamo airfield, once again carrying out a hazardous, lone reconnaissance. The enemy gunners found the range and his P-47D was badly holed but Knight managed to destroy six enemy aircraft in no less than ten strafing runs. His colleagues accounted for five more.

Early on 25 April, Lt Knight returned to Bergamo in company with 1st Lt William Rogers and 2nd Lt Roger Clement. Knight dived into a hail of flak to destroy an aircraft on the runway – but this time his Thunderbolt was so badly damaged that it was almost uncontrollable as he left the area. Mindful of the 350th Group's shortage of fighters, Knight elected not to bale out and instead attempted to nurse his P-47 back to base, which lay on the other side of the Apennine chain. Over the mountains, turbulence caused the heavy fighter to crash, killing Raymond Knight. He was awarded a posthumous Medal of Honor, the last bestowed on an A.A.F. pilot in the Second World War.

British troops entered Venice on 29 April and the Germans agreed to unconditional surrender. It had taken just seventeen days to complete the last offensive in Italy and nearly one million men laid down their arms. The first major German surrender of the war was signed on 2 May at Caserta.

All across Europe, Thunderbolt groups were flying their final missions at the culmination of the greatest air war in history. On 1 May 1945, twelve Comanche pilots of the 79th Group mounted a fighter-bomber strike against enemy shipping off Trieste. On their return, touching down without mishap on Cesenatico's steel mat runway, pilots naturally wondered what the next mission might be. Then came the heart-stopping news: there would be no more. It was all over.

For the 57th Group at Grosseto, 1 May was also the last full day of operations although the P-47s were out the following day on armed reconnaissance. Control tower personnel were delighted to call up the pilots and tell them to 'Return to base – the war is over'.

## EXEMPLARY RECORD

When the statisticians got around to compiling the combat records of the various A.A.F. fighters, the P-47 came out very well indeed – 3916 enemy aircraft destroyed in combat in Europe alone was impressive enough. Although it would be misleading to single out one group from so many, the 56th must stand apart as the only unit to fly P-47s throughout the conflict. By so doing, the Wolfpack produced the highest number of aces, an impressive thirty-nine. It followed that the group also achieved the highest number of aerial victories of any of the Eighth

*Thunderbolts continued to fly over Germany for months after their guns were stilled, the 368th F.G. at Straubing being one unit that stayed on as part of the occupation air forces. This was soon composed entirely of P-47 units, aircraft of which had red and yellow rear fuselage stripes to denote the fact that they, unlike their comrades in arms, were not yet heading Stateside. (J. Campbell)*

*Striking red heart emblem and the name* Dorothy K *on the cowling personalised the P-47D-28 (42-28473/R3-F) of ace Capt Talmadge Ambrose of the 373rd F.G. The aircraft is in a tidy, brick-lined dispersal, probably at Venlo, Holland. (J. Campbell)*

Air Force groups, with a final score of 664.5. By adding the total aircraft ground kills of 327, as the Eighth Air Force did to reflect the extremely hazardous nature of aerodrome strafing, the 56th's score reached 1006.5. During combat operations from the first escort mission on 4 May 1943 to 21 April 1945, the Wolfpack lost 128 P-47s.

More to the point than mere figures, impressive though these were, was the fact that the P-47 had held the line against the *Luftwaffe's* best in the days when there were no other U.S. fighters available. By courageously and skilfully defending the bombers, the pioneer Thunderbolt escort groups whittled down enemy pilot strength and gradually narrowed the gap in giving the heavy bombers 'all the way' fighter protection, paving the way for the Mustang to complete the task. In total, 110 U.S. aces flew P-47s during the war including the top E.T.O. pair, Francis Gabreski with twenty-eight aerial victories and Robert S. Johnson with twenty-

seven. Not all of them obtained all their victories while flying the P-47 but among those who did were Eugene Roberts of the 78th, Neel Kearby of the 348th and Robert Stone of the 318th.

Strafing claimed so many of the Eighth's top fighter pilots that the German *Stalags* became almost squadron and group reunion centres – fortunately very few men lost their lives. Many of them readily acknowledged rugged Republic construction for their high rate of survival when they were obliged to crash-land and, in many cases, await inevitable capture.

It was on ground-attack missions that the P-47 groups claimed the largest numerical successes. The figures included the destruction of 6,000 tanks and A.F.V.s, 9,000 locomotives, 86,000 items of rolling-stock and 68,000 trucks. In addition, untold numbers of enemy troops had been killed or incapacitated under the rain of bullets, bombs and rockets that P-47s had expended over the battlefields from Normandy to the Rhine and beyond.

# 11
# On to the Empire

Republic's continual effort to boost the P-47's overall performance, particularly range, resulted in a final wartime model which was arguably the most capable of the entire series. The P-47N represented a substantial redesign that was far more than merely cosmetic. It had been realised for some time that the only really effective way to increase the range of a single-seat fighter was for it to carry the maximum amount of fuel in internal tanks. In the case of the P-47, this meant more engine power and inevitably, another increase in an already high all-up weight.

While it was obviously impractical to disrupt production to undertake such a major change on the earlier model Thunderbolts,

time was available in the case of the P-47N. In designing what was to be the last model of the P-47, Republic introduced a 'wet' wing incorporating four interconnected (two each side) self-sealing fuel cells holding a total of 200 gallons. This tankage, plus the 370 gal in the standard fuselage tanks, brought the total for the P-47N to 570 gal which was far higher than the standard capacity of the P-47D and P-47M although an internal maximum tankage of 410 gal for the latter model was achieved with the XP-47M. The N could, in addition, carry 700 gallons externally.

Along with the internal changes, the P-47N wing was reprofiled. Gone was the familiar elliptical planform and in its place was a more

*P-47Ns of the 414th Fighter Group en route to Guam aboard CVE-88 in June 1945. (J. Lambert)*

*P-47N* Expected Goose *of the 463rd F.S., 507th Group flying in the vicinity of the Ryukus Islands in August 1945. (J. Lambert)*

squared off, angular mainplane spanning 42 ft 7 in, 2 feet more than that of the P-47D. A wider-track landing gear was fitted to cope with the aircraft's extra weight, this giving about 2 feet more 'spread' than that of the P-47D. It retracted into the wing proper, whereas on the D model the inner walls of the mainwheel doors formed part of the fuselage.

To increase longitudinal stability, a dorsal fin, substantially deeper than that fitted to the P-47D/M, was an integral part of the design of the P-47N. Ordnance load for the new model was impressive and the best of the entire Thunderbolt series. Bombs of up to 1000 lb could be carried on each wing rack, the belly shackles accommodating a third bomb of this weight or a drop tank. Fixed armament of the P-47N remained similar to that of all earlier Thunderbolts – eight 0.50in Colt-Browning machine-guns. This battery could be reduced to six guns without difficulty, the ammunition load consequently varying from 267 to 425 rounds per gun.

Most of the changes were incorporated on the single XP-47N (42-27387) which was a P-47D-27 taken from the production line and rebuilt. Somewhat earlier, Republic had modified the XP-47K (42-8702) to test the P-47N wing.

Powerplant for the N model was the R-2800-57 Double Wasp rated at 2800 hp, similar to that which had powered the P-47M – and had given considerable trouble when it was introduced to combat by the 56th Fighter Group in 1945. The valuable work done to rectify engine troubles in England helped Pratt & Whitney and Republic to install a similar but more refined engine in the P-47N; the result was a generally reliable powerplant, although engine failure was not unknown in service. A Curtiss Electric C642S-B40 propeller of 13 ft diameter was fitted to the P-47N-1, 550 of which were built. To lift off safely, the fighter that had now become the heaviest Second World War single-seater in front-line service anywhere and pilots became used to putting on power very early in the take-off run. Full throttle, full turbo and water injection as soon as possible became the norm.

Out in the central Pacific where the P-47N was destined to serve, the island of Ie Shima had a runway 1.5 miles long, as did those on Iwo Jima. With aircraft laden down with fuel and ordnance, pilots would soon get to appreciate every yard, for a maximum-loaded P-47N could gross as much as 20,700 lb. The aircraft needed 3800 ft to take off and clear a 50 ft obstacle.

Notwithstanding the significant weight increase, the P-47N had a very good maximum range of 2000 miles at 25,000 ft, normal range being 800 miles at the same altitude. In comparison, the P-51D had a normal range of 700 miles on internal fuel, drop tanks increasing this figure by 50 miles. When it came to fuel consumption the P-47N remained similar to earlier models by burning a maximum of 300 gal per hour whereas the Mustang's was a miserly average of 64 gals per hour, rising to 120 gals per hour at full power.

Production continued with 550 P-47N-5-REs which introduced ten zero-length H.V.A.R. launchers, tail warning radar, and a General Electric C-1 autopilot and ignition system on the R-2800-73 engine which was also introduced on this model and rated at 2800 hp. Alternatively, the aircraft could be fitted with the R-2800-57 which had a similar power rating. Farmingdale built the majority of the P-47Ns, 200 P-47N-15s similar to the N-1 following but with a K-14A or B gunsight replacing the 'basic' K-14. The S-1 bomb rack replaced the B-10 shackles used on previous Thunderbolt models.

There were also 200 P-47N-20-REs with the -73 or -77 engine, again with no rating change from previous powerplants. A radio change was made and other detail revisions compared to the P-47N-1 encompassed an emergency fuel system and provision for individual pressurisation of drop tanks. Evansville's solitary batch of the final series Thunderbolts was 149 aircraft designated P-47N-20-RAs. These were similar to examples built at Farmingdale although a revised cockpit floor with a smooth rudder pedal track was incorporated from aircraft 45-50051. Production was completed in September 1945.

The final P-47 batch of all was the 167 P-47N-25-REs from Farmingdale which could be fitted with the R-2800-81, again with no power change to that of the other two options, the -73 or -77. Otherwise similar to the P-47N-1 in terms of overall performance the -25 also had detail changes, including the revised cockpit floor (from 44-89294) and a new tailwheel linkage. Deliveries to the A.A.F. were extended to December 1945 although production had ceased in October.

## OPERATIONAL PROBLEMS

Thunderbolt groups assigned to the Pacific in 1944 in line with those elsewhere, had been equipped with improved models of the P-47D which still lacked the range to anticipate flying combat missions over Japan, no U.S. airfields being near enough. But the airfield picture had changed by the spring of 1945.

Generally good progress in the war against Japan allowed the A.A.F. to plan a long-range B-29 escort force built around the P-47N as early as July 1944 but it was not until 31 January 1945 that headquarters, 301st Fighter Wing and the 318th, 413th, 414th, 507th and 508th Fighter Groups were assigned to this duty under Twentieth Air Force jurisdiction. To that end, the 413th, 414th and 507th Groups had received early production models of the new Thunderbolt in October 1944. As the most experienced P-47 group in the

*Fully loaded, a P-47N was an awesome weapon.* Glori Gal *of the 73rd F.S., 318th Group has 1500 lb of bombs and ten 3-in rockets, not to mention full ammunition tanks, enough for any Japanese target still standing at that stage of the war. This aircraft was the mount of Lt Robert Redfield. (J. Lambert)*

*Yellow and black stripes were added to P-47Ns of the 318th Group around 1 August 1945, as well shown by the aircraft flown by Jack Russman of the 333rd F.S. (J. Lambert)*

western Pacific, the 318th Group would be the first to convert. The 508th Group was not assigned to a combat zone but remained in Hawaii when the Superfortress escort mission changed. Flying from Mokuleia, the group functioned as an R.T.U. under the command of Cols Frank Mears and Oswald Lunde between November 1944 and November 1945.

By April, the island of Ie Shima, 325 miles from the home islands, was in U.S. hands. Lying 3 miles off the coast of Okinawa, Ie Shima became home for fighter and bomber units which could attack numerous important tactical targets prior to the expected invasion of Japan in the autumn of 1945.

Maj Lew Sanders's 318th Fighter Group got its P-47Ns in March 1945. By then, the P-38Ls which the group had flown since November 1944 as a temporary measure to enable more distant targets to be reached, had been returned to air depots. Pilots were flown to Hawaii to pick up the new Thunderbolts and, after a few familiarisation flights, to ferry them in stages across the Pacific to Saipan and thence to Ie Shima. Apart from some apprehension about once more flying a single-engined fighter over long stretches of water, the 318th took to the P-47N, particularly now that with a full internal and external fuel load, the new Thunderbolt equalled the range of any other fighter in the inventory.

Having developed the primitive Japanese airstrip on Ie Shima, the Seabees mistakenly believed, through no fault of their own, that the 318th's P-47Ns could operate without problems. They were wrong. Lew Sanders was appalled at what he saw – 3700 feet of wet and sticky coral had been prepared for his group whereas the P-47N required at least 5800 feet of preferably dry surface.

The 318th now came under an integrated command structure within a new 301st Fighter Wing organisation which was in turn part of the Tenth Army Tactical Air Force. A Marine major-general was in charge of fighter operations. As the majority of the fighter units were Marine squadrons flying the F4U Corsair, the engineers were used to building runways that suited the far lighter Marine fighters. Army Thunderbolts with a take-off weight of up to 10 tons were something that they had not come across. Orders went out. Ie Shima's short runway would be extended.

Sanders was not impressed with the speed of the work, particularly as T.A.C. wanted the 318th to fly long-range night heckling strikes over Kyushu almost immediately. Night missions were hazardous enough without having to contend with a short runway, no homing devices, the weather – which could turn from poor to downright lethal in a matter of minutes – and the fact that the pilots had

*Alternate loads could be carried by the P-47N, including two pairs of heavier rockets inboard of the bomb rack. This aircraft was a 19th F.S., 318th Group machine in the earlier group markings. (J. Lambert)*

not been trained to operate at night. And then there was the enemy. With their backs to the wall, the Japanese had hoarded aircraft for defence of the homeland. While many continued to be expended as kamikazes, there were more than enough fighters to oppose U.S. strikes, particularly if these were carried out by only a few aircraft at a time.

Notwithstanding these annoyances, the 318th duly flew its first night sorties on 17 May. They were as predicted, quite unproductive and dangerous, for by the time the group was switched to daylight missions, it had lost four pilots and four P-47s. It was time for Sanders to employ a degree of cunning. Without actively disobeying orders, he would hold his fighters long enough for the weather to turn foul and simply scrub the mission.

Nobody questioned Sanders's decision to hold back futile nocturnal sorties over Japan, work that was more the province of the P-61

squadrons on Iwo Jima. The reason given for these strikes was (somewhat ironically in view of the quest for greater range for the P-47 which had gone on for about two years) that no other aircraft matched the P-47N for its ability to get to Japan and loiter for an hour or so to disrupt the favoured dawn take-off by the kamikazes.

On 24 May, the 318th's pilots heard that they would at last be sent on a daylight strike to attack airfields on Kyushu. Bombs, rockets and bullets were liberally spread around the targets which included railways, barracks and shipping. There were plenty of tactical targets in Japan left untouched by the B-29 bombing and fighters and medium bombers found more than enough to shoot at.

The following day, the 318th tried a repeat strike but the weather intervened. Bombs were jettisoned and the Thunderbolt force, still a substantial twenty-eight aircraft, turned for home. The weather was clear over Okinawa and the enemy had coincidentally planned a major night action against U.S. airfields. This was largely beaten off but in the morning the Japanese followed through with conventional and suicide sorties by an estimated 500 aircraft.

Tracked by the ever-alert radar picket destroyers patrolling off Okinawa, this force became a target for the remaining P-47Ns and Corsairs which were scrambled from Ie Shima. To add to the enemy's woes, the abortive Kyushu strike force of the 318th ran right into flocks of 'Zekes' and 'Vals'. And the P-47 pilots still had full ammo tanks. The results were predictable, given the low quality of the enemy pilots met in combat at that time. Trained for a one-way suicide trip, many individuals appeared to have little idea how to manoeuvre their aircraft when under attack. The 318th went to work with a will.

In separate combats ranging over a wide area, the Thunderbolt pilots estimated that out of about sixty enemy aircraft they encountered, they shot down thirty-four of them without loss. It was the 318th Group's best day of the war in aerial combat terms and gave the Seventh Air Force its first ace, a fact

in which it took understandable pride.

Lt Richard H. Anderson of the 19th Squadron was the pilot in question. He had scored the baseline five victories by downing five 'Zekes', a feat repeated on 28 May by Capt John E. Vogt of the same squadron. The Seventh's second ace also shot down five 'Zekes' on the same day. The carnage wrought among the Japanese flyers continued on succeeding days with the American team consistently claiming numbers out of all proportion to their own force. Interception was vital, for the enemy was still bent on wiping out the U.S. fleet by suicide attack and enough got through the fighter screen (and naval A.A. fire) to inflict many casualties and cause thousands of dollars' worth of damage. Many ships were so badly battered by kamikazes that they had to be pulled out for the remainder of the war. And some inevitably went down under the onslaught.

Engine failure now began to be a real threat to the 318th's P-47 operations, a factor easily traced to the necessarily harsh treatment of the Double Wasp in order to give the fighters enough lift to depart from Ie Shima's short runway. Weather problems were also never

*P-47N-5 44-88705/674 of the 413rd F.S., 414th Group being carted away after a crash-landing on Iwo Jima. (J. Lambert)*

*Butch of the 413th F.S., 414th F.G. on Iwo Jima shows to advantage the ten-point zero-length launchers for the full load of H.V.A.R.s. (J. Lambert)*

very far away and these dictated mission planning to a significant degree. Good instrument flying became, literally, a matter of life or death. Downed Army pilots had the consolation that by 1945 both their own service and the Navy had an efficient rescue organisation in place utilising aircraft, surface ships and submarines to pluck pilots out of the ocean. An encouraging number of men were saved when they went down to weather-related causes or the attentions of the Japanese.

A little variety for the 318th's pilots included photoplane escort. And on 10 June, the 333rd F.S. pilots found their cockpits full of packages of aluminium strips; their additional task on the mission was to toss out the bundles of *Chaff* to mask the presence of a PB4Y-2 Privateer from enemy radar – and hopefully to draw defending interceptors towards the P-47s. The patrol bomber's crew would be busily engaged on photographing possible landing beaches on southern Kyushu. The *Chaff* strips apparently worked, for the P-47s soon saw enemy fighters below, even though the Japanese pilots failed to note the threat. Seven 'Zekes', one entire formation, paid the price.

A similar ruse was tried on 11 June. A force

of thirty P-47Ns of the 318th met thirty 'Zekes', a potentially equal contest that should have given the Japanese at least parity. But the American pilots came home with a score of four destroyed, two probables and one damaged and no losses of their own.

**REINFORCEMENTS**

As the most experienced P-47N outfit by mid-June 1945, the 318th was then joined by the 413th and 507th Groups fresh from the U.S. Despite being trained under Twentieth Air Force jurisdiction for B-29 escort work, both Thunderbolt groups found themselves diverted to the Ryukyus and on attachment to the Seventh Air Force and the 301st Wing. Although most of their pilots had yet to make their combat debuts, both newcomer P-47N groups were led by European theatre veterans, none other than Colonels Harrison R. Thyng of the 413th and Loring F. Stetson jr of the 507th.

Early in April, the 413th Group's 1st, 21st and 34th Squadrons had left Hawaii, collected P-47Ns and headed out into the Pacific, bound for Ie Shima. The group reached Saipan where orders were received for it to carry out several strafing missions over Truk. Afterwards, the

413th flew to Ie Shima where it was established by mid-May, a few weeks before the 507th arrived. Flying its first mission on 1 July, the 507th had the 463rd, 464th and 465th Squadrons assigned.

These missions were of course different to those the pilots were anticipating but by the time the P-47N reached the Pacific the B-29 force had undergone some changes in operational deployment with many attacks taking place at night. Japanese fighter opposition had also proved to be lighter than expected, with the result that a 'full time' escort was not really needed, at least from P-47s. Two Seventh Air Force Mustang groups were in place to handle the majority of escort missions. The P-47Ns were assigned instead mainly to ground attacks on targets in Japan, Korea and China, although some escort missions were flown.

As it transpired, the second and third P-47N groups to go operational had a frustrating debut to combat. Under the guidance of the 318th, the pilots experienced mission after mission being either scrubbed or disrupted by bad weather. The war dragged on.

One good day in terms of the Thunderbolts actually being able to reach the home islands, was 21 June. Another 'Photo Joe' PB4Y escort began badly when two P-47Ns crashed on take-off, one pilot being killed instantly and the other dying of his wounds the next day. Four other aircraft failed to fly the mission, leaving thirty-two Thunderbolts to challenge the defences. Another pilot was then obliged to bale out due to engine failure.

Orbiting the downed pilot in his life raft until a Dumbo showed up, one 73rd FS P-47N dipped too low and crashed into the sea. No trace of the pilot was found. By the time the rescue was underway, the Thunderbolts were low on fuel and on return one pilot tried to put down on the less-crowded Yontan airstrip on Okinawa. His machine overshot and was wrecked although its pilot, James D. Handly, escaped with back injuries and a broken arm. The mission had resulted in five P-47Ns lost, three pilots killed and one injured. No enemy aircraft had been seen.

The combination of Ie Shima's difficult runway which, despite having been extended to 4200 feet, was still far too short for the P-47s, and frequent engine malfunctions, brought an absurd situation – how could airmen fight if they could not even take off? Few pilots minded the normal hazards of combat but the P-47N was simply too big to use a pokey little runway like Ie Shima's. Something had to be done if more men were not to become needless casualties.

Despite its operational problems, the 318th had acquitted itself well; in the nineteen days from 24 May to 11 June, pilots had claimed 102 victories for the loss of only three Thunderbolts. More ground attacks were carried out in late June and on the last day of the month the 301st Wing groups began flying bombing and strafing sorties on Japanese shipping. On 10 July, Japanese ground fire nailed the P-47N flown by the C.O. of the 319th Squadron, Frank Collins. No mean exponent of the P-47, he had become an ace while flying P-40s and P-47Ds with the Checkertails in the M.T.O. Collins survived to become a prisoner, a mercifully short incarceration.

In the meantime, the 414th Fighter Group – destined to be the last to fly the P-47N in combat and the last new U.S.A.A.F. fighter unit to see action in the Second World War – was establishing itself on Iwo Jima. The group, commanded by Col Henry G. Thorne jr, and comprising the 413th, 437th and 456th Squadrons, had begun moving across the Pacific in May. The group's Thunderbolts were transported by carrier and pilots were to spend the succeeding few weeks preparing for combat.

By that time the last A.A.F. groups sent to the Pacific could draw on a pool of experienced men who had seen combat in other theatres – it would be their last chance if they wanted to fly another combat tour and a number took the opportunity. The 414th's officers included Ben Drew, formerly of the 361st Fighter Group and victor over two Me 262s in a day in October 1944. Drew was impressed with the P-47N and could compare its qualities with the P-51. But considering each type's merits as an all-round combat aircraft, he admitted a slight preference for the Mustang.

Although Iwo Jima was a far more favourable location for the Thunderbolts, the island lay 900 miles east of Ie Shima and 660 miles from the nearest point on Kyushu. Pilots began to wonder exactly what they were supposed to do to aid the war effort; being stationed so far back

*Many P-47Ns were named – there was often time for groundcrew artists to carry out the work when bad weather prevented operations. This portrait appeared on a machine of the 414th F.G. on Iwo Jima where the next P-47N in line shows the group's yellow tail marking. (J. Campbell)*

they would have precious little fuel for combat over Japan. One reason why the 414th was not moved forward to Ie Shima was an acute lack of space. There were 250 plus P-47Ns stationed on the island by the time the 414th would have been ready to move in.

On 13 July, the 414th made its combat debut with a ground attack on the Japanese naval base at Truk, flying from its temporary base on Guam while it was still *en route* to Iwo Jima. It was not until the 22nd that the second mission, another foray to Truk, could be flown. A radar station on Chichi Jima, an island which served as a 'live' range for groups new to the Pacific Ocean Area, was duly attacked by the 414th which had in the meantime moved to North Field, Iwo Jima. In subsequent operations from Iwo Jima, the pilots rarely, if ever, saw a Japanese fighter for the rest of the war. In fact, only one enemy aircraft was confirmed destroyed by a 414th Group P-47N before the war ended.

Sharing Iwo Jima with the Mustang-equipped 15th and 21st Groups that had been given the B-29 escort role, gave the P-47N pilots the chance to find out exactly what their aircraft could – and could not – do in mock combat with the P-51. On many counts, the Thunderbolt lost out against the more agile Mustang but honour was redressed when the two types were put in a power dive from high altitude. The P-47N left the P-51 standing. Exceptionally stable, the Thunderbolt also proved to be the better gun platform and those extra two fifties made short work of numerous Japanese targets, irrespective of whether they were in the air or on the ground.

Taking off at maximum weight was always an anxious time in the P-47N but pilots, particularly the novices, were reassured by the very wide track landing gear. Getting a 10 ton aeroplane safely airborne, knowing that part of the weight included 900 gallons of highly volatile fuel in internal, wing and belly tanks, took considerable concentration, not to mention a very positive attitude to the job in hand.

The switch to general ground-attack work did not entirely remove the P-47N from B-29 escort missions, as on 8 August the 318th, 413th and 507th Groups accompanied the bombers to Yawata – and disturbed a hornet's nest of Japanese interceptors. Of 245 B-29s taking off for the mission, 221 attacked the primary target, dropping 1302 tons of incendiaries to destroy twenty-one per cent of the city. Bomber crews recorded fifty-three attacks by Japanese interceptors, their efforts resulting in the loss of but one Superfort.

American fighters fought both Japanese Army and Navy interceptors in a series of combats and were credited with twenty-one destroyed, four probables and six damaged for the day. In the vicinity of Yawata itself 2nd Lt William J. Cuneo of the 19th Squadron destroyed a Ki-84 and damaged a 'George'. South of the target city, 2nd Lt Harry M. Steinshouer of the 464th F.S. got another 'Frank' while 2nd Lt Edward V. Hollis of the 1st Fighter Squadron handled his P-47N to good effect to dispatch a 'Zeke' 52 for a confirmed kill.

The Yawata mission was, in addition to the Seventh Air Force's P-47Ns, escorted by the P-51s of the 348th Group, Fifth Air Force. Also operating from Ie Shima, the latter had traded its razorback P-47s for Mustangs in February, passing many of its faithful Thunderbolts to the 58th Group.

Although the Fifth and Seventh Air Force fighters were to see more combat before the end, the 8 August mission was the last in which the B-29s suffered casualties as a result of enemy action. Everyone knew that the Japanese were at their last gasp and that the end could not be delayed much longer.

A general move forward had been made by the Fifth Air Force fighter groups during 1944 and by September the 8th and 35th had reached Morotai. The landings in the Philippines gave the 348th a base on Leyte in November, to be followed there by the 8th and 49th. The 35th went to Mangaldan in January 1945, as did the 348th, concurrent with both units beginning to re-equip with P-51s. Some of the 35th's P-47D-25s were passed to the 58th which thus became the sole remaining Thunderbolt unit in the Fifth Air Force.

A.A.F. fighters remained in the Philippines only long enough for a Japanese defeat to be beyond doubt before they moved out to the Ryukus, for Kenney wanted his squadrons as far forward as possible to fly escort missions and conduct strikes on Formosa and the home islands. In June, the 35th moved to Okinawa with the 58th and 348th going to Ie Shima in

July. The P-38-equipped 8th and 475th Groups also went to Ie Shima in August.

## LAST ACE

On 13 August 1945, 1st Lt Oscar F. Perdomo climbed into the cockpit of his 464th F.S. P-47N named *Lil Meaties' Meat Chopper* and took off from Ie Shima. In company with forty-seven other Thunderbolts of the 507th Group, the young Texan pointed the nose of the big fighter towards Korea. It was Perdomo's tenth sortie. He had seen some action but had not yet had the chance to score a victory over the Japanese in aerial combat. With the enemy staggering from two atomic bomb strikes, it seemed unlikely that he would do so before the war ended.

Although Col Stetson's 507th Group had previously met J.A.A.F. fighters in combat during bomber escort missions, had scored victories and taken losses, it was impossible to predict how the backs-to-the-wall enemy would react to a particular fighter mission at that stage of the war. But that the enemy had serviceable interceptors with which to defend Korea was not in doubt.

The mission for the 464th Squadron that day was to strafe and bomb Japanese positions at Keijo. The Thunderbolts would be airborne for 8 hours to fly a round trip of 1580 miles. However, intelligence on the likely opposition in the target area had been incomplete – and as it approached the target, the P-47 formation was intercepted by some fifty enemy aircraft of assorted types.

Lt Perdomo sighted five Ki-43 'Oscars' and chased after one element of three. He shot down the 'tail end Charlie' in the formation, sent the second one down in flames and finally concentrated on the leader. In a tight turn, the American pilot fired and had the satisfaction of seeing his adversary stall and crash. As so often happened to individual pilots in combat, Perdomo had become separated from his colleagues. He turned towards Keijo and almost immediately sighted a pair of Yokosuka K5Y 'Willow' IJN intermediate trainers in close formation at 800 feet. Seeing the big enemy fighter coming at them, the Japanese pilots broke. This action saved one of them but the other biplane succumbed to Perdomo's fire. Four down in less than 30 minutes' combat.

Suddenly, the lone P-47N was jumped by three more 'Oscars'. Agile as it was and lethal with a good pilot at the controls, the Ki-43 had long been outclassed by the latest American fighters and Perdomo had little trouble in evading the pass. He turned, came in on the trio from behind and shot down one of them. Five. Perdomo was another Seventh Air Force ace-in-a-day. It might well have been six, for *en route* to rejoin his group Perdomo came

upon on two more 'Oscars' dogfighting with a Thunderbolt. He dived and thumbed the firing button but his guns quickly stopped, their ammunition troughs empty. Another 507th P-47N dispatched the 'Oscar'.

On return to Ie Shima, Perdomo and the rest of the pilots tallied the score – eighteen Japanese aircraft shot down for one P-47 lost to ground fire in the target area.

Perdomo, the last Army ace of the Second

*Top: The Seventh Air Force P-47N units had considerable operational input from pilots who had fought in other theatres. They included Ben Drew, 361st F.G. ace, who did a final tour in the Pacific with the 413th F.S., 414th Group. Drew named his P-47N-5 (44-88492/682)* Miss Detroit *while his Mustangs in Europe were* Detroit Miss. *(J. Lambert)*

*Above:* Cheek Baby *of the 333rd F.S., 318th Group, the P-47N flown by Lt Durwood B. Williams. Note squadron badge under the cockpit and three rising sun flags denoting enemy aircraft kills under the cockpit. (J. Lambert)*

*Nicely rendered nose art on a P-47N of the 463rd F.S., 507th Fighter Group on Ie Shima in 1945. (J. Lambert)*

World War, was awarded the D.S.C. for his combat achievement, and for the day's operation the 507th Group received the only Distinguished Unit Citation to go to a P-47 unit in the Pacific Ocean Area. For a fighter unit, there could hardly be a more fitting finale to a combat – and a war – as the 507th stood down the following day.

On Ie Shima, the war finally came to an end on 19 August when a Japanese surrender delegation landed a pair of Mitsubishi G4M 'Bettys' on the island, a stop *en route* to Manila to sign the necessary capitulation documents. Men of the Seventh Air Force were part of the estimated 55 000 spectators to that historic landing, which was escorted by P-38s. Pilots of the 318th Group were highly chagrined to be told that the twin-boomed Lightnings, rather than their P-47s, would fly this, the 'most memorable fighter mission of the war', because the P-38 stood less chance of being mistaken for an enemy fighter than anything else in the A.A.F. inventory. Lt-Col Harry McAfee, who had taken over the 318th when Lew Sanders returned to Hawaii, could only shrug and think up something to say to his men. It was not the easiest task he had ever had.

# 12
# Air Guardian

The end of the war in Europe found the U.S. obligated to station an occupation force of fighters and bombers in Germany alongside her British and French Allies. Taken together, the inventories of the four strategic and tactical air forces, the Eight, Ninth, Twelfth and Fifteenth, represented far more aircraft than were needed overseas; men were rotating home in their thousands and units were disbanding. Surplus aircraft, primarily fighters and medium bombers, that could not be flown back to the U.S. by the most direct route were scrapped, many of them in Germany. In the meantime, re-equipment programmes saw the latest Army aircraft being delivered to those units that remained on the continent.

The P-47, which had done so much to secure the victory, thus continued to be a familiar sight over the shattered cities and towns of Europe. German civilians who had a

few months previously hated the sight and sound of the big, low-flying American fighter gradually realised that it was now on their side. Allied aircraft were now based in western Germany as a bulwark against the rumoured – and real – excesses of communist governments and their supporters in the eastern European states.

The Thunderbolts used postwar were little changed from their wartime counterparts although the last surviving razorbacks were generally scrapped and replaced by P-47D-25s and subsequent bubble-top models. Production was as follows: P-47D-26 – 250 built at Evansville with R-2800-59 engine rated at up to 2300hp, otherwise similar to the P-47D-25; P-47D-27 – 615 built, similar engine but from aircraft 42-27074 power rating was increased by 64 hp without water injection and by 130 hp with injection giving maximum

*The P-47N served into the postwar period, this example exhibiting the large 'buzz number' intended to prevent unauthorised low flying (buzzing), and high-visibility markings to increase awareness for safety in the air. A P-47N-5 (44-88680), this aircraft has the early PE- (later FE-) letter prefix for the type.*

*This photo dated 17 February 1950 exemplifies the transition from piston engines to jets. These 2nd Air Division U.S.A.F.E. aircraft were over the Bavarian Alps during training for the aerial gunnery meet in Las Vegas due to begin on 29 March that year. The P-47Ds of the 86th F.B.G. were then commanded by Col John S. Chennault. (U.S.A.F.)*

power of 2430 hp. Three aircraft from this batch, 42-27385, 42-27386 and 42-27388, were completed as YP-47Ms and 42-27387 as the XP-47N; P-47D-28-RE – 750 built at Farmingdale, similar to P-47D-25-RE but with Curtiss paddle-bladed propeller of 36 ft 1.75in diameter to conform with Evansville production, and detail changes to cockpit ordnance controls, hydraulics and radio with provision for radio compass; P-47D-28-RA – 1028 built at Evansville, similar to P-47D-26-RE, some aircraft fitted with dorsal fin as field modification; P-47D-30-RE; - 800 built at Evansville, similar to P-47D-25-RE but with electrical release mechanism for external ordnance and permanent sway braces to improve stores carriage, and provision was made for two zero-length H.V.A.R. launchers under each wing. Dive flaps were extended to thirty per cent of chord from wing leading edge, blunt-nosed ailerons were fitted to improve control at maximum speeds, and

detail changes included elimination of ring-and-bead sight, improved fuel lines for external wing tanks and hydraulic oil filtering, and some instrument changes; P-47D-30-RAs – 1800 built, similar to those from Evansville production; P-47D-40-RA – 665 built, the final D model produced with dorsal fin fitted as standard, underwing dive brakes, provision for five zero-length launchers and a K-14 B or C gunsight in place of the Mk VIII and AN/APS-13 tail warning radar.

Before the end of the war, A.A.F. fighter units had generally been listed to re-equip entirely with the P-51D/K, with the P-47 and P-38 being phased out. In the event – and notwithstanding the advent of jets – the lightweight P-51H was used primarily as an interim type to modernise units in the U.S. while P-47s filled any gaps in inventory overseas by remaining in service until the late 1940s.

Albeit being considered technically 'old' in comparison with 'new' jets, the reciprocatingengined fighters that had entered service in the last years of the war represented an engineering peak, the best of their era. They remained modern in many respects including overall speed and could even outpace some of the straight-winged jets. But the process of re-equipment took time; Republic and Lockheed would supply respectively the F-84 Thunderjet and F-80 Shooting Star, the 'first generation' jet fighters to modernise the groups that survived the mass demobilisation and deactivation of the wartime air forces.

Activation of United States Air Forces in Europe (U.S.A.F.E.) on 16 August 1945 rationalised the operations of air units remaining in Germany and Austria as part of the occupation forces. These included a number of P-47 groups which became part of the regular United States Air Force when it replaced the old Army Air Forces on 18 September 1947.

## PEACE-KEEPERS
Six former Ninth and Twelfth Air Force groups contributed their P-47 strength to postwar peace in Europe, these being the 36th (based at Kassel – Rothwesten), 79th (Hörsching), 86th (Schweinfurt), 366th (Münster), 368th (Straubing) and 406th (Nordholz). The 36th and 86th were gradually run down in terms of personnel and both were deactivated in February 1946. By August 1946, the 366th and 368th and 406th had been redesignated as the 27th, 78th and 86th Groups respectively. The latter unit, based at Nordholz, became the 86th Composite Group and was the last U.S.A.F. P-47 group stationed in Europe, the other two having ceased to exist by June 1947. The 86th's P-47s were replaced by the F-84 in 1950.

In the continental U.S.A. surviving P-47 groups included the 332nd Fighter Wing which received both late model P-47Ds and P-47Ns and was based at Lockbourne A.F.B., Ohio until inactivation on 1 July 1949; the 81st Fighter Wing which flew P/F-47s from Wheeler A.F.B. Hawaii, Camp Stoneman, CA and Kirkland A.F.B., New Mexico until 1949, and the 52nd Tactical Fighter Wing which operated F-47s 1951-2 as part of First Air Force's Eastern Air Defense Force. The P-47 became the F-47 under revised U.S.A.F. designations introduced on 11 June 1948 and the substantial number of aircraft held on

charge by the Air Force were used to progressively modernise the Air National Guard until such times as jet aircraft became available. This extended lease of life in A.N.G. service represented the greatest postwar use of the Thunderbolt.

The first Guard unit to operate the F-47 was the 118th Fighter-Bomber Group (Connecticut) which received its new fighters in August 1946. Between then and February 1954 no less than twenty-eight Guard squadrons flew the Thunderbolt. Operating units were those based on the U.S. East Coast, in parts of the southern states, Puerto Rico and Hawaii. Both late-production P-47Ds and Ns were operated by the A.N.G.

## SCREEN STAR
The P-47's duty with the Air Guard saw some pilots returning to a familiar cockpit, one that in some instances they had relinquished years before. One returnee was Lee Gover who had flown Thunderbolts in the 4th Group. Gover re-enlisted in the Army in 1947 and transferred to the U.S.A.F. when it was formed on 19 June. In January 1948, Gover was reunited with the P-47 at Morris Field in Charlotte, NC, then home to the 118th F.B.G.

Gover became the regular Air Force instructor to the guardsmen pilots and that May he was detailed to fly sixteen Thunderbolts to California for a star role in the Warner Bros film *Fighter Squadron*. With its H.Q. at Nashville, Tennessee, the 118th F.B.G. controlled four Guard squadrons located in three states and, due to the tension created by the Berlin crisis, it was decided that only four aircraft from each squadron could be spared for film work. Thus the F-47s came from the 105th F.B.S. (Tennessee A.N.G.) at Berry, the 158th F.B.S. and 128th F.B.S. (both Georgia A.N.G.) at Savannah and Dobbins respectively, and the 156th F.B.S. (North Carolina A.N.G.) based at Morris Field, Charlotte.

Lee Gover's P-47 experience resulted in him flying extensively for the movie cameras and leading many of the low-flying sequences. Cloaked under a coat of camouflage paint, Gover flew his own Guard F-47D (44-20990) for the cameras. Cowling colours and fuselage numbers were frequently changed to give the impression of more aircraft than there actually were. Little did director Raoul Walsh realise that 'only' sixteen Thunderbolts was the kind of number that other film-makers would envy years later. In addition, he could call on the services of the Mustangs of the 195th F.S. (California A.N.G.) to play the enemy aircraft.

It was a shame then that *Fighter Squadron*, a third rework of the tired old *Dawn Patrol* storyline, did not cut out the clichés, the false patriotism and distinctly odd paint schemes. Much of the action was filmed at Oscoda, a disused air base in Michigan which had a rural setting somewhat reminiscent of England, complete with nearby Lake Huron which doubled for the English Channel. The story was based loosely on Eighth Air Force operations with the P-47 during 1943.

Despite the E.T.O. slant, when the unit painters had finished their task, the Air Guard Thunderbolts looked more like 12th A.A.F. ships, as the director had seen the colour footage of the wartime documentary *Thunderbolt* and, of course, had copied the markings. So much for well-qualified advisers; they were largely ignored, both on this aspect and the holes in the cringe-making script.

Filming was marred by the loss of Guard pilot Avary Mikell of the 158th F.B.S. whose F-47 broke up over Lake Huron after a loop during a regular Guard training flight. He baled out but was drowned in the freezing waters of the lake before anyone could rescue him.

Flying for the *Fighter Squadron* cameras was highly enjoyable for the participating pilots and Lee Gover was pleased to be working with pilots of the calibre of Fifth Air Force ace Maj Robert M. DeHaven who led the 'German' P-51s. But Gover was somewhat chagrined to have to bow out to film 'pilots' Robert Stack and Edmond O'Brien in all the close-ups!

**MORE ACTION**

When the Korean war broke out in August 1950, it might have seemed that the F-47 was a natural choice to equip those U.S.A.F. piston-engine fighter-bomber squadrons that were recalled to action. But it was not to be Thunderbolts that went to war again, but Mustangs. Air Force squadrons tasked with trying to stem the North Korean invasion were soon heavily engaged on ground-attack sorties and as in the Second World War, ground fire often proved lethal to the F-51's liquid-cooled engine.

The reasons for choosing the F-51 over the F-47 for Korea were almost certainly similar to those prevailing in the Second World War – fuel consumption versus range. Although the F-47N had as good a range as any fighter in the U.S. inventory in 1950, it hardly achieved it without a high fuel bill. And cost was a factor that could not be ignored within postwar military budgets. The unit cost of a F-47 was high; at 1945 prices the fly-away total for a single example was $83,000 compared to $50,985 for an F-51.

*One of hundreds of P-47Ds that served the Air National Guard after the end of the war, this machine has a bold red nose with swept-back blazes, although its parent state is unidentified. (P. Jarrett)*

## EAST INDIES UNREST

Unrest flared into open hostilities in other areas of Asia during the late 1940s and early 1950s where the end of the Second World War left something of a vacuum; nations freed from the yoke of the Japanese were not prepared to meekly accept pre-war colonial rule and while some nations recognised the widespread, deeply rooted desire for independence, others did not.

Dutch reluctance to relinquish the Dutch East Indies was to lead to a confrontation and that had the effect of drawing other nations into a deteriorating hostile situation. Britain initially backed the Dutch claim and resisted the early establishment of the Republic of Indonesia to little avail. Britain's primary concern was the repatriation of Allied prisoners-of-war and to this end Air Headquarters, Netherlands East Indies (A.H.Q.N.E.I.) was formed to protect the P.o.W.s and internees from any attempt to prevent them leaving the area. After this programme was complete, Britain dropped its veto of a republican government headed by Achmad Sukarno.

As the air element of A.H.Q.N.E.I., 904 Wing's two Thunderbolt units were Nos 60 and 81 Sqns but when H.M.S. *Cumberland* docked at Tandjoeng on 15 September, the aircraft had not arrived. The ship carried repatriation teams who were to link up with reconnaissance groups that had parachuted in,

and to cover them Mosquitoes were temporarily used. On 17 October, 904 Wing landed at Batavia; two days later both squadrons were operational, covering evacuation ground transports, protecting Dakotas flying in reinforcements and, from 29 September, flying air cover for British troops belonging to an occupation force.

Thunderbolts were in action from 1 November when nationalist transport was attacked at Magelang and on the 10th they were part of a force that bombed groups of buildings harbouring guerrillas. Sorties were more generally of a tactical reconnaissance nature, pilots dropping warning leaflets to minimise casualties and observing likely areas where ambushes of British and Dutch troops might take place. Other aircraft, R.A.F. and Dutch, joined in. No. 81 lost a Thunderbolt on 23 November when it went into the sea after attacking a gun-running ship off Djokjakarta. No.60 detached part of the squadron to Tanjong Prak, Soerabaja to be close to the ground forces, the squadron subsequently moving entirely to that location on 1 December. Another aircraft was lost on the 17th but the pilot, despite being captured by the enemy, was well treated.

Increasing numbers of prisoners were getting out of the area by whatever means. Flying from Batavia to Malaya remained hazardous, not least because airfield facilities were so limited.

*A Massachussetts Air National Guard P-47D-40 from the last production batch of Republic-built D models. (P. Jarrett)*

Escort had to be provided for air, road and rail transport to prevent ambushes. In 1946, the situation stabilised a little, although another drawback was the withdrawal of American aircraft supplied under Lend-Lease. The Dutch lost their long-range Liberators and under the terms of the agreement the Thunderbolts should also have been returned to the U.S. but as there was little or no use for them there a stay of execution was arranged – the alternative clause in the Lend-Lease Bill stating that aircraft could be destroyed in the theatre of war was undoubtedly brought into play in the case of the Thunderbolts. In the meantime, they were very useful in the East Indies.

The presence of Royal Netherlands Air Force squadrons eased the pressure on the R.A.F. to some degree and despite the Indonesian forces wanting anything but this situation to occur, they could do little to stop it. Locally the Dutch cooperated with their former colony but at home talks broke down and this in turn led indirectly to the formation of an Indonesian air arm. By May, the final evacuation of 10,000 former P.o.W.s began. No.81 Squadron disbanded on 30 June, leaving No. 60 in Java as the last operational Thunderbolt unit in the R.A.F.

With military control provisionally passed to the Dutch, there was now a wave of anti-British feeling and R.A.F. squadrons either withdrew from the region or were disbanded. No.60 was one of only two squadrons left in the East Indies by the end of August and further operations were flown before the autumn. A detachment operated briefly from Medan in northern Sumatra and another aircraft was lost. Finally, No. 60 got the word that it was to be withdrawn to Singapore to re-equip, leaving the trusty Thunderbolts to their fate. The squadron left the Indies on 28 November 1946. Very soon, the Thunderbolt was little more than a memory in the annals of the wartime R.A.F.

## LAST OF THE LINE
Few examples of the P/F-47 came on to the U.S. civilian market as a realistic recreational machine but one focus for surplus wartime fighters with a good performance was the peculiarly American sport of pylon air racing as exemplified by the annual Bendix event. Revived in 1946, the races saw a solitary

Thunderbolt entry, which was actually the first YP-47M. Stripped of military equipment and entered by Bill Odom, this machine was the fastest of all standard Thunderbolts and a potential race winner. But technical faults, albeit of a minor nature connected with fuel feed, kept it largely out of the running.

## OVERSEAS USE
With the phase-out of the F-47 from the U.S.A.F., there were more than enough surplus machines available to modernise the air arms of governments friendly to the U.S. Wartime agreements and Lend-Lease contracts had seen P-47s delivered to France, Brazil and Mexico, all of which retained some of the aircraft they had flown in combat pending the delivery of newer machines. Brief details of these and other nations that used P-47s are as follows.

## U.S.S.R.
Russia received just 196 P-47Ds from an allocation of 203 (three D-10s, 100 D-22s, and 100 D-27s) under Lend-Lease arrangements, seven aircraft being lost prior to delivery. The first three examples were sent via the Alaska-Siberia ferry route, four were shipped direct and the remainder were dispatched via the Persian Gulf. Fuller details of the P-47 in Soviet service remain to be fully documented. Recent information indicates, however, that the type was tested and/or used operationally by at least four units: 225 I.A.P. Fighter Regiment, 1 Dive-Bomber Aviation Division, 5 Mine-Torpedo Aviation Regiment and 5 Detached Reconnaissance Division of the *Voenno-vozdushnye sily Krasnoi Armii* (V.V.S.). Thunderbolts are understood to have operated alongside Soviet aircraft in mixed-type regiments, a common enough practice.

Russian design bureaux never created a fighter similar in size to the P-47 and it hardly fitted neatly into any V.V.S. category of combat aircraft. One might assume that, as in the U.S.A.A.F., it partly replaced the widely used P-39 Airacobra in Russian ground-attack units. Mention of the type's service in an anti-shipping regiment conjures up the fascinating possibility that the V.V.S. at least evaluated Thunderbolts carrying mines and even a torpedo.

## France
Some French combat units renewed their

*One of the P-47D-27s (42-27062) supplied to the Russians under Lend-Lease during the war in factory-applied national markings consisting of a red star on a white field, a simple variation on the U.S. national insignia. (M.A.P.)*

wartime association with the P-47 when the *Armée de l'Air* reformed a number of fighter and special role units during the 1950s, primarily as a result of her military commitments in Algeria and South-East Asia. The P-47s presented to the *Armée de l'Air* by the U.S. in May 1945 were, in common with other Thunderbolts around the world, to fly a last round of combat missions in support of the 'colonial wars' that broke out during the first decades of peace.

Of the wartime units, G.C. II/5 relinquished its P-47s in 1946 as did G.C. III/3 when both units were disbanded, to reform as an amalgamated unit (4e *Escadre*) to fly Spitfires in Indo-China. G.C. II/3 *Dauphine* relinquished P-47s for Spitfires when it was transferred to 4e *Esc.* in July 1947. G.C. I/2 *Cigognes* (Storks) flew Thunderbolts after the war, as did E.C.T.T. 2/30 which was the old *Normandie Niemen* unit. It became E.C. 2/6 in 1951 flying P-47s. To convert new pilots and to offer refresher courses to experienced individuals 314 *Groupement Ecole* – C.E.A.A. - had been established in December 1945 with three squadrons for training on P-47s, Spitfires and P-39 Airacobras.

The French determination to hold on to Algeria in the face of a growing independence movement led to protracted bloodshed over a period of eight years. Air power took on an increasing importance to French government forces, ground-attack aircraft being deployed both by the air force and navy. The F-47D was invariably operated by units which flew other types and during the early 1950s (the Algerian war beginning in May 1954), Thunderbolts were part of E.C. 2/6 (based at Oran), E.E.O.C. 1/17 (Oran-Telergma), E.C. 1/8 (Rabat, Oran), E.C. 1/20 and E.C. 2/20. All these were on active duty during the emergency or were placed on standby for operations in Algeria.

Among the Thunderbolt units that saw action was E.C. 1/20 which operated from Oran, Boufarik and Bone in the close-support role in company with AD-4N Skyraiders and Mistral jets. E.C. 2/20's Thunderbolts also operated alongside AD-4Ns and shared Oran and Bone with its sister unit during the same period, 1956 to 1963.

The Thunderbolt remained a core ground-attack type in the *Armée de l'Air* during the (sometimes lengthy) period of transition from piston-engined fighters to jets. In total, F-47s flew in the markings of twelve combat and training *escadrilles* plus a number of special-duty units before the American fighter was phased out during the mid-1960s in favour of jets.

*France was a major P-47 user and her aircraft served in two wars, Algeria being one of the last operational areas for the Thunderbolt. This machine, still with 'invasion stripes' was part of G.C. I/4 in 1950. (M.A.P.)*

## Italy

When Italy became a republic in June 1946, her air arm became the *Aeronautica Militaire Italiana*. European nations whose forces had been shattered during the Second World War became eligible for limited aid, part of which included military aircraft. Italy had also been allowed to retain its armed forces infrastructure under the 1947 Paris Treaty of Peace. Although there was some international urgency to have jets in all European air forces, other commitments meant that the main supplier, the U.S.A., was obliged to provide older types as a stopgap measure. Italy accordingly received P-38s, F-51Ds and F-47s,

the first twenty-three examples of the latter arriving at Treviso in December 1950.

The fighters, 100 of which were allocated to the A.M.I., were assigned to the 20º and 21º *Gruppi* of 51º *Stormo* despite an acute shortage of spares and auxiliary equipment including armament. In view of this, it was decided that only seventy-seven of the F-47s would be used by operational units.

All allocated pilots had converted to the F-47 by the first quarter of 1951, but serviceability was relatively poor due not only to the spares situation but to technical problems with the Thunderbolts. Nevertheless, the A.M.I. maintained a

*Italy used all three U.S. wartime fighter types for a period when she was coming out of the doldrums of the conflict. The Thunderbolts passed on by the U.S. suffered a spate of technical troubles leading to accidents, which did not make for high reliability. These 5º Gruppo P-47Ds were photographed in 1952, some months before they were replaced by F-84s. (Italian Air Force)*

comprehensive training programme which included a number of high-altitude and long-range sorties, army cooperation flights and, in 1951, an important visual and photographic reconnaissance of the flooded River Po. Accidents continued to plague the Italian F-47s and, in 1952, 51º *Stormo* converted to the F-84, its Thunderbolts being passed to 5º *Stormo*. More Thunderjets arrived and the F-47s were progressively withdrawn. By February 1953, the forty-five surviving aircraft were passed to the 23º *Gruppo Caccia* at Taranto-Grottaglie. This unit flew the type until the following March when it returned to Treviso. By October, the forty-three remaining F-47s were overhauled at Bresso which had retained twenty-three aircraft for spares before being returned to U.S. depots in Germany.

## Iran

In May 1948, the Iranian government took advantage of the good terms offered by the U.S.A. for military equipment. The Imperial Iranian Air Force became a separate air arm in August 1955 and among the aircraft supplied were at least fifty F-47Ds. These were deployed by a single fighter-bomber Wing which based its aircraft at different locations including Shiraz, Mashhad, Isfahan, Tabriz and Ahwaz. During the late 1950s, the I.I.A.F. comprised four wings, to direct fighter-bomber, transport, training and air depot functions. The P-47s were largely replaced by F-84s during 1957-8.

## Nationalist China

Having largely flown types other than the P-47 in combat during the war, the Nationalist Air Force inherited an unknown number of Thunderbolts left in China by the U.S.A.A.F.'s Chinese American Composite Wing. This unit had begun to receive P-47Ds in mid-1945, shortly before the Japanese surrender although none are believed to have seen any action. Postwar, the Chinese activated the 11th Fighter Group which had sufficient F-47s to equip three component squadrons. Along with further examples supplied to the country under M.D.A.P. these older F-47s were pressed into service in order to build up the Nationalist forces, particularly when the country underwent a mass conversion to communism. The Nationalist government moved to Taiwan in 1950 and maintained a largely Western-equipped air arm.

There were enough F-47s to equip two fighter-bomber Wings by 1954 and when the military action expected by Peking failed to materialise, the C.N.A.F. settled down to an uneasy peace. Eventually, the air force received U.S. jets and the Second World War types, which are understood to have been replenished by the U.S. to make good attrition, ultimately passed into a second-line training role as they were declared obsolescent.

## Communist China

Former Nationalist combat aircraft acquired by the armed forces of the People's Republic of China included at least one P-47D which survived to become a current museum exhibit at Beijing University's magnificent collection of rare and, in some cases, unique aircraft types.

## Portugal

In July 1952 when the *Forca Aerea Portuguesa* (F.A.P.) was formed, fifty F-47D-25s were acquired under M.D.A.P. These were flown in the operational training role, equipping *Esquadra* 10 with twenty-five aircraft and *Esquadra* 11 with the other twenty-five, both units being based at *Bases Aereas* 2 at Ota. These were in fact first-line units, staffed by the country's top pilots but the days of the piston-engined fighter were then numbered and in January 1953 Portugal received her first F-84s. The F-47s were subsequently amalgamated into one unit, *Esc.* 10 which continued to provide transition training for jet-fighter pilots. On 25 April 1952, *Esc.* 10's F-47s provided an escort to the aircraft carrying Field Marshal Montgomery, then NATO C.-in-C., on a visit to Portugal. A move was made to Tancos in 1953 and the Thunderbolt remained a familiar sight in Portuguese skies for another three years before giving way to another Republic product, the F-84 Thunderjet.

## Turkey

The U.S. Congress approved military aid to Turkey on 22 May 1947 and the country thereafter received a substantial number of aircraft, including F-47Ds. These were delivered in 1948 and were, it is believed, based at Diyarbakir prior to the country joining NATO. Jet aircraft were then delivered in order that Turkey could fulfil a commitment to guard the 'southern flank' of treaty-aligned countries in collective defence against the Eastern Bloc.

## Yugoslavia

With the signing of a Mutual Assistance Pact on 14 November 1951, the Yugoslavian government took delivery of U.S. and British military aircraft, including 150 F-47Ds. These equipped ten front-line squadrons of the *Jugoslovensko Ratno Vazduhoplovstvo* (J.R.V.) until 1958 when jets more or less rendered them obsolete and surviving examples were used as advanced trainers. The F-47s shared

this duty with the T-33A and S-49C, some Thunderbolts remaining in service until 1961.

The greatest postwar utilisation of the F-47 was in Latin America, where a squadron of Thunderbolts was a prestigious acquisition for both large and small air arms hungry to modernise and fly contemporary warplanes with outstanding combat records. Generally, these countries turned to the U.S. which in the main did not let them down. By introducing various schemes under which surplus warplanes could be acquired on favourable terms, F-47s became at worst the toys of dictators and at best a tangible

*Turkey was among those countries that received P-47s as an interim type pending a build up of pro-Western air arms with jets as a bulwark against Eastern Bloc communist expansion. These machines, with two-digit rear fuselage codes, have the red square insignia used by Turkey before the current roundel was adopted. (R.L. Ward)*

*Yugoslavian P-47D with a serial that is believed to be of national rather than U.S. origin. The Il-2 in the background emphasises the East-West pull of countries in the Balkans and elsewhere as regards military equipment, particularly during the decade after the Second World War.*

defence force, a very real counter to internal and cross-border aggression that threatened stability.

## Brazil

As detailed earlier, Brazil became the earliest Latin American user of the P-47 with its service in the M.T.O. during the Second World War. Postwar supplies ensured that the country also became the largest user of the Thunderbolt outside the U.S.A. After the war, the Brazilians disassembled and shipped home the twenty-six aircraft it had on hand at its base at Pisa. A further nineteen machines, nominally the property of Brazil, had had to be used as replacement combat aircraft by other U.S.A.A.F. units but these were soon replaced by almost brand-new aircraft under Lend-Lease arrangements.

A further delivery of F-47Ds was made in 1947, twenty-three being accepted between June and December. These were based at Santa Cruz to back up the strength of the 'original' F.A.B. Thunderbolt unit, the 1º *Grupo de Aviacao* which, although having been redesignated, succeeded in retaining its identity through a reorganisation and was based at São Paulo. Spares to service thirty aircraft were also delivered.

Thus by February 1952, the F.A.B. had fifty-one F-47s on hand. A year on and the U.S. was not only offering jets to Brazil but the

Thunderbolt fleet had inevitably suffered from the passage of time. Held in very high esteem both inside and outside the country, 1º *G.Av.Ca* was allowed to stay loyal to its wartime combat aircraft as long as practicable. But the arrival of Gloster Meteors in 1953, favourable terms for the F-80 Shooting Star and the better overall economics of jet operations, could hardly be ignored.

The surplus F-47s remained intact in Brazil however and there were still about forty as late as 1958. These soon began to be snapped up by museums and no less than nine were earmarked for preservation in Brazil, while others were inevitably struck off charge or used by the air force as instructional airframes. Today, the Brazilians still hanker after seeing their sole wartime fighter in the air and to that end a long-term restoration project is being undertaken on P-47D-30RE 44-20339.

## Chile

Beginning in September 1947, the *Fuerza Aerea de Chile* (F.A.Ch.) received a total of twenty-four F-47Ds under A.R.P./M.D.A.P., these being firstly integrated into a mixed *Grupo de Aviacion* No.2 at Quintero. This unit had all Second World War type aircraft and represented almost the entire strength of the F.A.Ch. Two years later, the F-47s were reorganised into a fighter unit, No. 5, and finally No. 11 the 'definitive' Chilean fighter

*Brazil's great affection for the P-47 is reflected in a number of preserved machines. Pride of place must go to the example displayed in the Museum of Aeronautics in São Paulo, pictured here some years ago marked as the aircraft flown by Nero Maura, the 1º G.Av.Ca commander in Italy.*

formation. Two aircraft were lost in accidents and a lack of spares reduced serviceability to one F-47 by late 1949. The situation improved slightly and, although only seven F-47s remained by 1952, that August the Chileans received fourteen F-47D-40s. These had low utilisation in the next two years or so, due to Vampire jet trainers being on hand and pending delivery of F-80s in 1958 when the twelve remaining Thunderbolts were finally struck off charge. Two were retained for preservation.

## Colombia

Eventually taking delivery of a total of thirty-five F-47s, the F.A.C. formed a single fighter unit, 1º *Escuadron de Caza*. Due to the country's lack of experience in operating high-performance military aircraft, Colombia's pilots found the Thunderbolt quite a handful. Variants of the AT-6 Texan trainer had been delivered, yet none of the latter were apparently on F.A.C. strength by the time the first F-47s arrived in July 1947. This apparently caused few problems as the fighters were extensively flown without loss for some three years. Border tensions saw the F-47s in limited action including one aircraft dropping a single bomb — which failed to explode — on a guerrilla H.Q., causing the rebels to surrender. More F-47s were acquired

in the early 1950s and thirteen were on strength by June 1952 and twenty-two by May 1953. High utilisation continued with an admirably low attrition rate until, in late 1954, the F.A.C. took delivery of T-33s. Flying hours on the F-47s invariably dropped to a low level due to a lack of sufficient pilots to fly both types and by 1955 the F-47s were grounded. They were finally scrapped in 1958, one example being retained for museum display.

## Cuba

Deliveries of F-47D-30s and D-35s to the *Fuerza Aerea Ejercito de Cuba* (F.E.A.C. or Cuban Army Air Force) began in May 1952 and extended until January the following year. Soon after the 1953 formation of the *Escuadron de Persecucion '10 de Marzo'*, Cuba's first combat-worthy fighter squadron, there were twenty-five F-47s and one TF-47 on hand. Weathering an agreed but poorly executed delivery of spares from the U.S., Cuban pilots put in many F-47 hours during the next few years, the aircraft being used for hostile action during a Navy-inspired revolt against the Batista regime in Cienfuegos in September 1957. Down to ten machines by 1958, the F-47 was all but retired by mid-1958, one possibly surviving the Bay of Pigs invasion and into the Fidel Castro era.

*F-47D-30 on display at the Colombian Air Force Museum is 45-49102/F.A.C. 861. For some reason the F.A.C. identity has since been changed.*

## Dominica

Taking delivery of twenty-five F-47D-30-RAs under the Mutual Defense Assistance Program in 1953, the *Aviaçion Militar Dominicana* (A.M.D.) mixed its single- and twin-engined fighters in a single massive unit, the 1º *Escuadron de Caza Bombardero*. The Thunderbolt was the primary F.A.D. tactical type although the air arm also boasted F-38s, F-51s, Mosquitoes and Beaufighters. This diversity proved unweildy particularly from the maintenance viewpoint, and limited pilot numbers also caused problems, leading to lower utilisation of the F-47s than was required by the A.M.D. Nevertheless, from 1955 to 1957 the number of Thunderbolts remained steady at nineteen. The latterly renamed *Fuerza Aerea Dominicana* (F.A.D.) had acquired Vampires which proved highly popular. The F-47s languished until November 1957 when they were declared surplus and scrapped.

## Ecuador

Chronologically the third Latin American country to operate Thunderbolts, the *Fuerza Aerea Ecuatoriana* (F.A.E.) took delivery of twelve F-47D-30-RAs under the American Republics Project (A.R.P.) aid programme in mid-1947. Also the first modern combat aircraft acquired by Ecuador, the F-47s were based at Quito in the Andes foothills. Aircraft utilisation, while not high, bred a fine *espirit de corps* and the Ecuadoreans managed to keep accidents down to an acceptable level. Serviceability and spares were, however, a problem. Four more F-47s were acquired in 1949 to replace two lost in accidents, followed by eleven F-47D-40s under M.D.A.P. in June 1953. These latter machines enabled the formation of a single unit, 10 *Escuadron*, 100º *Ala de Caza-Bombardero*. Maintaining high standards through perseverance, the F.A.E. faced a major crisis with F-47 turbocharger failure. This was addressed by lengthy rebuilding, a process overtaken by the arrival of T-33s in 1956. The Thunderbolts finally served out their time as target tugs for F.A.E. F-80s and were retired in 1958-9.

## Mexico

Having flown combat missions as part of the 58th Fighter Group in the Philippines during the war, personnel of the *Fuerza Aerea Expedicionaria Mexicana* did not, like the Brazilian expeditionary force, bring their aircraft home. But soon after they arrived back in Mexico, twenty-five nearly new F-47D-35-RAs were delivered by the U.S. These machines were flown by *Escuadron de Pelea* 201, the original numerical designation of the small wartime force being retained. It was practical for men experienced in flying and servicing the F-47 to remain in this unit and many individuals did so until retirement or a higher calling occurred in the early 1950s. Time took its inevitable toll on the Thunderbolts and by 1957, retirement loomed. Two examples were retained as gate guardians.

## Nicaragua

Relatively few Thunderbolts fired their guns in anger after the Second World War but they included the F-47N, examples of which were delivered to Nicaragua in 1954. All drawn from stocks held by the Puerto Rico Air National Guard, they were used in the Central Intelligence Agency-backed invasion of Nicaragua to depose the communist-backed government of Jacobo Arbenz and install Castillo Armas. Under the codename Operation *Success*, the C.I.A. engineered the movement of some thirty aircraft including six F-47Ns into Nicaragua.

The Thunderbolts that survived this operation passed into *Fuerza Aerea Nicaragua* (F.A.N.) service, all apparently being fitted with only six guns on delivery. When the military coup, the backing for which included strafing by F-47s, got Armas installed, F-47s were passed to the F.A.N. Fighting flared again in 1955, with a small-scale invasion of Costa Rica launched from Nicaragua by anti-communist 'Calderonistas'. This venture, which had some air support in the form of the F-47Ns had by 18 January all but fizzled out – but overhead the last F-47Ns to see action anywhere were completing their final sorties. By late 1959, the F.A.N. machines were all but grounded and the Confederate Air Force bought the last three in 1962.

## Peru

Second largest Latin American operator of the F-47 after Brazil, Peru's examples were also supplied under A.R.P., deliveries beginning in

July 1947 with twenty-five F-47D-30-RAs. Flown at first by the *Escuadron de Caza* 11 (redesignated *Esc de Caza* 12 in 1949) the F-47 was mastered quickly by the Peruvians, who could draw on useful previous experience of operating U.S. piston-engined fighters. Subsequent deliveries of twenty-five refurbished F-47D-40s enabled a second unit, *Esc de Caza* 13, to be formed in 1953, the national air arm then having been renamed as the *Fuerza Aerea del Peru* (F.A.P.) in 1950.

With twenty-one aircraft each, the two operational units continued to train until turbocharger problems occurred in August 1953. All F-47s were grounded temporarily pending inspection and repair. Remedial work put most of the aircraft back into service but other technical problems arose. By June 1958, F-80s had arrived in Peru and the F-47s, by then used as fighter trainers, carried on, complementing the jets as no suitable replacement for the Thunderbolt could be found. It was 1969 before the last six machines were sold to the Confederate Air Force, thus marking the final demise of the F-47 in Latin American service.

## Puerto Rico

The use of F-47s by Puerto Rico came within the U.S. Air Guard structure. Many A.A.F. personnel hailed from Puerto Rico and these veterans returning home after the Second World War represented an excellent pool of experience for the new A.N.G. unit, which was established on 23 November 1947. As the 198th Fighter Squadron (Augmented) P.R. A.N.G., it was headed by Maj Alberto A. Nido, a highly experienced F-51 pilot who had served in the 9th W.R.S., Ninth Air Force, during the war.

Puerto Rico's Thunderbolt models were mostly the long-range F-47N, although one D-30 was initially assigned, followed by twenty-three F-47Ns of various subtypes. The unit took up the 'lineage and honours' of the F-47N-equipped 507th Fighter Group, Seventh/Twentieth Air Force, as per U.S.A.F. tradition and, in the event, flew F-47s until 1954, making the P.R. A.N.G. the last U.S.A.F.-associated organisation to officially operate the Thunderbolt.

That the unit was needed was proven in October 1950 when Puerto Rican nationalists staged a jailbreak. The 198th F.S. was mobilised and a well-ordered show of strength was laid on for the 31st. It included two flights of four F-47Ns, led in by a B-26 Invader, diving low over two towns held by the rebels, and opening fire. The pilots were not however out to kill anybody. They merely hoped to scare the escapers into surrendering by firing high but ensuring that streams of brass shell cases clattered off the roofs of the shanty-town dwellings. The noisy show of force was enough to unnerve the rebels and the trouble was over in four days.

*Puerto Rico's A.N.G was called up to quell unrest in the country and P-47Ns opened fire briefly to bring rioters to heel. This machine, an N-25 named* Wild Hair, *was one of the last Thunderbolts built. Note red lightning bolts on tail and mainwheel doors. (P. Jarrett)*

The P.R. A.N.G. was demobilised on 7 November after the only action in which the organisation was called upon to answer a genuine threat to U.S. internal security. Some two years before the P.R. A.N.G. changed its F-47Ns for jets, the unit became the 198th Fighter Interceptor Squadron; its Thunderbolts were sold to Nicaragua and some were later returned to the U.S.

### Venezuela

Six F-47Ds were received under the A.R.P. project in August 1947, the type representing a quite radical but not unique departure for the Venezuelans in that the air arm had previously operated multi-purpose aircraft. Only one 'single role' fighter type had previously been purchased, the Hanriot HD 1 in 1923. T-6 trainers eased the conversion process to the mighty Thunderbolt, as did Fiat CR.32s, although two pilots were killed in crashes during that first year of operations, which reduced the inventory of F-47s to a meagre four machines. One replacement was delivered and the F.A.V. still had five on strength by the following May.

As the country became more political stable, military aid from the U.S. was forthcoming in 1949, including a further twenty-two F-47s. These equipped the *Grupo Aereo* 9 based at Maracay. All examples had been delivered by late in the year to make up the bulk of the peak F.A.V. inventory of twenty-four Thunderbolts recorded in April 1950. On that date, de Havilland Vampires were also in evidence, these and other jet types helping to sound the death knell of the F-47 in numerous Latin American air arms as other jets had inevitably done elsewhere. This situation was compounded by an ever-dwindling number of Thunderbolt spares, a difficulty only partially alleviated by cannibalisation and the original supply (in some cases) of complete airframes intended entirely for use as spares.

By June 1950, accidents had also reduced the F.A.V. F-47 inventory and by late 1951 no more than eight examples serving in the sole operational unit, *Escuadron de Casa* No. 36, were known to be serviceable. For the next four years, the F-47 situation remained more stable, to the point of allowing the Venezuelans to successfully operate a Thunderbolt aerobatic team. Inevitably, phase-out had to occur in the not too distant future and in 1952 with the country turning more to Britain than the U.S.A. for military equipment, the F-47 unit was deactivated on 10 December.

### STILL THUNDERING?

Of the total of 15,683 P-47s built during the Second World War, it has been estimated that about one-third were expended in combat, a third were scrapped after the war and the remaining third served with Air Guard units and/or were sold abroad. During the war the 'home front' training circuit, which could be rough on aircraft, accounted for no less than 3049 P-47s destroyed or damaged between 1942 and 1945, with 455 pilots being killed. The accident record of the P-47 was rated at 127 aircraft per 100,000 flight hours. Relatively few P/F-47s of the 'remaining' third (some 5000 aircraft) survived, the majority being scrapped in intervening decades.

By the mid-1990s, despite the international 'warbird' movement being as strong as it has ever been, the Thunderbolt is far from numerous. About fifty-four airframes are known to exist throughout the world in all states from full flying trim to a collection of rusting parts rescued from obscure corners of the globe. The majority are naturally enough in the U.S.A., the current civil inventory including a substantial number that were once in service with Latin American air arms.

The U.K. boasts three P-47s, the flyable example being maintained by the Fighter Collection at Duxford, Cambs which began life as 45-49192, and two static airframes, one at Duxford for restoration for the American Air Museum and one currently stored by the R.A.F. Museum, presumably for eventual display at Hendon.

As far as subtypes go, the razorback models are represented by three P-47D-2s, one D-15, a G-10 and a G-15. Late-production bubble-top D-versions make up the remainder, along with the P-47N. The bubble-top models include at least two D-27s, three D-30s, twelve D-40s and four N-25s.

Virtually all surviving Thunderbolts have interesting, not to say chequered, careers which invariably include more than one civilian owner and U.S. civil registration, the latter being commonplace for many warbirds, with a sale to a foreign country often beginning the long road to exhibition or

*Full circle. After service in Latin America, P-47s brought back to the U.S. were sold to private collectors. Invariably repainted in U.S.A.A.F. markings, these are the most active survivors of the Thunderbolt that can be seen today. Organisations such as the Confederate Air Force have been a driving force in maintaining historic combat aircraft in flying trim.* Unadilla Killa *of the C.A.F. represents a P-47D of the 354th Fighter Group, Ninth Air Force. (Al Lauer)*

display flying today. Aircraft of fifty plus year's vintage are, however, quite prone to malfunction, damage and loss, even with a highly experienced pilot at the controls and it is to be hoped that the current P-47 inventory does not drop very much lower, from whatever cause. There is not much further to go!

Surviving Thunderbolts in Asia, Central America and Europe include display examples in France (P-47D-30, 44-20371) in the Musée de l'Air, Paris Le Bourget; in Turkey (P-47D-30, 44-33712) in the Air Force Museum, Istanbul, and in Italy (P-47D-30, 44-89746) formerly at Pisa University before passing to the military aeronautical museum at Vigna di Valle for refurbishing. Mexico holds two P-47s, the aircraft of course recalling – and indeed dedicated to the memory of – the wartime service of her airmen in the Pacific. P-47D-30 44-90205 is displayed at the Colegio del Aire while P-47D-35 44-90217 can be seen at Santa Lucia's Base Aerea Militar No.1.

Brazil's primary museum exhibit is probably P-47D-25 (42-26450) 44-20339 painted in the colours of the wartime Brazilian 1º *G.Av.Ca* and representing the aircraft flown by the group commander, Nero Moura. Displayed in the Museum of Aeronautics, São Paulo, this machine duplicates the serial number of a P-47 used in combat but struck off charge in Brazil in March 1958. At least three other Thunderbolts and almost certainly more, are held by Brazilian museums and the air force.

China has a P-47D on display in Beijing, the

aircraft being one of a fine collection of rare historical types held by the Aeronautical Institute. An interesting example in New Zealand is 42-8066, a razorback P-47D-2 recovered from a swamp in Papua New Guinea in 1968 and a third example of the earliest surviving Thunderbolt model. The remains of this one arrived in New Zealand in 1992.

**KEEP 'EM FLYING?**
A special effort appears to have been made to restore the early razorback models to flying condition in the U.S.A. and both the P-47Gs have been seen in their 'natural element' painted in well-rendered wartime markings. Numerous restorations, either to static museum condition or to full flying condition, are constantly underway with aircraft of historic importance and the P-47 is no exception. But there is no denying that the appeal of the Thunderbolt and Mustang, once complementary first-line combat aircraft wherever the U.S.A.A.F. or its Allies saw action, has long since diverged, with the P-51 dominant.

The relative rarity of the Thunderbolt can arguably be traced to a substantially shorter period of first-line U.S.A.F. service compared with that of the P-51 which also had an upsurge in use in the Korean War and other operations of foreign air forces. Indeed, many warbirds currently flying in the U.S.A. and Europe today owe their survival to low operational utilisation rates by budget-restricted South American air arms.

The same is true for some of the surviving P-47s and were it not for these far-flung countries even fewer Thunderbolts would now be seen by the general public. It is also not overstating the case to say that the 'out to pasture' policy adopted by certain countries for former military aircraft no longer in use has saved rather more airframes for posterity than the mass scrapping followed by others.

Flyable P-47s in the U.S. at the time of writing include *Big Stud*, Bob Baseler's wartime mount with the 'Checkertails'. Cared for by the Champlin Fighter Museum, this P-47 must be a pulse-quickening sight to veterans who flew with this or any other Thunderbolt outfit during the Second World War. The Curtiss-built G-15 model represents the Eighth Air Force by carrying the markings of the second wartime Thunderbolt (42-8487/UN-M) of 56th Fighter Group ace Walker Mahurin, complete with the War Bond subscriber dedication 'Spirit of Atlantic City, NJ'.

The 78th Group at Duxford is represented by another G-10 painted as Walter Beckham's 42-8476/YJ-X *Little Demon*. The exploits of the Eighth are further recalled by two of the P-47D-40s flying in Wolfpack schemes, 42-26418/HV-A and 42-28473/HV-P.

Ninth Air Force markings have appeared on various P-47s and currently the *Big Ass Bird II* alias 44-32773/4P-S is the scheme worn by

another of the surviving D-40s. As impressive today as it was over the European battlefields in 1945, the original was flown by the then Lt Howard W. Park of the 406th Group.

By flying these veterans for the delight of millions, a younger generation of pilots is finding out the exhilaration of being at the controls of a Second World War heavyweight. At their best, fighters like the P-47 have so good a power-to-weight ratio that in capable hands they must take the adrenelin level way off the scale. And if there are problems with the old war horses there are plenty of equally old, bold pilots and crew chiefs to give sound advice based on experiences of sadder times when the P-47 and its ilk was a weapon of war, pure and simple.

That the P-47 was loved by many men whom it carried safely through combat is shown by the degoratory (ie affectionate) nicknames bestowed upon Republic's 'Jug'. To that most common handle was added 'Repulsive Scatterbolt', 'Thundermug', 'Thunderjug', 'Superbolt' and probably others but the best one of all appeared on P-47N-1 44-88119 which was dubbed 'Repulsive Thunderbox' by an irreverent Wright Field individual. Few aeroplanes ever thundered so effectively.

*The original* Grumpy *was a P-47 flown by Lt Tom Ellis of the 527th F.S., 86th Fighter Group in Italy and the replica paint scheme on this warbird Thunderbolt (for once) does it justice. The subject aircraft was photographed at Harlingen, Texas, first home of the Confederate Air Force. (Al Lauer)*

# Appendix I
# Production Details

## RAZORBACK MODELS

| Model | A.A.F. serial number | Quantity | Remarks |
|---|---|---|---|
| XP-47B | 40-3051 | 1 | |
| P-47B | 41-5895 to 41-6065 | 171 | |
| P-47C-RE | 41-6067 to 41-6163 | 57 | |
| P-47C-1-RE | 41-6066; 41-6124 to 41-6177 | 55 | |
| P-47C-2-RE | 41-6178 to 41-6305 | 128 | |
| P-47C-5-RE | 41-6306 to 41-6667 | 362 | |
| P-47D | 42-22250 to 42-22253 | 4 | First Evansville examples |
| P-47D-RE | 42-22254 to 42-22363 | 110 | |
| P-47D-1-RE | 42-7853 to 42-7957 | 105 | |
| P-47D-2-RE | 42-7958 to 42-8402 | 445 | |
| P-47D-2-RA | 42-22364 to 42-22563 | 200 | |
| P-47D-5-RE | 42-8403 to 42-8702 | 300 | |
| P-47D-3-RA | 42-22564 to 42-22663 | 100 | |
| P-47D-4-RA | 42-22664 to 42-22863 | 200 | |
| P-47D-6-RE | 42-74615 to 42-74964 | 350 | |
| P-47D-10-RE | 42-74965 to 42-75214 | 250 | |
| P-47D-11-RE | 42-75215 to 42-75614 | 400 | |
| P-47D-11-RA | 42-22864 to 42-23113 | 250 | |
| P-47D-15-RE | 42-75615 to 42-75864 | | |
| | 42-76119 to 42-76364 | 496 | |
| P-47D-15-RA | 42-23143 to 42-23299 | 157 | 42-23297 and 42-23298 became P-47Hs |
| P-47D-16-RE | 42-75865 to 42-76118 | 254 | |
| P-47D-16-RA | 42-23114 to 42-23142 | 29 | |
| P-47D-20-RE | 42-76365 to 42-76614 | | |
| | 42-25274 to 42-25322 | 300 | |
| P-47D-20-RA | 43-25254 to 43-25440 | 187 | |
| P-47D-21-RE | 42-25323 to 42-25538 | 216 | |
| P-47D-21-RA | 43-25441 to 43-25664 | 224 | |
| P-47D-22-RE | 42-25539 to 42-26388 | 850 | |
| P-47D-23-RA | 43-25665 to 43-25753 | | |
| | 42-27389 to 42-28188 | 889 | |

## BUBBLE CANOPY MODELS

| Model | A.A.F. serial number | Quantity |
|---|---|---|
| P-47D-25-RE | 42-26389 to 42-26773 | 385 |
| P-47D-26-RA | 42-28189 to 42-28438 | 250 |
| P-47D-27-RE | 42-26774 to 42-27388 | 615 |
| P-47D-28-RE | 44-19558 to 44-20307 | 750 |
| P-47D-28-RA | 42-28439 to 42-29466 | 1028 |
| P-47D-30-RE | 44-20308 to 44-21107 | 800 |
| P-47D-30-RA | 44-32668 to 44-33867 | |
| | 44-89684 to 44-90283 | 1800 |
| P-47D-40-RA | 44-90284 to 44-90483 | |
| | 45-49090 to 45-49554 | 665 |
| XP-47E | 41-6065 | 1 |
| XP-47F | 41-5938 | 1 |
| P-47G-CU | 42-24920 to 42-24939 | 20 |
| P-47G-1-CU | 42-24940 to 42-24979 | 40 |
| P-47G-5-CU | 42-24980 to 42-25039 | 60 |
| P-47G-10-CU | 42-25040 to 42-25119 | 80 |
| P-47G-15-CU | 42-25120 to 42-25273 | 154 |
| XP-47H | 42-23297 to 42-23298 | 2 |
| XP-47J | 43-46952 | 1 |
| XP-47K | 42-8702 | 1 |
| XP-47L | 42-76614 | 1 |
| YP-47M-RE | 42-27385 | |
| | 42-27386 | |
| | 42-27388 | 3 |
| P-47M-1-RE | 44-21108 to 44-21237 | 130 |
| XP-47N | 42-27387 | 1 |
| P-47N-1-RE | 44-87784 to 44-88333 | 550 |
| P-47N-5-RE | 44-88334 to 44-88883 | 550 |
| P-47N-15-RE | 44-88884 to 44-89083 | 200 |
| P-47N-20-RE | 44-89084 to 44-89283 | 200 |
| P-47N-20-RA | 45-49975 to 45-50123 | 149 |
| P-47N-25-RE | 44-89284 to 44-89450 | 167 |
| XP-72 | 43-6598 | |
| | 43-6599 | 2 |
| **Total P-47 production** | | 15,683 |

# Appendix II
# Wartime P-47 Units
# and Operational Dates

| Air Force/Unit | Motto/Nickname* | P-47 Combat Debut | Model |
|---|---|---|---|
| Fifth Air Force | | | |
| 8th F.G. | | Nov. 1943 (36th F.S. only) | razorback only |
| 35th F.G. | | Nov. 1943 | razorback/bubble-top |
| 49th F.G. | | Nov. 1943 (9th F.S. only) | razorback |
| 58th F.G. | | Feb. 1944 | razorback |
| 348th F.G. | | July 1944 | razorback/bubble-top |
| Seventh Air Force | | | |
| 318th F.G. | | June 1944 | razorback/P-47N |
| 413th F.G. | | June 1945 | P-47N |
| 414th F.G. | | July 1945 | P-47N |
| 507th F.G. | | July 1945 | P-47N |
| Eighth Air Force | | | |
| 4th F.G. | Eagles | March 1943 | razorback only |
| 56th F.G. | Wolfpack | April 1943 | razorback/bubble-top |
| 78th F.G. | | April 1943 | razorback/bubble-top |
| 352nd F.G. | Bluenosers | Sept. 1943 | razorback |
| 353rd F.G. | Slybird Group | Aug. 1943 | razorback/bubble-top |
| 355th F.G. | Strafers | Sept. 1943 | razorback |
| 356th F.G. | | Oct. 1943 | razorback/bubble-top |
| 359th F.G. | | Dec. 1943 | razorback |
| 361st F.G. | Yellow Jackets | Jan. 1944 | razorback |
| Ninth Air Force | | | |
| 36th F.G. | | May 1944 | razorback/bubble-top |
| 48th F.G. | | Apr. 1944 | razorback/bubble-top |
| 50th F.G. | | May 1944 | razorback/bubble-top |
| 354th F.G. | Pioneer Mustang Group | Nov. 1944-Feb.1945 only | bubble-top |
| 358th F.G. | Orange Tails | Dec. 1943 | razorback/bubble-top |
| 362nd F.G. | Mogin's Maulers | Feb. 1944 | razorback/bubble-top |
| 365th F.G. | Hell Hawks | Feb. 1944 | razorback/bubble-top |
| 366th F.G. | Hun Hunters | Mar. 1944 | razorback/bubble-top |
| 367th F.G. | | Feb. 1945 | razorback/bubble-top |
| 368th F.G. | | Mar. 1944 | razorback/bubble-top |
| 371st F.G. | | Apr. 1944 | razorback/bubble-top |
| 373rd F.G. | | May 1944 | razorback/bubble-top |
| 404th F.G. | Tin Hornets | May 1944 | razorback/bubble-top |

| Air Force/Unit | Motto/Nickname* | P-47 Combat Debut | Model |
|---|---|---|---|
| 405th F.G. | Thunder Monsters | April 1944 | razorback/bubble-top |
| 406th F.G. | Stardusters/Raiders | May 1944 | razorback/bubble-top |
| Tenth Air Force | | | |
| 1st A.C.G. | | Sept. 1944 | razorback/bubble-top |
| 33rd F.G. | Nomads | Sept. 1944 | razorback |
| 80th F.G. | | Sept. 1944 | razorback |
| Twelfth Air Force | | | |
| 27th F.G. | | June 1944 | razorback/bubble-top |
| 57th F.G. | America's Flying Circus /The Gang | Jan. 1944 | razorback/bubble-top |
| 79th F.G. | | March 1944 | razorback/bubble-top |
| 86th F.G. | | June 1944 | razorback/bubble-top |
| 324th F.G. | | July 1944 | razorback/bubble-top |
| 350th F.G. | | July 1944 | razorback/bubble-top |
| Fourteenth Air Force | | | |
| 33rd F.G. | Nomads | April 44 | razorback/bubble-top |
| 81st F.G. | | June 44 | razorback/bubble-top |
| Fifteenth Air Force | | | |
| 325th F.G. | Checkertails/The Clan | Nov. 1943 | razorback |
| 332nd F.G. | Red Tails | April-July 1944 only | razorback/bubble-top |
| **Royal Air Force** | | | |
| No. 5 Sqn | Thou mayest bend but shall not break me | Oct. 44 | Mk I, Mk II |
| No. 30 Sqn | All out | July 1944 | Mk I, Mk II |
| No. 34 Sqn | Wolf wishes, wolf flies | March 1945 | Mk I, Mk II |
| No. 42 Sqn | Bravely in action | July 1945 | Mk II |
| No. 60 Sqn | I strive through difficult skies | July 1945 | Mk II |
| No. 79 Sqn | Nothing can withstand us | Sept. 1944 | Mk I, Mk II |
| No. 81 Sqn | Not only but us | June 1945 | Mk II |
| No. 113 Sqn | Swift and vengeful | April 1945 | Mk II |
| No. 123 Sqn | Swift to strike | Sept. 1944 | Mk I, Mk II |
| No. 131 Sqn | Invicta | June 1945 | Mk II |
| No. 134 Sqn | We will fly through hardships | May 1944 | Mk I, Mk II |

| Air Force/Unit | Motto/Nickname* | P-47 Combat Debut | Model |
|---|---|---|---|
| No. 135 Sqn | We show our wings everywhere | May 1944 | Mk I, Mk II |
| No. 146 Sqn | The watchful panther strikes | Sept. 1944 | Mk I, Mk II |
| No. 258 Sqn | In the thick of things | Sept. 1944 | Mk I, Mk II |
| No. 261 Sqn | I always fight | June 1944 | Mk I, Mk II |
| No. 615 Sqn | By our united force | June 1945 | Mk II |
| **Armée de l'Air** | | | |
| II/3 Groupe de Chasse | Dauphine | 1 May 1944 | razorback/bubble-top |
| III/3 Groupe de Chasse | Ardennes | Oct. 1944 | bubble-top |
| I/4 Groupe de Chasse | Navarre | Sept. 1944 | bubble-top |
| I/5 Groupe de Chasse | Champagne | 31 Dec. 1944 | bubble-top |
| II/5 Groupe de Chasse | La Fayette | 8 May 1944 | razorback/bubble-top |
| III/6 Groupe de Chasse | Roussillon | 1 Feb. 1945 | bubble-top |
| **Brazilian Air Force** | | | |
| 1 Grupo de Aviacao de Caca (attached 350th F.G.) | The Ostriches | 31 Oct 1944 | bubble-top only |
| **Mexican Air Force** | | | |
| 201 Escuadron Aereo de Pelea (attached 58th F.G.) | | May 1945 | razorback/bubble-top |

*These were usually unofficial titles

# Appendix III
# Ninth Air Force
# P-47 Group Bases

36th F.G. Kingsnorth, Kent; Brucheville, France (A16); Le Mans, France (A35); Athis, France (A76); Juvincourt, France (A68); Le Culot, Belgium (A89); Aachen, Germany (Y86); Niedermendig, Germany (Y62); Kassel-Rothwesten, Germany (R12)

48th F.G. Ibsley, Hants; Deaux Jumeaux, France (A4); Villacoublay, France (A42D); Cambrai-Niergnies, France (A74); St-Trond, Belgium (A92); Kelz, Germany (Y54); Kassel-Waldau, Germany (Y96); Illesheim, Germany (R10)

50th F.G. Lymington, Hants; Carentan, France (A10); Meautis, France (A17); Orly, France (A47); Laon-Athis, France (A69); Lyon-Bron, France (Y6); Toul-Ochey, France (A96); Gibelstadt, Germany (Y90)

354th F.G. (P-47s Nov. 44 to Feb. 45 only) Rosières-en-Haye, France (A98); Ober Ulm, Germany (Y64)

358th F.G. Raydon, Suffolk; High Halden, Kent; Cretteville, France (A14); Pontorson, France (A28); Vitry, France (A67); Mourmelon-le-Grand, France (A80); Toul, France (A90); Mannheim, Germany (Y90)

362nd F.G. Wormingford, Essex; Headcorn, Kent; Liggerolles, France (A12); Rennes, France (A27); Prosnes, France (A79); Rouvres, France (A79); Frankfurt, Germany (Y73); Fürth, Germany (Y39); Ullesheim, Germany (R10)

365th F.G. Gosfield, Essex; Beaulieu, Hants; Azeville, France (A7); Lognerolles, France (A12); Bretigny, France (A48); Juvincourt, France (A68); Chievres-Mons, Belgium (A84); Metz-Frescaty, France (Y34); Florennes-Juzaine, Belgium (A78); Aachen, Germany (Y46); Fritzlar, Germany (Y86)

366th F.G. Membury, Berks; Thruxton, Hants; St-Pierre-du-Mont, France (A1); Dreux, France (A41); Lauon-Couvron, France (A70); Asch, Belgium (Y29); Münster, Germany (Y94); Bayreuth, Germany (R26)

367th F.G. (P-47s from Feb.1945) St-Dizier, France (A64); Jarney, France; Conflans, France (A94); Frankfurt-Eschborn, Germany (Y74)

368th F.G. Greenham Common, Berks; Chilbolton, Hants; Cardonville, France (A3); Chartres, France (A40); Laon-Athies, France (A69); Chievres-Mons, Belgium (A84); Juvincourt, France (A68); Metz, France (Y34); Frankfurt, Germany (Y73); Fürth, Germany (R10)

371st F.G. Bisterne, Hants; Beuzeville, France (A6); Perthes, France (A65); Dole-Tavaux, France (Y7); Tantonville, France (Y1); Metz, France (Y34); Frankfurt-Eschborn, Germany (Y74); Fürth, Germany (R10)

373rd F.G. Woodchurch, Kent; Tour-le-Bessin, France (A13); St-James, France (A29); Reims-Champagnes, France (A62D); Le Culot East, France (Y10); Venlo, The Netherlands (Y55); Lippstadt, Germany (Y98); Fürth, Germany (R10)

404th F.G. Winkton, Hants; Chippelle, France (A5); Bretigny, France (A48); Juvincourt, France (A68); St-Trond, Belgium (A92); Kelz, Germany (Y54); Fritzlar, Germany (Y86)

405th F.G. Christchurch, Hants; Picauville, France (A8) St-Dizier, France (A64); Ophoven, Belgium (Y32); Fritzlar, Germany (Y86); Straubing, Germany (R68)

406th F.G. Ashford, Kent; Cretteville, France (A14); Tour-le-Bessin, France (A13); St-Leonard, France (A36); Mourmelon-Le-Grand, France (A80); Metz-Frescaty, France (Y34); Asch, Belgium (Y29); Münster-Handorf, Germany (Y94); Nordholz, Germany (R56).

# Index